Advanced Persistent Security

Advanced Persistent Security

A Cyberwarfare Approach to Implementing Adaptive
Enterprise Protection, Detection, and Reaction Strategies

Ira Winkler

Araceli Treu Gomes

Dave Shackleford, Technical Editor

AMSTERDAM • BOSTON • HEIDELBERG • LONDON
NEW YORK • OXFORD • PARIS • SAN DIEGO
SAN FRANCISCO • SINGAPORE • SYDNEY • TOKYO
Syngress is an imprint of Elsevier

Syngress is an imprint of Elsevier
50 Hampshire Street, 5th Floor, Cambridge, MA 02139, United States

Notices
Knowledge and best practice in this field are constantly changing. As new research and experience broaden our understanding, changes in research methods, professional practices, or medical treatment may become necessary.

Practitioners and researchers must always rely on their own experience and knowledge in evaluating and using any information, methods, compounds, or experiments described herein. In using such information or methods they should be mindful of their own safety and the safety of others, including parties for whom they have a professional responsibility.

To the fullest extent of the law, neither the Publisher nor the authors, contributors, or editors, assume any liability for any injury and/or damage to persons or property as a matter of products liability, negligence or otherwise, or from any use or operation of any methods, products, instructions, or ideas contained in the material herein.

Library of Congress Cataloging-in-Publication Data
A catalog record for this book is available from the Library of Congress

British Library Cataloguing-in-Publication Data
A catalogue record for this book is available from the British Library

ISBN: 978-0-12-809316-0

For information on all Syngress publications
visit our website at https://www.elsevier.com/

  Working together
to grow libraries in
developing countries

www.elsevier.com • www.bookaid.org

Publisher: Todd Green
Acquisition Editor: Brian Romer
Editorial Project Manager: Anna Valutkevich
Production Project Manager: Punithavathy Govindaradjane
Cover Designer: Matthew Limbert

Typeset by TNQ Books and Journals

To my mother, and my wonderful co-author - Ira

*To those who raised me personally (my parents), professionally
(Kim Jones), and patiently (my wonderful co-author) - Ari*

Contents

About the Authors

Ira Winkler, CISSP (Certified Information Systems Security Professional), one of the world's most influential security professionals, is the president of Secure Mentem and co-host of The Irari Report. He is the author of *Spies Among Us* (Wiley, 2005) and *Zen and the Art of Information Security* (Syngress, 2007) among other books, a regular contributor to numerous security publications, and an active public speaker. He has been featured in *Forbes*, *USA Today*, *Wall Street Journal*, and other media. Mr. Winkler began his career at the National Security Agency where he served as an intelligence and computer systems analyst. He can be reached through the book website at http://www.advanced-persistentsecurity.com.

Araceli Treu Gomes serves as a cybersecurity strategist and subject matter expert and co-host of The Irari Report. She provides strategic security expertise to leadership teams, and counsels global organizations on preventing advanced attacks. Previously, she held technical and leadership positions including Strategic Security Advisor for a Fortune 100 company. She served as Engineering Director at a large defense contractor, Deputy CSO for a multinational financial services organization, and Chief Security and Privacy Officer at a major content delivery network. She designed early DDoS, extrusion prevention, and network forensics tools for Internet backbone providers. She holds certifications in privacy and computer forensics, and serves on IEEE Cybersecurity SIGs and ISSA boards locally and nationally. Araceli also writes for several industry publications and speaks around the world on many topics related to advanced and strategic security topics. She can be reached through the book website at http://www.advancedpersistentsecurity.com.

Introduction

This book is something neither of us originally thought of writing. However, it turns out that this was the book we were meant to write. Both of us wanted to write a book and when approached by Syngress to write this book, we both described the book we thought our friends required, and we thought our descriptions were identical. Then as we began writing the proposal, it was clear that what actually sounded identical was subtly, yet critically, different. Although this sounds almost impossible, you have to understand us to know how that can happen. What is immediately important is that the book is incredibly valuable to the intended readers.

While the story and background follows, what is important is the driver for this book. We are tired of hearing devastating attacks being proclaimed as "sophisticated" based on either the perpetrator or the resulting damage. The fact is that when you examine almost any attack that was proclaimed sophisticated, you can observe that it was completely preventable with available countermeasures.

In short, the personally identifiable information (PII) and credit card numbers of 110,000,000 people should not have been compromised at Target and Sony should not have been devastated by North Korea. Few, if any, of the likely dozens of proclaimed sophisticated attacks that have occurred since the time of this writing should have been successful. We are not clairvoyant, but we do not see the current pattern of attacks changing any time soon.

We have delivered presentations on this concept around the world. We published and promoted *The Irari Rules for Sophisticated Attacks*, which described specific criteria for what would really qualify an attack as sophisticated. For a detailed description of The Irari Rules, please visit www.AdvancedPersistentSecurity.com.

What came out of the presentations and discussions with other professionals is that the Irari Rules define good, basic security practices. Although the Irari Rules are sufficient for the defined purpose of determining whether an attack may be sophisticated or not, and the rules imply a starting point for a good security program, it again is just a starting point. A program based solely on the Irari Rules would be insufficient. Imagine it as measuring someone's body temperature; although body temperature is a sign of general health, an elevated temperature does not define the problem itself. At the same time, it is possible that even a person with a normal temperature has some illness or injury.

So when we were approached to write a book, we were in agreement that the book would essentially expand on the Irari Rules to define comprehensive security programs that address what are now normal attacks that attack known attack vectors, but somehow go unabated. This is a very critical and valuable concept. It, however, provided multiple methods for addressing the problem.

Although this will be expanded in the body of the book, we both perceived a way of describing the current attack landscape and attacks on Target, Sony, and the Office of Personnel Management (OPM) as traditional cyberwarfare attacks that target nonmilitary targets. Although this sounds ominous, it really just implies that attackers are more than script kiddies who know a single type of attack methodology. Attackers will use multiple attack vectors and different types of attacks at different phases of the attack. There will be detailed reconnaissance and a methodic approach to the attack.

As important, in all the major cases, there were gross failures in detection. Although it is admittedly inevitable that a malicious party will gain access, and just as inevitable that an insider will do something that causes damage, it should be equally inevitable that the acts are detected. Even if the attacks cannot be prevented, the resulting damage should at least be contained to some level. This focuses on the fact that security involves protection, detection, and reaction. Without planning for and implementing each aspect sufficiently, you cannot have an adequate security program.

While we both had the same intent for the book, it turns out that we had distinct approaches for satisfying that intent. Ari (Araceli goes by Ari) defined an approach that mimicked defensive cyberwarfare. Her approach was fairly low level to implement specific sets of countermeasures. Ira proposed a programmatic approach that focused on implementing strong processes.

Obviously, the result you are reading now is essentially the best of both worlds. We both have a broad range of experience in technical and nontechnical aspects of implementing security programs, but although our areas of knowledge overlap, we are individually stronger in different areas.

We do have to make a special note about the title. Both of us believe that a title is crucial to the book. There are so many similar sounding titles that it is easy to be confused about which book best satisfies your needs. Ari gets full credit for the title, *Advanced Persistent Security*. The title is incredibly simple, yet perfectly captures our intent. When Ari proposed the title, after many hours of thought and discussion, it was clear that it was perfect from the start.

While people love to hype the advanced persistent threats (APTs) and to make them sound unstoppable, the reality is that the term is not unreasonable. Being persistent implies that an attacker will not stop when he/she runs into basic countermeasures. The attacker clearly is a threat by definition. Whether the threat is advanced or not depends on your perspective.

The problem with the use of the term, APT, is that people equate that with unstoppable. As has been mentioned, APT-related attacks can be prevented. The problem is that most security programs implement an insufficient level of countermeasures in a piecemeal manner. Advanced Persistent Security is about a conscious effort to implement a complete and coordinated security program.

Although this may sound like a simple concept, the reality is that it is not the norm. Frequently, organizations buy individual products that might or might not be coordinated with each other. There might or might not be an adequate detection capability in place. As we do not intend to cover the entire book in the Introduction, we will leave it here for now.

We are proud to introduce the concept of Advanced Persistent Security. The defenders should be as properly organized and coordinated as the attackers, and although it may be a Pollyanna goal, we intend to at least start to level the playing field to allow our readers an opportunity to not fall prey to completely preventable and simple attacks that otherwise could lead to tremendous losses.

Ira Winkler and Araceli Treu Gomes

CHAPTER 1

What Is Advanced Persistent Security?

We recently spoke at a major security conference, where there was a keynote panel talking about the infamous Sony hack and what it meant for the future of security. The panel was moderated by former presidential cybersecurity advisor, Howard Schmidt, and the panelists include chief security officers of some of the top entertainment companies in the world. During the panel discussion, one of the panelists stated that the Sony hack was essentially unpreventable.

The author, Ira Winkler, challenged the panelist during the question and answer session. Ira stated that the Sony hack resulted from exploiting a variety of vulnerabilities that should have not existed. Specifically, there was no multi-factor authentication in place on critical systems, there was improper network segmentation, there was insufficient antimalware software in place, and several other elements of what would be considered basic cyber hygiene were missing.

The panelist then replied that although he agreed that the attack should have been prevented, he meant to imply that eventually a knowledgeable insider or a dedicated nation-state, such as North Korea, would have been able to bypass otherwise sufficient security in place.

Although Ira was tempted to continue arguing with the panelist, it was not his session to hijack. However, from our perspective, with a proper security program in place, in other words, one that employs the Advanced Persistent Security principles, it is possible that the attack could have been stopped completely. There is, however, no such thing as perfect security, so it is possible that the North Korean attackers would have eventually found some attack path into Sony.

However, even if they found a successful path into Sony, the resulting damage could have been significantly contained with a proper security program in place. For example, if better network monitoring and intrusion detection were in place, the attack would have been detected earlier in the intrusion; malware could have been prevented from being installed on as many systems; and email systems and file servers might not have been compromised, maybe only one movie would have been stolen.

Advanced Persistent Security. http://dx.doi.org/10.1016/B978-0-12-809316-0.00001-4

It also appears that Sony ignored what we would describe as threat intelligence. According to a *Fortune* magazine article that detailed the Sony attack, Sony was warned on multiple occasions that North Korea would consider retaliating for their distribution of the movie, *The Interview*. The threat intelligence gave Sony an indication on where they should have beefed up security countermeasures.

The Sony hack demonstrated a complete breakdown, or arguably an absence, of an effective security program.

Although you can categorize a security program in many ways, a comprehensive security program takes into account protection, detection, and reaction. Failing to effectively incorporate all these elements into a security program will result in failure.

PROTECTION

Clearly, protection must be robust, but it will never be perfect. Frankly, it cannot be perfect. Although you do need to protect information, computer systems, and everything else under your charge, you need to actually make them vulnerable to be useful.

For example, you cannot have a webserver that you remove from the Internet. You cannot refuse to grant users access to computer systems or information, because users are the greatest source of security failings. Although security needs to be integrated into business functions, it is secondary to business functions.

This will be discussed later, but security programs are doomed to fail by definition. The actual definition of security is freedom from risk. You can never be free from risk, and that is ok. No element in life is free from risk. As the saying goes, a ship in port is safe, but that is not what it is meant to do. Likewise, your information and computer systems were not meant to be safe, but were meant to provide a service. The services expose them to interactions with other forces.

At the same time, we would also add that a ship in port is not perfectly safe. For example, the ships at Pearl Harbor were supposedly safe in port on December 7, 1941, until they were attacked. When a hurricane is predicted for a port, the ships are sent out to the sea, so that they will not be subjected to traumatic conditions that might slam the ships into the piers. There is even the possibility of a ship in otherwise safe conditions being boarded and robbed, so there is no such thing as freedom from risk, even with a ship docked in port. There is clearly less risk, but not security.

We frequently challenge people to describe perfect computer security. Someone will eventually say, "Turn the computer off," or something similar. However, in the first place, a computer that is turned off is useless. So in trying to provide security, a denial of service attack was created. After we point that out to people, we then ask how many computers were potentially sitting in the World Trade Center and Pentagon on September 11, 2001? How many computers are destroyed in fires? How many computers suffer accidental water damage? How many laptop computers, which are turned off, are lost or stolen every year? So even a computer that cannot be theoretically hacked is still exposed to potential loss. Clearly the risk is lower, as the 9/11 style attacks are thankfully extremely rare. However, even this lower risk of hacking is accomplished by compromising the actual purpose of the computer itself; this is unacceptable.

So in this chapter, we are stating that perfect security is unattainable. The only people who will ever offer you perfect security are fools or liars. If any book tells you that by implementing the material in the book, you will achieve security, put the book down and walk away.

Before going on, though, this does not excuse putting insufficient protection mechanisms in place. Risk reduction means that all reasonable and cost-effective countermeasures should be implemented. You cannot throw up your hands and proclaim that your security program will fail, so you might as well give up in advance. You need to have a comprehensive and effective protection program in place. To the best of your ability and within reason, you want to stop incidents from happening in the first place. The problem that we see with most security programs is that they do not stop even basic attacks, and basic attacks can create massive losses as easily as the most sophisticated attacks.

DETECTION

This is why detection is as important, if not more important, than protection; There will always be a failure. That is a given. However, a failure in protection does not have to result in an actual loss. In case of a successful attack (where a successful attack is defined as an attack that made it past the security counter-measures in place and the attacker now has potential access to a network, information, computer, or other assets you intend to protect), it does not necessarily mean that there will be a loss.

For example, if an attacker gains access to a network, it does not mean that he or she will end up compromising information. If some form of intrusion detection system detects the attacker, a reaction can occur to kick he or she off the network before information is compromised, or at least a complete compromise of information can be stopped.

With the Edward Snowden case, although Snowden was a systems administrator at the National Security Agency (NSA), and arguably he was a de facto part of the NSA network security program that failed, there were many chances to detect his crimes before the bulk of the data thefts were accomplished. Arguably, if his actions were detected early enough, he could have been arrested before providing the information to reporters and other parties.

Examples of missed detection opportunities with *Snowden* include the fact that he downloaded data for several years. He accessed systems that he had no reason to access. He asked coworkers for their passwords. The background check performed on Snowden was apparently grossly lacking and missed past actions, as well as other indications that meant he should not have received a clearance. He might have been arrested for a variety of activities related to his previous employment at the CIA, and at a previous NSA contractor. The NSA officials actually stated that misuse and abuse detection was rolled out throughout NSA, but not to the Pacific theater, where Snowden worked.

With the Sony hack, better network monitoring tools, actually any network monitoring tool, would have likely detected the malicious traffic going across the network. Although we will discuss the importance of reaction later, it is already clear that with detection, reaction can then occur.

Besides monitoring network activity, Sony should have been able to detect the movies being downloaded from their systems. They should have detected the access to their email servers and file servers, as well as the downloading of critical information. Although the details have not been made fully public, when you consider the damage and the available security tools, among other things, it is clear that there were dozens, if not hundreds, of missed opportunities to detect the North Korean attack before significant damage was perpetrated.

It can be argued that Sony should have had all the detection mechanisms, even applying the available threat intelligence, which actually would have told Sony that they need to be on the alert for a certain type of malware. Detecting that malware on the system proactively would have allowed Sony to remove it before their infrastructure was destroyed. This is one detection mechanism that could have been put in place.

Clearly, though, Sony is expected to be under regular attack from a variety of malicious parties. Although North Korea was the source of a devastating attack, it is very likely that other parties were and are attacking Sony on an ongoing basis. For this reason, detection should be as robust as reasonably possible, and not deficient on so many fronts.

When you look at most of the attacks that have been proclaimed, "Sophisticated," by the victims or the consultants whom they pay to speak for them, you see insufficient protection combined with insufficient detection capabilities. In this chapter, to this point, we have just touched upon two of the most notable case studies; the Sony hack and the Snowden crimes. Despite the media and the victims, and even other security professionals who do not consider the details, trying to hide behind a supposed "sophisticated attacker," it is clear that the actual skill of the attackers is irrelevant.

The damage caused by North Korea was more because of poor protection and detection than because of the potential skills of the North Korean hackers. Likewise with Snowden, although the media loves to portray him as a computer genius, there is no indication of any exceptional skills on his part. Despite the fact that his victim was the NSA, whom anyone would assume to have the strongest security program in the world, there were clearly gross failings at many levels in their internal security posture.

Ira worked at the NSA, and he attests to the fact that the security measures that the NSA relies on the most is its background check and its people. The NSA relies not only on the background checks and the choice of personnel whom it allows access to data as a form of protection, but also on the personnel to detect suspicious behavior on the part of coworkers as a form of detection.

Edward Snowden was a contractor, so he did not have to go through a full-scope polygraph test to obtain an NSA clearance. Snowden resigned from the CIA in 2009, before being scheduled for an expected polygraph examination, which is standard for employees and would have questioned him about counterintelligence-reacted activities and tendencies. So it can be argued that the NSA security policies that do not require contractors to go through the same level of security screening as the actual NSA employees enabled Snowden's actions.

Thus it is clear that the contractor who was supposed to perform Snowden's background investigation failed to contact the CIA, where it was reportedly noted on Snowden's personnel file that he was suspected of attempting to break into systems to which he was not granted access.

Despite that, Snowden left clear signs to his coworkers, the most obvious of which was asking other people for their passwords, so he could comb through the NSA systems that he would otherwise not have access to, as well as conceal his identity by browsing the network as other people.

Again, there were a wide variety of failings with Snowden as much as Sony.

REACTION

Clearly reaction cannot occur without detection; however, it is still a distinct task. There are way too many cases where organizations detect harmful actions, but fail to take the appropriate, if any, actions in response. Reaction can take many forms, which can vary greatly.

It might be a legitimate reaction to do nothing. When you have an attack that appears trivial, and involves a basic scan, you just might want to note that a scan is taking place and perhaps use it as an indicator to be on the alert for potential other attacks and scans that might be more focused. This would be reasonable given that most organizations are regularly scanned by Internet-based attackers, who are mostly not even aware of the specific organization they are scanning.

However, there is definitely a continuum depending on the nature of the event detected, the target (system, person, network, facility, etc.) of the possible attack, etc. For example, an attack that is targeting the new movie database at Sony from internal systems, using administrator credentials, would deserve an immediate and massive response. Clearly, an attack of a high-value target, and the presence of some unusual resources, especially and including administrator credential, implies a serious chain of failings, with the strong potential for massive damage.

In general, though, a reaction needs to be measured and appropriate for the event detected. Your environment can also impact what is measured and appropriate. There is no perfect answer; however, the one wrong answer is that there is no proactive consideration of what a reaction to expected attacks would be.

Example reactions include (and will likely include multiple reactions) the following:

- do nothing
- blacklist an IP address
- disable a user account
- shutdown a system
- tighten the rule set on firewalls and other perimeter devices
- monitor traffic or a user
- back up all data immediately
- call in a team of outside experts
- alert law enforcement
- examine all user accounts for signs of compromise

In many cases, reactions can be straightforward. However, you have to consider that if a system is compromised, it likely needs to be considered completely compromised. For example, when Ira investigated a computer-based bank robbery, he discovered a compromise of another electronic funds transfer system. He contacted the administrator of the system, who replied that he noticed the attackers and kicked them off. Ira then told him to check option 13 of the login menu. The administrator replied that there was no option 13. Ira then told the administrator to type 13 at the login prompt, and the administrator continued to pushback on Ira, until he finally and dejectedly said, "Oh."

Although the administrator may have noticed the attack, and believed he kicked the attacker off the system, he did not consider the possibility that the attacker installed a backdoor on the system, in case he/she was discovered. This type of behavior is common if the attacker is minimally skilled, and the systems should be considered completely compromised, until proven otherwise.

We will discuss reaction in more detail later in the book. However, it is critical to understand that although strong protection is required, and that as protection will inevitably fail, you need to have strong detection capabilities in place. However, detection is just the beginning. Reaction, a.k.a. an incident response plan, must be in place proactively to provide a strong and robust security program, or more specifically, a strong risk management program.

DEFENSE IN DEPTH

Hopefully, most people reading this book would have heard of the concept of Defense in Depth long before picking it up. However, there may be some confusion as to what it actually means. It can be argued that this book is Defense in Depth by another name. However, we would disagree. At a high level, Defense in Depth implies protection.

Defense in Depth is a broad term that generally means that you do not create a single point of failure. You do not rely on a firewall for perimeter security and assume that your firewall will keep out all bad people, so you do not need any more security countermeasures. You assume that attackers will come at you from many attack vectors, so you keep layering security around the most critical systems. This is a strong form of protection and something that we advocate strongly for in future chapters.

However, Defense in Depth does not necessarily imply that you maintain constant vigilance, but that you throw many layers of protection around the critical systems, such as the proverbial onion model. The most critical systems and data requiring the most protection get many security countermeasures, whereas the systems of lesser importance get comparatively less protection.

What this does not have by definition is a comprehensive management structure that tightly integrates detection and reaction. Creating an environment without a single point of failure is critical, but it is just the starting point.

WHAT IS ADVANCED PERSISTENT SECURITY?

As a concept, Advanced Persistent Security is Defense in Depth that is enhanced with a comprehensive methodology for integrating the appropriate and properly configured detection capability, along with proactively implementing and executing a reaction capability. Although this may sound like common sense to many security practitioners, the sad fact is that most organizational security programs are not designed this way.

Advanced Persistent Security is an ongoing process of constantly examining potential incidents detected and reacting appropriately to those incidents by further tailoring the program. This includes monitoring threat intelligence, so that you can proactively adjust the program to remain strong and resilient to potential and/or likely attacks.

The NSA likely had Defense in Depth to prevent would-be Snowdens; however, it clearly failed. They had background checks, which were flawed. There was a security awareness program in place, which should have alerted Snowden's co-workers to be suspicious and report his requests to them to disclose their passwords. There were likely several forms of authentication that Snowden was able to bypass. They had policies that stated that people should not be allowed to place USB drives in classified systems and take them home. There was auditing in place, so the NSA could see what Snowden stole after the fact. To a large extent, this is very robust Defense in Depth. It still failed miserably.

The system lacked the detection capability that should have identified many questionable activities. Although many people want to paint Snowden as a computer genius, the reality appears to be that he has some talent, but no exceptional ability. Minimally, if he had any exceptional ability, he did not have to use it much, as the security in place appears to have failed on multiple levels. This is more a case of an unsophisticated security program, and not a sophisticated attacker.

Advanced Persistent Security provides an environment where you implement the appropriate protection measures. Although none of them provides perfect security, they make it exponentially easier for an attack to be detected. As attackers attempt to bypass security countermeasures, it provides another opportunity to detect the malicious activities. The more opportunities to detect the actions, the more likely your organization can stop the attacker before any damage or loss occurs. Even if loss occurs, you have more opportunities to mitigate and control the loss.

Advanced Persistent Security is essentially creating a security environment that is as dynamic as even the most advanced of the Advanced Persistent Threat (APT)-related attacks. This is a very powerful concept that needs to be considered for creating a security program that addresses where the current state of computer-based crimes and attacks have evolved.

As you go through this book, you will see that we are not advocating just throwing a lot of countermeasures into your organization, but proposing an overall process to design, implement, and maintain a strong security environment.

Yes, the process must include the appropriate tools, but as Snowden demonstrated all too clearly, tools (including background checks and awareness), even in the most secure organization in the world, can be completely useless.

ADVANCED PERSISTENT THREAT AND ADVANCED PERSISTENT SECURITY

Clearly, we came up with the term Advanced Persistent Security to imply it counters APT. Typically, APT refers to China or some other nation-state, such as Russia, Iran, North Korea, or well-funded and established criminal entities.

Let us examine what this means. Breaking down the term backwards, the organizations or entities who want to compromise you are a threat by definition. So the word, threat, applies.

Persistent is a relative term, but if you assume it to mean that an attacker will not give up when met with trivial countermeasures, then, yes, the attacker is persistent. You need to consider that just about any organization has something of value. You need to assume that you are going to face an attacker that is not going to test default passwords and give up.

A persistent attacker will probe a network, scour social networks for information they can find about the target's employees, and perform extensive reconnaissance. To a large extent, they might know the target organization better than most employees. When there is a lot of money, or other reward, such as the treasure trove of information from the Office of Personnel Management (OPM) hack, should it not be expected that an attacker will go through all of this effort?

Consider that the Target hack yielded the criminal, or criminals, millions of dollars. Why would a criminal not devote several months of effort to the crime? Every organization should consider that they hold more than enough value to motivate any criminal to be persistent.

Any organization that does not think they have enough value to motivate a criminal to be persistent should be out of business.

Then considering the term advanced, it is almost irrelevant at some point. The term APT includes advanced by default; however, most persistent threats do not have to be advanced to be successful. When you consider the Sony hack, although North Korea may have advanced technologies, the attack itself did not utilize any advanced techniques. Spear phishing messages were sent to trick administrators to divulging their passwords. The malware they used was previously known and should have been detected by most antimalware software. The attackers did not have to compromise any authentication beyond passwords. There was no network segmentation that the attackers had to compromise. Hard work was exponentially more valuable than anything that would be considered advanced.

So while attackers such as China, Iran, Russia, and the United States might have zero-day attacks, which might be considered unstoppable attacks, assuming you are actually running the software, rarely do they have to use those techniques.

However, the key point is that any motivated attacker will go beyond the trivial attacks that most organizations design their security programs to prevent. The organizations implement countermeasures that are specific to a given attack vector and are not frequently coordinated with other countermeasures. The motivated attacker will quickly adapt to countermeasures in place and try other attack vectors. They will eventually get in, and without a proper detection program in place, they will be successful.

Advanced Persistent Security creates an overall program to address motivated attackers by being persistent in proactively defending against attackers, while simultaneously searching for signs of successful attacks. Of course, there is a comprehensive response program in place, so that there is a rapid reaction when potentially successful attacks are detected.

Although we wish we did not have to propose this concept as something new and revolutionary, most security programs do not have this level of sophistication.

APPLYING ADVANCED PERSISTENT SECURITY TO THE SONY HACK

At the beginning of this chapter, we discussed the countermeasures that would have prevented the Sony hack. Again, Ira let stand the comments that an attacker would have eventually compromised the organization. As you can tell, we actually agree that a motivated attacker would eventually have gained entry to the organization's network and infrastructure.

However, by applying the Advanced Persistent Security principles, the inevitable penetration would have been detected. No matter how the attacker gained entry into the Sony network, monitoring the log files would have detected that outside parties were attempting to remotely access the network as administrators. Anti-malware software would have detected the installed malware. Behavioral analytics software would have detected the attempts to access date files and personal emails. Users would have reported the phishing messages and that would have helped to alert the company to delete unopened email messages and be on the alert for other attacks. Data leak prevention software should have detected the exfiltration of movies, emails, and critical files. The security team would have applied threat intelligence to know to block certain IP addresses. Threat intelligence would have allowed the company to know that they need to focus on protecting the pre-released movies.

Again, there was a great deal that could have been done to stop the inevitably successful intrusion from causing major damage. This is the key that the panelist missed. Just because a criminal can compromise an organization, it does not mean that it has to be a complete loss.

Advanced Persistent Security is a methodology that ironically assumes that there will be a failure, much in the way that an APT assumes that they might be unsuccessful at many attempts to compromise an organization, before they eventually get in. Security is not a static program that implements a set of tools, but an ecosystem that is constantly evolving to the latest threats.

The remainder of this book discusses the methodology to design, implement, and maintain a comprehensive security program that implements protection, detection, and reaction with a process that creates a living program. Again this program will definitely not provide perfect security, but you will have fewer incidents, and those incidents that do occur, will be significantly more contained. Advanced Persistent Security will save your organization time, money, and other resources.

Concepts/Foundation

Before going into the heart of Advanced Persistent Security (APS), it is useful to understand the fundamental concepts that comprise implementing an APS program. Clearly, we cannot anticipate and write about every situation and circumstance you will encounter. However, with an understanding of these concepts, you will be able to make better decisions in the absence of other guidance.

It is also important that we establish a common language to avoid confusion. Even a word as fundamental as security can have different meanings to different, equally qualified security professionals. Although some definitions and interpretations might be more commonly used, none are inherently right or wrong.

Additionally, we performed extensive research to enhance our own knowledge bases. This research involved nation-state cyberwarfare strategies, as well as talking to people who run some of the best security programs in the industry. We both came away with new foundations that helped us to evolve our thought processes and recommendations that we give others. We are excited to share that with our readers.

Although some readers may already have a firm understanding of the content in this section, we want to ensure that we do not make assumptions about every potential reader's base level of knowledge. Therefore, providing a base of common knowledge allows readers to exercise common sense. It also creates an environment that allows people to implement strong security programs that are resilient to successful and unsuccessful attacks against their organization.

CHAPTER 2

Cyberwarfare Concepts

Cyberwarfare is an overused term, but there are many related concepts that are applicable to Advanced Persistent Security (APS). The US military has started to refer to cyberwarfare as a component of Information Operations. Cyberwarfare is literally the subject of volumes of books. However, for the sake of brevity and practicality, we will focus this discussion on the important principles as they apply to APS.

An accepted definition of war is, "The use of military force to achieve a political goal." The key concept is that the purpose of war is to achieve a political goal. Cyberwar can have two potential definitions. The first is, "The use of computer-based force to achieve a political goal." The second is, "The use of computer-based force to support a military action."

In the first definition, cyberwar can be used as asymmetric warfare, where a weaker party can take on a more powerful party or engage in attacks without fear of significant retribution, and the computer-based attacks are the entirety of the potential conflict. In the second definition, computer-based attacks are used as a tactical component of a traditional military operation. Neither definition is right or wrong in all cases.

At the 2014 Black Hat conference, General Keith Alexander, then director of the NSA, used the phrase Computer Network Operations (CNO). CNO is the umbrella term for the different components involved in traditional cyberwarfare. There are three components that comprise CNO: Computer Network Defense (CND), Computer Network Exploitation (CNE), and Computer Network Attack (CNA).

For the remainder of this chapter and this book, we will refer to CNO as synonymous with cyberwarfare. Cyberwarfare is composed of offensive cyberwarfare and defensive cyberwarfare. As previously described, CNO has three components. CND is the equivalent of defensive cyberwarfare. CNE and CNA combined are the equivalent of offensive cyberwarfare.

CND is essentially APS. Although we will cover all elements of security, this book is intended for the technical audience and that is where the focus of

Advanced Persistent Security. http://dx.doi.org/10.1016/B978-0-12-809316-0.00002-6

our discussion and countermeasures will be. CNA and CNE are what you are protecting yourself from.

Although the connotations of cyberware and CNO seem large and potentially overkill for what you believe your organization must deal with, the concepts are relevant to security programs of all sizes. The fundamental principles of security are applicable whether you are dealing with nation-state actors or script kiddies. Your security program must have an established process that is capable of dealing with threats of all capabilities.

Your organization is really an implementation of business processes. Your security program must likewise be a business process. Cyberwarfare and CNO should not necessarily imply scope, but process. The NSA and governments approach warfare and security as a process, and that should be emulated. The scope of the process is clearly determined by the scope of the risk your organization faces, but it must be an established process to be successful.

CONFIDENTIALITY, INTEGRITY, AND AVAILABILITY

Before continuing the discussion on CNO, we need to discuss the components of security. It is a generally accepted principle that security of data is defined as protecting confidentiality, integrity, and availability of data. Although there are variations of this paradigm, it represents a good framework for detailing the components of CNO.

Confidentiality means that you are trying to keep the data confidential. You want to ensure that only the appropriate people have access to the information in question. Confidentiality can also imply that functions are only available to authorized users. When you think some aspect of a computer requires access controls, the implication is that you are trying to ensure the confidentiality of some aspect of the computer, network, and/or system.

Integrity means that you want to ensure that the data is not manipulated. You want to ensure that the data is accurate, or at least as accurate as it was when it was entered into the system. Although accurate data entry is a legitimate risk consideration, for the purpose of CNO, the implication is that an attacker will attempt to modify the data. For example, an attacker can add money to or take money from a bank account, can change the launch codes for missiles, or may change the targeting of the missiles.

Availability means that you want the data to be available to the people who need it and computer-based services to be available to all legitimate users. Clearly if the data or services required from a computer system are not available, they are worthless.

It is important to note that gaining illegitimate access to a system potentially compromises any aspect of security. There is a principle that you do not care if a person breaks into a computer; you care about what they do once they are in. By definition, illegitimate access is irrelevant until the perpetrator takes some action. If the attackers look at data, they are compromising confidentiality. If they modify data, they are compromising integrity. If they take the system down, they are compromising availability.

Clearly all malicious actions begin with accessing the computer-based systems. Security programs begin by preventing illicit access, whereas attackers begin their activities by gaining access.

COMPUTER NETWORK ATTACK

CNA is what most people think of when they think of cyberwarfare. They envision attacks taking down power grids. They envision cars being stopped in their tracks. They envision planes coming down. Those are all possibilities in theory.

CNA is the compromise of computer-based assets and manipulating the systems. The systems can be taken down, data can be modified, resources can be misused for botnets, or any other action that compromises the integrity or availability of a system can be done. The computer system is either used against the organization or its resources or data are made unavailable.

To perform a CNA, attackers will likely not only gain access to the network, but also perform reconnaissance on the network, before taking action. The reconnaissance will allow them to learn the configuration of the network and determine how to best perform their malicious activities.

Preparation of the battlefield may also be considered a CNA. Although the damage may not be immediate, attackers manipulate the system to allow for future damage at a time of their discretion. For example, when you see reports that Russia, China, and Iran have invaded the US power grid, and the implication is that they have the finger on the button, although they might not actually have caused any damage, they are essentially one step away. It might not technically be considered an attack; however, it is more than just information gathering, which is what is involved in CNE, which is explained later. It does, however, create a quandary for the victims who discover the attack, as it creates the need to determine an appropriate response.

A realized case of CNA occurred during the invasion of Iraq in 2003. The United States reportedly hacked the Iraqi air defense network and manipulated the displays on the Iraqi radar screens to make it appear that aircraft were in different locations than where they actually were.

The Stuxnet attack that caused the destruction of the Iranian nuclear centrifuges is a clear CNA. The Sony hack by North Korea is an example of CNA.

There are many versions of CNA, but for the purpose of this discussion, we consider the most critical aspect: once an attacker gains access to the system, they compromise the integrity or availability of a system.

COMPUTER NETWORK EXPLOITATION

CNE is best described as the attack on the confidentiality of the targeted computer system. CNE is the theft of data, with no other functions affected. With CNE, there is specifically no intent to cause damage to the targeted systems. Ironically, the integrity (with the exception of the compromise of system integrity required to gain and maintain illicit access) and availability of systems are critical to a successful CNE. After all, if you cannot gain and maintain access to the desired information, you cannot maintain your espionage efforts.

CNE is essentially computer espionage. The goal is to spy in one form or another. The attacker is basically attempting to gather information. To accomplish this goal, the attacker needs to gain access to the network, perform reconnaissance, identify and gain access to the relevant systems to compromise, and find and compromise the targeted information. There is typically a need to maintain access to continue to collect the information. You also want the information you compromise to be accurate.

In many ways, CNE is more complicated than CNA, because more effort is required for the attacks to be surreptitious. With CNA, although the attackers might want to maintain their anonymity, the attack itself would become obvious. With CNE, the value of the attack is frequently dependent on nobody knowing information was compromised. For example, with the Snowden leaks, it was apparent that the NSA had reliable access to terrorist communications channels. When that information was divulged, further access was denied.

In the 2012 Target hack, during which 110,000,000 credit card numbers and related information were compromised, the attackers first had to gain access to the Target network, which they did through a vendor network. They then performed reconnaissance to understand the network and determine which systems needed to be compromised to accomplish their goals. When the point-of-sale (POS) systems were finally compromised, it was to the attackers' benefit for the attack to remain unknown for as long as possible, so that they could gather as many credit card numbers as possible.

In short, the difference between CNA and CNE is that there is no damage to the underlying systems with CNE; however, when there is damage, it could be much more critical and long lasting. You may consider that you can quickly recover from a computer outage, but if your competitor knows all your data, you can lose a great deal of value over an extended period.

COMPUTER NETWORK DEFENSE

CND is defensive cyberwarfare. It is security. Simply, the goal of CND is to prevent CNA and CNE. CND is APS.

The goal of this book is to discuss how to put together CND that is proactive, robust, and essentially a living security program.

CND involves protection, detection, and reaction. Protection provides a foundation for the program. It is the base of operation. From the base, and detected incidents, the reaction includes taking immediate steps to stop an incident in progress.

To implement a proactive and capable CND, you need to understand the motivations and methods used in CNA and CNE. This will allow for the most relevant countermeasures (a.k.a. protections) to be put in place, as well as allow you to implement better detection and reaction capabilities. While it is important to understand CNA and CNE, the focus of this book is on CND.

CHAPTER 3

What Is Proaction?

Security programs are typically inherently responsive. As practitioners and leaders, we consider operational challenges as they relate to responding to threats, analyzing trends in protection methodologies and attacker techniques, and reviewing breaches to glean some elusive detail that we might have overlooked while crafting and implementing our own defenses. We do this, even as we endeavor to stay ahead of adversaries and techniques that constantly emerge. Security is a reactive concept, even when it is addressed proactively. Its primary mission is to establish defenses and controls that will withstand and respond to an endless stream of affronts and nefarious activities committed by countless nameless adversaries, who look to thwart our efforts and gain access to the assets we seek to protect.

Security needs to account for changes and states that occur over time. This holds true for any strategy meant to address a constantly changing threat landscape, and it should apply to a security program across its very spectrum. This is the foundation for the concept of proaction.

Habitual proaction is regarded as being among the holy grails of security practices. Vendor pitches, trade magazines, and other venues that propagandize fluff and jargon frequently highlight predictive security tools and robust intelligence gathering methods. These tools account for events that have not yet occurred, adversaries that have not yet mounted an offense, and assets that have not yet been compromised. This panacea is a stunning and evolved place to be for an organization to aspire to be. Unfortunately, the reality is that it is not only as ephemeral state of existence as is being secure, but also largely impractical, if not downright impossible. Whether you want to lump the state of emerging threats as being inherently a series of ever-moving targets or not, you accept the premise that these elements of protection are in constant motion.

For this reason, we aim to set aside the futile concept of proactivity by contrasting it to a similar sounding but critically different concept of proaction. Unlike proactivity, which is defined as acting in preparation for possible future occurrences, proaction is defined and characterized as being active or in a state of conscious action or habit and, moreover, as something that is engaged with

21

Advanced Persistent Security. http://dx.doi.org/10.1016/B978-0-12-809316-0.00003-8

the intention of initiating change instead of reacting to it. Being conjugates of the same root words, the notions are very similar in origin. However, the subtle differences are profound when considered as a foundation for a comprehensive security program. Consider this: to be proactive is to be constantly preparing to react to an expected occurrence. As opposed to having to react on the terms of an event that requires a response, proaction endeavors to bring about the change on your own terms, enabling continued action instead of requiring a response secondary to an event.

Imagine if your security program set out to define cybersecurity battles and bring them to bear on its own terms? This chapter focuses on some of the principles that change the way we regard adversity and construct defenses with that posture in mind.

KILL CHAIN BASICS

We discuss kill chain analysis in detail in Chapter 16, however we want to stress the importance of the principle in the discussion of proaction. Proaction involves taking action in advance of a potential attack, while also facilitating faster reaction in the event of a detected attack. This requires understanding how attackers approach their attacks.

The kill chain specifies the phases of an attack from an attacker's perspective. By understanding the attack phases, you can anticipate the sequential actions of an attacker. This information provides the opportunity to know what vulnerabilities might be most vulnerable to attack and assist in the determination of countermeasures that should best prevent an inevitable attack.

When an attack is then detected, understanding kill chain analysis allows you to anticipate the attacker's next actions, so you can attempt to prevent those actions. It also allows you to look back in the kill chain to examine the attacker's earlier actions. This can help you find potential damage. Kill chain analysis can also assist in identifying how the attacker gained entry into the organization, and allows you to find the egress points, so that you can shut it down. Alternatively, it may also help in observing the attacker, so that you can determine how far they got, the extent of the compromise of your organization, what their actual goals are, and the most effective methods for stopping them.

Proaction requires anticipating your adversaries actions so that you can take action to prevent the attacks in the first place, as well as creating a security program that has an effective reaction program built into it. Kill chain analysis facilitates both of those activities.

CHANGING THE GAME

The theory behind use of the kill chain to aid in development of defenses suggests that detective capabilities can be inserted earlier in the chain, rather than waiting for attacks to manifest and trigger defenses at later stages. By identifying attack methodologies and organizing events into chains of events that create a series of leading and trailing indicators of compromise, defense actors can theoretically engage earlier in the attack cycle. Like the original military kill chain on which it was based, according to this model, the earlier the defense actors engage, the better.

However, there are several challenges posed by this mentality, and they should be considered philosophically when trying to operationalize a kill chain defense strategy. First and foremost, establishing a picture of the complete attack chain and order of adversary operations can be very difficult, if defenses are not perfectly orchestrated or real-world communication challenges exist between system owners.

Let us be realistic about incident investigations: infighting is as much of problem as the reacting to the incident itself. Disagreements among process and resource owners, blaming users for enabling entry, improperly classifying detecting an intrusion as a failure of protection rather than a success of detection, and other failure-intolerant and blame deflecting practices can stand in the way of implementing the visibility requirements necessary to reverse-engineer an advanced intrusion, even if the raw technical challenges can be overcome.

Looking at the "earlier is better" logic in the kill chain mentality from another practical perspective, does it really make sense for an organization with finite resources to engage at the earliest possible opportunity? Is it the best use of your fiscal and personnel capital to hunt down and eradicate every port scan, publicly available string of email addresses, and social media account owned by one of your employees, because it could be used as part of the reconnaissance phase by an adversary? Is it even technically feasible to implement a defense somehow, somewhere that will challenge an adversary's own software development life cycle, as it endeavors to develop a code that targets your environment specifically?

It is right around this point that traditional security organizations find themselves chasing proverbial wild geese or consuming fractured solutions that, although well-marketed, do not do a whole lot to address the concern they last identified, before their collective eyes glazed over. If security is an evolutionary process and its growth is often preceded by failure, then there has to be a calculated but practical approach to purposefully assess, reassess, and respond to failures, with improvement as a goal rather than perfection as an endgame.

One part of this agenda is to understand what failure really means to an organization or a given asset and what success equals to the adversary. Redefining the objectives on both sides, based on what the immediate and measurable threats, events, or objectives are, applies a clarifying moment to the evaluation of an exposure. In kind, we are able to align and focus our alerts and investigations on areas that are more likely to yield results, even if those results are just to thwart the adversaries' objectives.

Consider this: if an adversary's aim is to exfiltrate data, but is caught and stopped on the way out, is that the same level of failure as not having caught him/her at all? If his/her ultimate objective was to leave with intellectual property of some sort, but the data, although accessed, was never transmitted outside the enterprise borders, it could constitute a defensive success. But when was the last time you developed a security program element that was focused on extrusion prevention versus intrusion prevention?

THREAT HUNTING

We mentioned earlier that security programs are doomed to fail by definition, and there are conditions where failure is acceptable. Modern threats provoke and arguably require a more active role in detecting and responding to attacks. Foundational security elements, such as perimeter defenses, event monitoring, and endpoint protection are focused on prevention and detection and are thereby limited in how they inform your security program. An emerging trend that aims to come at the security problem from the other side is threat hunting. Threat hunting typically couples high-level anomaly detection with iterative drilling down into systems and data in search of incidents that have gone undetected. Threat hunting solutions, services, tools, experts, and methods have evolved recently as the next level in a progressive security program. However, we would argue that threat hunting should be one of the earlier steps in program development.

Hunting defies or exceeds signature-based detection in favor of a hypothesis-driven approach paired with analysis. After all, the adversary activities typically spawn from creative human offenders, so our defenses should be supported by creative human defenders. Many organizations engage in cursory levels of threat hunting when they manually comb through logs and alerts in search of activity for which a rule did not exist or did not fire. However, APTs and, moreover, advanced persistent security programs are defined in part by not only practices but also perspectives that transform these basic hunting activities into fundamental hunting habits. This goes against the traditional security grain of assuming a program's objective to be successful and measuring its successes to confirm. Using threat hunting as a foundational and early phase practice assumes that no matter the level of a security program, the most impactful measure of its evolution is to measure where it is unsuccessful.

Hunting is an iterative, cyclical, and informative process that begins by "jumping in the middle" and iterating out continuously to look for evidence your security program has failed and the failure went undetected. To do this, a series of hypotheses as to what may have gone wrong must be established and sought proactively. Practitioners should take an honest look at their environments and assets and think in terms of risk, and then work backward from there to find adversary activity that would look to exploit these weaknesses.

From a strategic perspective, threat hunting hypotheses should derive from one of five primary foci: external intelligence, internal intelligence, institutional knowledge, asset awareness, and advanced analysis. We discuss these foci further in the chapter on Threat Intelligence.

External intelligence is just what it sounds like; there are any number of open- and closed-source intelligence feeds, services, and channels that can be combed and interpreted for risks and exposures that may be present in your environment. These intelligence feeds should be consumed and evaluated, and use cases should be developed that allow you to evaluate your environment for cases that slipped through defense.

Internal intelligence is interpreted information you have about your own environment and may include internal log data to internally collected event details from homegrown rulesets and monitoring habits. Use cases designed to look for the opposite of what is expected of existing defenses are good places to start when devising hunting hypotheses meant to address weaknesses in internal intelligence.

Institutional knowledge combines a fuzzier value of intimate knowledge we all have about our own organizations. Many times, this category includes easy-to-qualify but hard-to-quantify holes in process, politics, or priority that may be blends of comparing internal intelligence to external intelligence or knowledge of weaknesses based on where you know you have struggled or failed before. Use cases that seek to detect past or people-oriented failures may be informers of institutional knowledge-based hunting.

Asset awareness refers to criteria like an organization's appetite for risk, risk assessments, perceived assets, and perceived threats based on corporate profile. Development of use cases and threat manifestations that would target what an organization values, what it believes makes it valuable or vulnerable, or what it cannot afford to have happen gives rise to hunting hypotheses in this domain.

Advanced analytics is a catch-all category for any automated, risk-scored, or machine-learned statistics or threat scenarios that have been derived through advanced analytics. In many cases, the solutions and devices generating these statistics can create use cases to test hypotheses for analytics systems and as a part of the risk scoring process.

It is important to note that a hypothesis is not unbiased and does assume a specific outcome, for which it sets off to prove. Regardless of what hunting methods and perspectives you choose to use in developing a hunting program and culture, the mindset going in should be that the unthinkable has already happened and that the threat has been successful. Regardless of the outcome, your results should become part of an internal intelligence and institutional knowledge base, which will go on to inform future investigations and will be discussed in Section 4 of this book. In the nearer and arguably more important term, the outcomes of your hunting exercises provide a roadmap for immediate and impactful changes to your security program.

SUMMARY

Proaction is the difference between a traditional security program that puts in place static defenses with cursory detection and reaction capability and a program that is as dynamic and adaptive as the attackers. Security programs need to account for, in advance, the inevitability of attack, and ensure that their defense program reacts appropriately. This means that detection detects the attacks in progress, and reaction rapidly improves defenses. Remember, security programs only fail when the adversary achieves their goal. Even if an attacker is successful in defeating protection, they are not successful until they accomplish their goal. Proaction is the act of ensuring adversaries do not achieve their goal.

CHAPTER 4

Risk Management

Security is about risk management. Security itself is unattainable. The actual definition of security is being free from risk. You can never be free from risk. If you have anything of value, there is always risk.

There is always a risk of value being compromised. As described in an earlier example, even if you bury a computer in a hole, it means that the data and computer are unavailable, so you have lost all your value. In this case, the loss is self-inflicted. However, frequently the loss is neither complete nor self-inflicted.

DEATH BY 1000 CUTS

When you think of loss, you think catastrophic losses. You think of a total loss that costs hundreds of millions of dollars, like the infamous Target and Sony attacks. The reality is that most losses are small and individually inconsequential. However, when considered in the aggregate, they can be more devastating than a single loss of the nature of the Sony attack.

It is the philosophy of *Death by 1000 Cuts*. The analogy goes that an individual cut is inconsequential and maybe slightly painful. However, when you have 1000 cuts, it is 1000 times more painful and the blood loss becomes critical. This is representative of the losses experienced by most security programs.

A virus incident. A lost USB drive. A file accidentally sent to the wrong person. A power outage that takes down an operations center for a few hours. All these experiences are common and frequent. Unfortunately, most organizations see these losses as something to deal with, but do not consider them a major problem worthy of significant efforts.

Several decades ago, there was the principle of total quality management, which revolved around the concept that when a small defect percentage in each phase of a process, although seemingly inconsequential, is aggregated over many phases of the process, it creates a significant defect rate. So, for example, if there was a 1% defect rate at each of the 10 phases of a manufacturing process, it results in a 10% overall defect rate, which is significant. Security programs and their resulting losses are similar in nature.

27

Advanced Persistent Security. http://dx.doi.org/10.1016/B978-0-12-809316-0.00004-X

So as we start discussing risk management, it is important to understand that a security program has to account for small losses as much as the large losses.

UNDERSTANDING RISK

You need to understand the components of risk, so that you know how to manage those components and therefore risk as a whole. Although there are many ways to describe and quantify risk, we use the simple formula that uses value, threat, vulnerabilities, and countermeasures as the components of risk.

The following formula represents those components mathematically. Although a formula implies that there can be a quantifiable number or dollar figure representing loss, this is not the purpose of this book. There are specific disciplines that attempt to quantify risk, such as actuarial science, for business purposes. It would, however, behoove the reader to look further into being able to quantify risk.

$$Risk = \left(\frac{Threat * Vulnerability}{Countermeasure} \right) * Value$$

Consider value as the entire value of an organization that is at risk. The combination of threat, vulnerability, and countermeasures represents the probability that the value can be lost. Threat and vulnerability add to the probability of loss, whereas countermeasures decrease the probability of loss. So essentially, how much you have at risk is a function of how well you mitigate your vulnerability and threat.

Value

Value is left outside the base equation because it represents the maximum loss. The other factors are only relevant in that they either increase or decrease the risk to your overall value. Either way, value is what you have to lose. Value can take many forms, and you need to consider all forms of value when you consider the risk that you need to address.

Each form of value creates a different type of loss and can be compromised by different types of vulnerabilities. For example, monetary value can be compromised by physical vulnerabilities, whereas reputation value can be compromised by lack of computer availability. For the purpose of this book, we are not going to go into detail on all forms of value. However, it is important to be aware of the general principle of where loss can originate and to truly understand business concerns.

It is also important to consider that value can be lost in multiple categories from a single incident. For example, when an airline computer system goes down, planes can be grounded, incurring a monetary loss. However, the airline will also take a reputational hit, as people will associate decreased reliability with the airline.

Monetary Value

Monetary value is the simplest to understand. It is the clear loss of money in one form or another. Monetary loss equates to a clear and immediate loss of money. For example, if you lose cash, you lose the value of the cash. If the computer network goes down and you cannot charge people for the services provided by the network, you lose the money you would have made from the network being up.

When a tangible loss can be potentially attributed to a security-related incident, it is considered monetary loss. When you think of risk as a whole, it is easy to say that the potential monetary losses can justify a security budget. For example, if you are protecting $1,000,000 in a safe, you can justify a reasonable amount to invest in the safe. It is therefore to a security program's advantage to determine all potential monetary values being protected it to justify the maximum potential security budget.

Reputation Value

Reputation value, sometimes referred to as brand value, is the perceived value of a brand or organization. Brands such as Tylenol, IBM, Coke, and Apple have very significant value. When Tylenol was the victim of product tampering, there was actually an insignificant monetary loss. However, the damage to the reputation of the brand almost created a complete loss of $100,000,000 per year revenue stream for Johnson & Johnson.

In this case, in 1982, someone went into the stores and placed Tylenol packages on the shelves with legitimate packages. The tampered packages contained Tylenol doses laced with cyanide. To protect the brand, Tylenol spent millions to recall all products on the shelves around the United States. They spent more to redesign their packaging to protect future tampering. They likewise spent millions of dollars to publicize everything they were doing. So for not having actually experienced a direct loss to any of their own assets, there was almost a loss of billions of dollars.

When consumers or others place trust in a company, the potential for the trust to be lost must be a consideration in risk planning. It is admittedly difficult, if not impossible, to predict all potential areas or incidents where trust or reputation can be lost. Tylenol would have never predicted exactly how the product tampering would have occurred, as such incidents never happened before. Subway would have never predicted that its spokesperson, Jared Fogle, would have been arrested for something as heinous as child sexual abuse. However, you do need to at least consider and brainstorm as many areas as possible. But remember, just because there is a potential risk to the value, it does not necessarily mean that you need to account for the risk. You should at least attempt to consider it.

Sometimes there is dilution of reputation or trust, where another party misappropriates your brand. Counterfeit parts are a significant problem in the manufacturing field, with fake chips and other computer parts making their way into a legitimate supply chain. The counterfeit chips can result in revenue loss, and they are also less reliable and can cause the breakdown of systems.

Counterfeits with inferior quality plague many industries. Pharmaceutical companies face revenue loss as well as potential liability because of counterfeit drugs. Even Beachbody, a company that produces widely successful DVD-based exercise programs such as P90X and Insanity, is subject to reputational damage, because many counterfeit DVDs are of inferior quality, and the purchasers of counterfeit DVDs blame Beachbody, because the counterfeit DVDs frequently do not play properly.

Reputation value can take many forms and you need to attempt to determine how the value can be compromised in the design of your security program.

Opportunity Value

When considering value, you need to consider the value of opportunities that could be gained or lost. For example, if you make a choice that you are not going to allow the use of personal devices in a corporate network, you are missing the potential productivity value obtained by having the extra ability to communicate with employees, or you need to decide that you will pay for the employees' devices.

If you fail to enter a market, because you cannot provide the appropriate security, you are losing value. For example, many companies delayed e-commerce activities, because they were afraid that they could not handle online attacks. Some organizations cannot be compliant with the Payment Card Industry (PCI) Data Security Standard or other standards, so they cannot go into different lines of business.

Although there are clearly many different opportunities to be gained or lost, it is critical to determine if security can provide additional value or if the lack of security can inhibit value. In some cases, such value is clear. More frequently, it does take some creativity to examine the different potential areas where value can be created or lost by security controls.

Threat

Threat is another element that adds to risk. Threats are essentially entities or events that can cause you harm given the opportunity. Although threat will be discussed in detail in Chapter 6, here it is important to understand how threat contributes to risk.

Threats require an opportunity to cause you harm, and you must consider that they are always there. Some threats are there because of who you are or what you do. These threats arise because of the value that you have innately or that you create. For example, a bank has money and criminals who want the money will attempt to steal it. An organization with personally identifiable information (PII) has information that an identity thief might want. Oil exploration companies have computer models that help them determine where oil reserves are and how large those reserves may be, which attracts the attention of governments wanting to obtain the best price for drilling rights, competitors who want to know the same information, and countless other parties.

Then there are threats that will always exist no matter who you are or what you do. For example, hurricanes, earthquakes, floods, and other natural disasters will always exist. They can potentially cause you harm, if you leave your assets vulnerable to their effects.

There are also categories of people or entities common to all organizations. For example, well-meaning employees will make mistakes and create damage of some sort. There are also malicious insiders, who are inevitable. These individuals will attempt to cause as much harm as possible, or in other words, ruin the value of your organization. The value they compromise is determined by what is available to be compromised.

The higher the probability of the existence of threats to exploit an organization, the higher the potential risk. To determine the overall Risk, it is important to determine which threats potentially exist.

Once you know they exist, you can then use that information to determine the methods and resources used to compromise an organization. For example, if you assume that there is a likelihood of power outages because of natural events, you can determine the potential need to install generators or uninterruptable power supplies. If you know that the Chinese government may target your organization, you know that they might expend unlimited resources and begin their attacks with phishing methods. Knowledge of the threats will help identify the potential countermeasures to be implemented.

Vulnerability

Vulnerabilities are essentially the weaknesses that allows threats to exploit an organization. Vulnerabilities are covered in Chapter 9 in detail, but regarding risk, it is important to understand that vulnerabilities enable risk. Threats will always exist, and an organization or other entity will innately have value, but vulnerabilities are those that create the inevitable compromise of value.

In short, a threat may exist, but if there are no vulnerabilities for the threat to exploit, then there would be no risk. For example, although there will always be hurricanes in Florida, if you do not have any facilities or critical assets in Florida, you are not susceptible to the damage a hurricane can cause. On the other hand, if you have a data center, a large number of employees, supplies being shipped through Miami, or other resources, you have left your organization extremely vulnerable to suffer loss. The vulnerabilities can be poor power supplies, poor connectivity and communications, supply chain issues, limited data availability, etc.

People are not necessarily considered a vulnerability, but poor awareness on the part of the users is. What is the difference? Such person is an actor who is neither good nor bad, and will always exist. However, the person's behavior is the vulnerability. If the person chooses a weak password, the password is the vulnerability. The person can choose to click on a phishing message or not. The action of the person can be either a countermeasure or a vulnerability. Poor awareness, a vulnerability, will cause the person to create a potential loss. Strong awareness, a countermeasure, will cause the user to report the message, or at least not take a harmful action.

However, not all vulnerabilities need to be mitigated. It might be too expensive to mitigate a vulnerability. For example, the potential loss might not justify the cost of mitigating the vulnerability. Likewise, although a vulnerability might exist, it might not be likely exploited or it might not yield a loss.

For example, if you have a forklift in the middle of a large warehouse in a secluded area, it is unlikely that leaving the keys in the forklift would result in damage or loss. It is unlikely to be stolen, and few people would take it for a joyride.

Categories of Vulnerability

Vulnerability can be divided into four different categories: physical, operational, personnel, and technical. Physical vulnerabilities are broadly vulnerabilities that require a physical presence to exploit. For example, locks that are not locked are a physical vulnerability. Computers left logged on and otherwise unprotected are physically vulnerable to compromise.

Operational vulnerabilities relate to how organizations do business. Excessive information posted on a website is an operational vulnerability. A weak process that allows for someone to change the password on an account is an operational vulnerability.

Personnel vulnerabilities relate to the recruitment, hiring, and termination process. Although these are clearly operational issues in some ways, as organizations rely heavily on the trust they place in their employees, it is something to consider separately. There are also frequently legal and ethical questions that distinguish this category of vulnerabilities.

Technical vulnerabilities relate to a weakness that allows for an attack against computers, networks, and related technologies. These are generally related to how the technology is designed, configured, or maintained. For example, you can set up a computer to be accessible to the world. There are bugs in commercially available software and in custom-developed software that provide holes to attackers.

Again, all these vulnerabilities will be discussed in Chapter 9, so here they are introduced, so that you are aware of how vulnerabilities essentially create risk.

Countermeasures

Countermeasures are what you do to mitigate threats or vulnerabilities. In theory, you can reduce risk by mitigating the value. After all, if you have nothing of value, you have no risk. However, reducing value to reduce risk is basically destructive. Again, security programs want to optimize risk and retain value. Anyone who consciously attempts to reduce value should be removed from their position.

Regarding mitigating threat, the reality is that it is difficult to mitigate threat. For example, you can never mitigate the occurrence of a hurricane. Unless you are a government agency, you cannot really mitigate the existence of a terrorist group or even script kiddie hackers. Admittedly you can fire employees, but that is a single type of threat within your control. This implies one of the most critical issues for a countermeasure; it has to target something that is within your control.

Vulnerabilities are frequently within your control, and are more readily mitigated. For example, although you cannot mitigate a hurricane in Florida, you can reduce the critical assets that could be susceptible to the effects of a hurricane, such as you can avoid placing a computer operations center in the area that would be susceptible to flooding and power outages and be difficult for employees to get to the facility during the hurricane.

Although you cannot stop entities from targeting computer accounts, poor passwords, which are considered a technical vulnerability, can be prevented through various countermeasures. When the vulnerability is mitigated, it prevents the opportunity for any threat to exploit it. So, for example, if there is a bank account that has a bad password, any bad actor can attempt to exploit it. This includes hackers, foreign intelligence agencies, malicious insiders, or any other parties. Removing vulnerabilities removes the opportunity for the threats to cause harm.

Countermeasures can be categorized into the same four categories as vulner-abilities: physical, operational, personnel, and technical. Physical counter-measures involve putting physical controls in place. For example, locks and fences restrict access. Guards can stop people from entering buildings. Infor-mation in a locked desk is not readily available to people wandering the facilities.

Operational countermeasures are processes in place to mitigate vulnerabilities. Poor awareness can be addressed by awareness training. To ensure administra-tors cannot cause excessive damage, a process can be implemented to separate administrative functions between two people. Reviews of information releases is also an operational countermeasure.

Personnel countermeasures may resemble operational countermeasures, but they focus on personnel-related issues, such as hiring, human resources pol-icies, and separation procedures. Background checks are considered a personnel countermeasure. Policies to ensure collection of information on employee sep-aration is a personnel countermeasure.

Technical countermeasures are as broad as technology. We will go into these in detail; however, they include technologies for protection, detection, and reac-tion to attacks. Poor passwords are considered an operational vulnerability and they can be addressed by using password policies, which are an operational countermeasure. Token authentication is a technical countermeasure that can also mitigate poor passwords. Technical countermeasures will be discussed in more detail throughout the book.

As previously noted, it is important to realize that countermeasures do not have to be in the same category as the vulnerabilities that they address. Again, token-based authentication (a technical countermeasure) can mitigate an operational vulnerability of poor passwords. An operation process of regular data backups can mitigate the technical vulnerability of hard-drive crashes. It is therefore important that when you consider risk as a whole, you consider all forms of countermeasures in determining how to mitigate a vulnerability.

Possibly the most important consideration for countermeasures is that they are not expected to be perfect. There is no such thing as a perfect countermeasure. You must realize that all countermeasures will eventually fail.

The real test of a countermeasure is whether it mitigated more loss than the cost of implementing it. For example, if you spend $100,000 on implementing an awareness program and there are an estimated six incidents prevented, with each incident estimated at costing $50,000, the awareness program created a net savings of $200,000. Countermeasures are not expected to be perfect, but to be less expensive than the losses incurred.

Although a failure in a countermeasure and the resulting loss is not desired, the reality is that every failure and loss has to be looked at in perspective to the other incidents prevented. There are admittedly many cases where an organization grossly underestimates the potential loss. For example, the Sony CIO was quoted years ago as saying that he did not want to spend $10,000,000 to prevent a $1,000,000 loss, and that makes complete sense. However, the loss from the hack by North Korea, with all the residual effects, is estimated at well above $100,000,000. The countermeasures in question would have likely cost well under $10,000,000. Clearly, if you are making grand claims, you need to ensure that there is a legitimate examination of the real potential costs and the real losses.

RISK OPTIMIZATION VERSUS RISK MINIMIZATION

When people hear about risk management, they assume that it means to get rid of as much risk as possible. In other words, they assume the goal is to minimize potential loss or risk, but this is not the case.

The goal is to *optimize* risk.

Minimizing risk implies that you will try to reduce every potential loss. You will implement every possible countermeasure that you can think of. The cost to protect against a loss can outweigh the potential loss. In an extreme example, you might want to protect a piece of jewelry from theft. You can theoretically hire a team of guards to guard the jewelry 24 hours a day. If you are talking about a $500 necklace, you would be wasting money. There might be some sentimental value tied to the necklace, so it might be worth some extra protections; however, it is likely not justification for the expense of hiring guards.

Risk optimization requires making a conscious decision about what is the appropriate balance between loss and the level of effort you are willing to put into mitigating the loss. Ideally, you find the optimum balance.

Fig. 4.1 depicts the relationship between countermeasures and vulnerabilities. When there are no countermeasures, both vulnerabilities and potential loss are at their maximum. The area below the vulnerabilities curve represents potential loss or value at risk.

As countermeasures are implemented, and the assumption is that the countermeasures are relevant, vulnerabilities are mitigated and potential loss is reduced. Generally, a significant amount of risk can be mitigated with simple and basic countermeasures. For that reason, the potential loss quickly decreases.

There is the 80/20 rule that implies that 80% of problems can be solved with 20% of effort. With security, it is much more like the 95/5 rule, where 95% of problems can be solved with 5% of effort. Although this does not intend to

FIGURE 4.1
Vulnerabilities versus countermeasures.

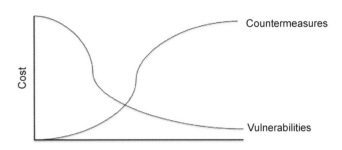

imply that you ignore the 5%, it does imply that the appropriate countermeasures can quickly mitigate a substantial amount of loss.

If the goal of a security program is risk minimization, the implication is that they would want to go as far to the right on Fig. 4.1 as possible. That would theoretically reduce potential loss to near zero. The graph specifically implies loss will never be zero. However, when you look at the countermeasure line, you see that the cost of countermeasures is significantly more than the potential loss. Your security program is therefore costing your organization more money than it would save. So risk minimization is not a reasonable goal.

An obvious point on the graph that represents the appropriate balance between countermeasures and vulnerabilities is where they both intersect, which is not ideal. In other words, you are investing as much on your security program as you can possibly lose. The reality is that except on very rare occasions, an organization will not lose complete value. So even at the point of intersection, you are spending more money on security than you are likely to lose.

Fig. 4.2 highlights the concept of risk optimization, where you are making a conscious determination of the appropriate level of risk you are willing to accept and determine the cost of the security program that will get you there. It is important to note that the level of potential loss is greater than the cost of the countermeasures being implemented. There should be a notable difference between these entities, as a complete loss is not likely.

FIGURE 4.2
Risk optimization.

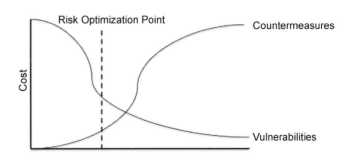

You must first determine the amount of loss you are willing to accept. Currently, it is typical that a security program is provided with a random budget, sometimes a specific percentage in the overall information technology (IT) budget, without regard to the losses the security programs are expected to prevent. There is, therefore, no relationship between the security program's budget and the actual requirements that the security program is supposed to satisfy. This is important to understand, as it is a critical issue that will lead to the failure of the security program.

It is important to understand that the IT budget, a traditional indicator of a security budget, should be irrelevant to the funding of a security program. If you run the security program of a bank, you need to understand that you are not protecting the computers, but the money that flows through your computers. If a bank has a $100,000,000 IT budget, it is of course substantial. However, those computers are likely handling hundreds of billions of dollars of transactions a year, which the bank needs to protect and budget accordingly.

Clearly, the bank should not invest that much money into their security program. However, basing it on the IT budget is ludicrous.

PRACTICAL IMPLEMENTATION

Although it would admittedly be outstanding for all organizations to reengineer their security programs and budgets, it is unlikely to imminently happen. It is easier to execute risk optimization and budget justification on a vulnerability-by-vulnerability basis. For example, if you know the Chinese are likely to attack you, and can use a phishing campaign, you might want to implement multi-factor authentication to mitigate the damage caused by a user divulging their password. Multifactor authentication prevents a wide variety of social engineering attacks, and also mitigates a large number of requests for password resets.

You can then estimate the cost for the multifactor authentication, such as token authentication, which might be $1,000,000. You then need to estimate the cost of likely incidents, as well as the costs associated with password resets. So, from the previously described Sony hack, the cost of a single incident was in excess of $100,000,000. There are also more regular small-scale incidents to include. You then have a business case, where the investment of $1,000,000 can mitigate potentially more than $100,000,000 of damage.

GETTING THE BUDGET YOU NEED, NOT THE BUDGET YOU DESERVE

Finally, we need to discuss the problem with many security managers who typically complain that they are not provided with enough of a budget to implement what they believe are adequate security programs. Our response tends to be sympathetic, but we advise them that they get the budgets they deserve, not the budgets they need.

Although this is clearly a bit of a Pollyanna statement, we believe that, in general, security managers can get a sufficient budget, if they can make a good business case. Typically, security managers are asked to prepare a budget, and they put a budget together based on what they have and what they want. Barring any significant incidents, they will usually get their current budget and maybe a more specific percentage. This makes sense because security is typically considered an operational expense without a return on investment.

As we previously described, organizations have to look logically at all the values that are at risk. They can look at the vulnerabilities that place that value at risk and begin to prioritize the vulnerabilities that need to be mitigated. Simultaneously, they need to consider the threat. Although threat cannot be mitigated for the most part, it tells you the likely methods of attack, as well as the resources that will be invested in the attack.

If you know that China is a likely threat to your organization, you can assume that a large amount of resources will be invested in targeting your organization. You know that it will likely attempt to begin an attack with spear phishing messages and that it will plant malware in the network, and likely compromise critical servers, such as the email and other communications servers.

This information also helps to prioritize which vulnerabilities should be mitigated, as you know the likely vulnerabilities to be targeted and how to potentially detect attempted and successful attacks.

Using the previous example justifying the cost of multifactor authentication, you can see that there is a tangible benefit in implementing the countermeasure.

In this way, you are making a case for your budget. You are deserving of your budget. If you do not get the budget, then you have at least made the best case and your management is assuming the responsibility for any loss.

You need to be able to go to your management for each and every countermeasure and say, "I would like $XX,XXX, so I can specifically purchase this countermeasure. With that countermeasure, I will save $YYY,YYY,YYY." At that point, you are making a business case to have your budget raised. This puts your management on notice that they are making decisions that will either save or cost money for the organization.

If, however, you cannot make your case, you should not buy the countermeasure in question, as it is a waste of money.

So when we describe that people get the budgets they deserve, and not the budgets they need, they are doing an insufficient job making the business case for what they need the budget for.

You may not always get the budget you deserve, but the goal is to deserve more. When you receive the budget that you actually need, you know you are successfully deserving the budget you need.

At the time of this writing, cybersecurity is one of the top concerns for organizations in all industries. There is a perceived need for better security, so make sure you take advantage of that by being deserving of the budget you need.

CHAPTER 5

How to Hack Computers

This content was initially intended to be a piece of another chapter; however, it is hard to talk about securing computers, networks, and other technologic assets without a fundamental understanding of how they can be compromised. Although this chapter is comparatively small, it is important to understand this concept before talking about how to protect computers. Although many people might know this material, it is important to establish a baseline of knowledge.

It is important to note that we almost oversimplify what hacking is, and for the purpose of understanding the rest of the material, it is acceptable. Most studies indicate that 97% of hacks should have been prevented, if basic countermeasures, such as keeping software updated and properly maintaining the software, were in place. Most hacks were embarrassingly simple to accomplish and relied more on the insecurity of the victim rather than on the genius of the perpetrator.

Even when you are dealing with nation-state attacks, they typically compromise an organization with as little sophistication as possible. Clearly after initially compromising an organization, the sophistication exhibited by an attacker can vary greatly. A greater indication of the sophistication of hacking is the effectiveness of accomplishing desired goals and maintaining the secrecy of the compromise.

For now, we will define a "hack" as gaining unauthorized access to a system or the data stored on the system. Once an attacker has compromised a system, there are likely other activities performed. This chapter specifically refers to how to break into (gain unauthorized access to) computers and computer networks.

SECURITY RESEARCHERS

People who focus on finding new ways of exploiting computers are called *security researchers*. In a pure sense, a security researcher should examine products

41

for the existence of vulnerabilities. A true security researcher has a great deal of technical talent. As discussed in Chapter 4, vulnerabilities are built into software or enabled by system configurations. Security researchers find those vulnerabilities that are not yet known. This is a critical contribution to all major hacking efforts.

It is common for researchers to specialize in a specific type of hardware or software. Some researchers work for an organization that pays them to perform their research, whereas most researchers are independent and do it for a sense of accomplishment and/or money. There are bug bounty programs that pay for previously unknown bugs, or the researcher may sell the information to a party who will use it for their own purposes.

These people might create hacking tools or scripts to automate the attack against the vulnerabilities that they find. These tools allow someone with no skill to exercise what might otherwise be a highly complex attack. It is common for many of these tools to be used by criminals of all skill levels, as there is no reason to duplicate the effort.

However, we do not generally have a great deal of respect for the typical hacker who downloads these tools and runs them. Security researchers have a great deal of talent. How they choose to demonstrate their talent is, however, controversial. Some researchers exercise what is referred to as "responsible disclosure," and provide the information to the affected software vendor or to a bug bounty program such as, HackerOne, so that the problems can be fixed before they are exploited. Other "researchers" seem to want the pride of publicly claiming the vulnerability discovery and issue what they refer to as "proof of concept" code, which is essentially a hacking tool to exploit systems that have little chance of being protected.

TWO WAYS TO HACK A COMPUTER OR OTHER TECHNOLOGY

There are many methods to break into a computer or computer network, but they all can be grouped into two broad methods: compromising software vulnerabilities and compromising how a computer is configured, used, or maintained. All other hacking methods are different variations of these methods.

Although this material is intended to describe how to get a foothold in the targeted computer, network, or system, as an attacker proceeds, he/she is likely to take advantage of other software vulnerabilities or configurations issues. Typically, attacks involve a string of exploitations. For example, the Sony attack, discussed in Chapter 1, involved a spear phishing attack targeting administrators to get initial access and exploiting various configuration issues to get to the business network, various technologies to gain access to servers and other systems, and exploited other issues to evade detection and exfiltrate large volumes of data. There are clearly many simple attacks, such as an attacker exploiting a vulnerability on a website and then downloading all data on that system; however, all systems may be attacked.

Software Vulnerabilities

Software vulnerabilities involve bugs in software. Bugs are coding errors that cause the system to make an unwanted action. All software has bugs of one form or another. Some bugs cause the system to crash, some cause connectivity to fail, some do not let a person to log in, and some cause printing not to work properly.

Some bugs create information leakage or elevate user privileges or grant otherwise unauthorized access. These are security vulnerabilities. If all software has bugs and it is inevitable that some bugs will be security vulnerabilities, all software will have security vulnerabilities.

It is important to consider that just about every device has software, and therefore security vulnerabilities. Operating systems are composed of software, as are web browsers, word processing programs, spreadsheets, video players, websites, and every other application. Even computer hardware includes a form of software called firmware. Networking equipment and cell phones also have software, and therefore inevitably security vulnerabilities.

In the technical media, you will hear about "buffer overflows." Buffer overflows are forms of security vulnerabilities that frequently give a potential attacker full control of the computer. Cross-site scripting (XSS) errors are a type of coding error where a malicious party can trigger execution of software from their browser. SQL injection attacks are also an attack against websites that allow illicit access to or manipulation of the back-end databases.

An easy example to understand is when the author Ira Winkler found a vulnerability on the website of a popular computer industry publication. He received a link to renew his subscription and noticed that the link contained a six-digit number. When he clicked the link, his subscription information appeared, including his personal details and contact information. He then changed the six-digit number and someone else's information appeared. He realized that he could write a program that could download the entire subscriber base by sequentially entering all numbers in the range of 1—999,999. The website was not written in a way to encrypt the subscriber number.

Some software comes from vendors, such as Microsoft, Adobe, and Cisco. However, a good portion of software is written by website owners and other parties. This custom software is also vulnerable to security vulnerabilities. XSS and SQL infection attacks are often enabled by custom-designed software.

You do not expect a company to knowingly release software with security vulnerabilities. Most bugs are found only after use by millions of users. Security vulnerabilities are generally found after the software has been released to the public. Some vulnerabilities might never be found, and there is no way of knowing when a vulnerability will be discovered. When a vulnerability is found, in the ideal situation, the vulnerability will be reported to the software developer, who will release a correction. For example, Microsoft AutoUpdate automatically installs updates for Microsoft Office when fixes for security vulnerabilities are available.

However, some vulnerabilities are not properly reported and a fix (a.k.a. patch) is not available. These vulnerabilities are called zero-day vulnerabilities; in other words, if you are running that software and if an attacker can access your computer or system, then the attacker can successfully hack you. It is important to state that even if a patch is available, if you do not install that patch, you can likewise be hacked. This will be discussed further in Chapter 10.

Depending on which study you read, software vulnerabilities enable approximately 30% of all successful attacks. This number is highly substantial, as it implies billions of dollars of loss occurring because of what is mostly a preventable problem.

The Vulnerability Life Cycle

We will operate under the assumption that a vendor does not release software knowing that there is an existing security vulnerability. We realize that this does happen, but that is a separate issue. After the software is released, in some way, the vulnerability is discovered. Once it is discovered, in the ideal world, the developer is notified of the vulnerability and can then create a patch.

If the patch is on the developers' own systems, such as a website, the problem has been successfully avoided. But if the patch involves the software in a user's computer, the vendor has to make the patch available to the end users and notify them, and then the end users have to install the patch.

The last part is where problems occur. It is very common for users, including administrators within organizations, to not implement the patches in a timely manner, if at all. Billions of dollars have been lost because of criminals exploiting vulnerabilities that should have been patched.

One of the most widely publicized bugs was the Heartbleed vulnerability discovered in April 2014. The headlines blazed, "Foundation of the Internet Vulnerable." It was the top news story on national news programs. It was discussed widely throughout social media. It was impossible not to hear about it. Patches were then quickly made available. However, in April 2015, *Fortune* magazine reported that 74% of the Fortune 2000 companies still had systems that were vulnerable to the Heartbleed attack. In September 2015, *The Register* reported that more than 200,000 Internet-connected systems were still vulnerable to Heartbleed. Remember, this is for a vulnerability that was a top international news story. Imagine what happens with vulnerabilities that are nowhere nearly as widely publicized.

Also consider that if the problem is not properly reported, the vulnerability allows for zero-day attacks, and potential victims have no opportunity to protect themselves.

Configuration Vulnerabilities

Configuration vulnerabilities relate to how systems are configured, maintained, and used. As implied in the previous section, approximately 70% of all hacks result from configuration vulnerabilities. With these vulnerabilities, the software itself does not have any known vulnerabilities. It is dependent completely on the implementation of the systems.

For example, an otherwise secure computer system can grant users too many permissions. Servers may share their directories too broadly. Data is placed on a website available to the public. There are unlimited methods to take an otherwise secure system and configure it to be insecure.

The previous examples involve how administrators configure their systems. There are many ways by which users also put data at risk. For example: (1) users can click on phishing messages and download malicious software or divulge their login credentials, (2) they can download data to a USB drive and lose it, (3) they can leave a laptop computer in their car for it to be stolen, or (4) they can leave their computer unlocked and unattended, and let a malicious person walk up and access the system.

In the ideal world, there are formal processes in place to establish and maintain a secure configuration, or software baseline. There is regular testing to ensure that system configurations are not modified and remain secure over time. There should also be regular awareness training and audits to ensure that users are aware of proper behaviors. However, as previously stated, 70% of all successful hacks result from configuration vulnerabilities.

TECHNOLOGY IS IRRELEVANT

Although many people will say that we are oversimplifying computer hacking, and to a certain extent that is true, the reality is that all hacks result from compromising the underlying software, or the way the software is implemented and maintained. It does not matter if you are talking about a Windows or Unix computer or about a router or a PC, the software needs to be written properly, implemented properly, and patched properly. If any aspect of this cycle fails, the computer or system can be hacked. This is also frequently referred to as practicing good cyber hygiene.

Just about any, if not all, potential hacks can be grouped into these two categories. Although there may be exceptions, they provide a working model for the importance of proper maintenance and administration, and a good foundation for Advanced Persistent Security (APS).

CHAPTER 6

Threat

Threats are the *who* or *what* that can do you harm, if provided with the opportunity. Although this sounds fairly simple and straightforward, there are many considerations when discussing threats. The implications of threats can determine how you design your program, respond to incidents, and handle everything related.

The intent of this chapter is not to provide an exhaustive list of potential threats that an organization may face. If that was the goal, there could be an entire book on the subject, let alone an individual chapter. More importantly, although it might provide general interest with some clear value, such a comprehensive description would not be a good use of your time.

To be proactive, you need to be able to understand and potentially anticipate the actions of your potential and actual attackers. You need to be able to adjust your countermeasures not only in a reactionary manner, but also in a manner that is most likely to disrupt the attackers and reduces losses.

Although we provide the definition of some specific threats, the focus is on threat categorization and concepts. If you come away from this chapter with an understanding on the categories of threats you face, the general motivations of threats, the resources attackers can use to target your organization, and the damage they intend to inflict, you should have sufficient understanding to create Advanced Persistent Security.

WHY THREATS ARE IMPORTANT TO CONSIDER

Threats determine the likelihood for a vulnerability to be exploited. They determine the resources that may be expended to compromise your value. The reality is that if a vulnerability fundamentally exists, any threat can exploit it, but knowing the threats you face can better help you prioritize vulnerabilities that need to be mitigated and the resources you need to put toward the countermeasures you choose to implement.

Advanced Persistent Security. http://dx.doi.org/10.1016/B978-0-12-809316-0.00006-3

Although the Chinese government is frequently maligned and overused as a threat actor, it is a legitimate and potential threat. If you can assume that you are a potential target of the Chinese cyberespionage, you can determine likely attack vectors. For example, China has been known to unknowingly co-opt Chinese nationals who work inside a targeted organization. Therefore, you know that the possibility of a malicious insider, with legitimate access, is a source of concern.

Another common attack vector is to use spear phishing messages targeting specific users. If the messages are successful, the attackers will then install malware on the targeted network. Communications and file servers will be compromised and monitored. Other systems will be compromised to serve as exfiltration servers. When you know the modus operandi, you know how to mitigate the appropriate vulnerabilities and to set up detection capabilities.

You also know the potential damage the threat intends to inflict. For example, although the Chinese have sometimes retaliated out of anger, and intended to cause random damage, they usually do not intend to inflict obvious harm on the victim. Their intent is frequently information gathering, which they can do without damaging the underlying network. In some cases, the Chinese may have actually stabilized the targeted network to ensure that their own software runs properly.

Thus it is not likely that there will be direct damage caused by Chinese hackers. They will not steal money. They will not damage the network. The information thefts will not be leaked to the general public. If there are losses, they will generally be due to lost revenues months or years later. There are also intelligence-related hacks that may compromise the identity of spies or allow China to create advanced weapons. You can assume that if China has successfully attacked you, all information on your network can expected to be compromised. The effects might not be immediate, but can be felt for decades to come.

You can compare these goals with those of hacktivists, who intend to embarrass or create immediate damage to their targets. They might not care about critical information, but want to damage your assets as best they can. However, the results are very short term. In many ways, North Korea's attack against Sony seems to be much more similar to a hacktivist attack than an attack by a nation-state. As you can see, being aware of the specific threats targeting you can tell you the scope of the potential loss, the targets, and the likely defense and detection strategies.

WHO THREATS VERSUS *WHAT* THREATS

When people think of threats they typically think of people, governments, criminals, and other people. *Who* threats are important to consider. These are entities that can take specific actions to cause harm. There is intelligence behind their actions. Although many actions may be purposeful, actions that are non-purposeful can also cause harm. Anyone with access, or can obtain access, can potentially cause damage to information or other computer assets.

You cannot underestimate the potential damage caused by a person who can take either intentional or unintentional actions. A person who can take intentional acts can significantly damage an organization and potentially cause irreparable harm that can completely destroy an organization.

An example of who threat includes the terrorist attack by Osama bin Laden, who masterminded the destruction of the World Trade Center and caused significant damage to the Pentagon. Besides the 3,000 deaths, there was an economic impact of up to $13 billion.

But consider the damage caused by Hurricane Sandy in 2012, which also affected New York. Although the loss of life was not nearly as large as the terrorist attack, the total damage was estimated at approximately $75 billion. Thousands of people were displaced, with many being permanently displaced. Hurricane Sandy, however, caused only a fraction of the damage caused by Hurricane Katrina in 2005, which caused approximately $125 billion in damage. In total, since the September 11, 2001, attacks, hurricanes have caused more than $350 billion in damage.

Hurricanes are thus considered as *what* type of threats. The *what* threats, including random power outages, car accidents, spills, snowstorms, and water main breaks, can cause damages beyond a terrorist's wildest dreams.

What threats have no intent. Although some *what* threats are man-made, such as foreseeable power failures caused by poorly maintained equipment, unless they are intentionally caused, they are more events than acts.

It is important to understand that these threats contribute to the risk you face. They need to be accounted for within your security program. What you might also need to consider is that sometimes *what* threats create opportunities for *who* threats. For example, after Hurricane Katrina, looters and a general state of lawlessness created even more risk to organizations.

In designing security programs, you need to ensure that you consider both the *what* and *who* types of threats.

MALIGNANT THREATS VERSUS MALICIOUS THREATS

When you consider threat, you need to understand the difference between malignant and malicious threats. There is too much focus on malicious threats, which ironically cause a relatively small percentage of the losses that organizations experience.

It is easiest to start the discussion with malicious threats. Malicious threats are those threats that intentionally cause you harm. They actively target you and look for ways to inflict damage.

Malicious threats are again the most obvious. These include petty criminals, organized criminals, hacktivists, competitors, vendors, customers, nation-states, and especially, malicious insiders. Although some of these threats target you solely because you exist and have something of value, others are motivated by political or personal goals. These threats are likely to attempt to cause you the most harm; however, they may or may not be capable of inflicting the damage they intend to.

Malignant threats are threats that just exist. These include weather-related issues, faulty equipment, flooding, unreliable technical infrastructures, and accidents. Malignant threats can frequently be predicted to one level or another. As previously mentioned, hurricanes cause a significant amount of damage throughout the Atlantic coastal region of the United States. Tornados are a major threat primarily to the central US region.

As described with Hurricanes Katrina and Sandy, malignant threats have caused more damage than malicious threats ever could. Human error is a major source of loss as well. Although people may be involved, they are not malicious, but can unintentionally cause immense damage. Every administrator has likely caused substantial data loss because of carelessness, fatigue, poor training, and countless other issues. Users have accidentally spilled coffee on countless computers, costing the world's economy likely hundreds of millions of dollars of damage. Lost computers, USB drives, or other computing assets have likewise created immense loss.

We have both received and sent emails that had people on the distribution who should not have received the emails. Mail clients make it too easy to accidentally enter an inappropriate recipient onto an email message. For example, when you start typing the name "Michael", into the recipient field, it is likely that many Michaels come up because of autofill, and it is easy to choose the wrong one. Sometimes the sender might choose the right recipient, but with an outdated address, which will go to the recipient's former employer instead of the intended recipient at the new employer.

Although people fear terrorists, throughout the first-world countries, automobile accidents cause exponentially more deaths and losses than terrorists. The same is true for obesity. When considering overall risk, you need to ensure that you account for malignant threats as much as, if not more than, malicious threats.

Prioritizing Malignant Threats Over Malicious Threats

After the September 11 attacks, there was a thorough review of potential threats to large urban areas. A threat that was identified was that railroad cars that carry chemicals are required to have a Hazardous Material, or HAZMAT, placard on the car, with a number that identifies the type of chemical the car is carrying. Homeland security officials realized that a terrorist could potentially identify a railroad car that is transporting harmful chemicals, such as chlorine, and attack that specific car, which could potentially kill hundreds or thousands of people in populated regions. They, therefore, wanted the HAZMAT placards removed from the railroad cars.

First responders heard about this and fought the effort to remove the HAZMAT placards. Although terrorists may someday resort to such an attack, the attack is still theoretical. However, first responders actually respond to train derailments on a regular basis. If there is a derailment, or other incident, that involves a car that contains potentially dangerous materials, first responders need to know this information immediately, which is why there is a requirement to have the placards. Although terrorist attacks are a potential concern, derailments are an active concern, as they happen frequently and need to be addressed. A train derailment is clearly a malignant issue, as it happens unintentionally on all, but extremely rare, occasions.

Addressing Malignant Threats

Although the remainder of this chapter addresses malicious threats, we just want to highlight that malignant threats have created more damage than malicious threats. When designing your security program, and implementing Advanced Persistent Security, you need to ensure that you consider the malignant threats as much as, if not more than, malicious threats.

The good thing is that the same countermeasures will prevent damage caused by both malicious and malignant threats. For example, access controls will prevent a user from accidentally deleting data or gaining access to data they should not have access to, just like it would prevent a malicious actor from causing damage or compromising information. But malignant threats do contribute to the likelihood of a vulnerability being exploited and therefore add to the need to mitigate that vulnerability.

ADVERSARY CATEGORIZATION

Adversary is the term we use to describe malicious threats. Although many people prefer to use the term enemy to describe a malicious entity, the term adversary is used in the intelligence and military world, and also seems more appropriate for readers of this book. The word enemy has an emotional component to it; it implies battle, which is not necessarily inappropriate if an organization is not actively attacking you. However, the word adversary implies that they have competing interests, which is generally more appropriate for defining security programs.

For example, consider that you have a business competitor who is sometimes a partner on different projects. It would be inappropriate to consider them an enemy. However, they do have competing interests, sometimes even when they are partnered with you. Companies frequently have joint ventures, by which they cooperate and may even create a new business together; however, it does not mean that they might not compete in other market segments.

As of this writing, Russia and the United States are cooperating in some areas to fight the Islamic State of Iraq and Syria (ISIS). Clearly both the countries still have adversarial interests around the world, but calling each other an enemy will impede the goal of combatting the ISIS.

When designing a security program, or making any other important decision, it is important to keep emotions out of planning. So as we proceed further on how to consider malicious threats, we specifically want to establish the use of the term adversary in our discussions.

Adversary Versus Attacker

Although it is important to keep emotions out while planning for a security program, you need to delineate between a threat that is potentially causing harm and one that is actively attacking you. Clearly, an attacker needs your immediate attention and should be treated as a hostile entity.

This can become extremely problematic when the attacker is also a business partner. Such is the case with the Chinese entities on many occasions. For example, many companies have active business dealings in China with the Chinese government, yet they may find themselves compromised in a traditional advanced persistent threat (APT) style attack, where the entire network is compromised. This is clearly troublesome, and the issue needs to be incorporated into a reaction strategy.

In many cases, the attack is clearly by a malicious party, and an appropriate response plan needs to be initiated.

It is important to note that when you detect an attack, the threat has been realized, and you need to determine the likely attack methods, the level of intended damage, other systems likely compromised or will be attempted to be compromised, and the appropriate reactions strategy.

This will be discussed further in Section 4 of this book, but for now consider an incident that the authors responded to involving a large financial institution.

In this case, it was determined that an attacker compromised a system responsible for initiating electronic funds transfers (EFTs). However, in watching the attacker's activities and looking at the actual damage inflicted and the work performed, it was quickly determined that the attacker did not realize, or at least care, that an EFT system has been compromised. The attacker was using the system as a site to exchange pirated software. Although the attacker could have theoretically attempted to steal millions of dollars, he/she did not seem to care. It was determined that the best course of action was to simply kick the attacker off and reconfigure the system. If the attacker had actually attempted to compromise the EFT system for monetary gain, or for purposes specific to EFT systems, the reaction would have been clearly different.

This example demonstrates how you need to understand your attacker to determine the appropriate response and reaction.

Malicious Insiders

Although there is a great deal of focus on the external threat, and enhanced connectivity makes external threats much more relevant to your organization, be aware that malicious insiders represent perhaps the greatest threat that you face from a malicious party.

Malicious insiders know what you have of value. They know what would inflict the maximum harm possible. They know whom you consider your greatest competitors. If they have minimum knowledge about exploitation principles, they can likely determine how to compromise vulnerabilities that often go overlooked. They may also know what detection capabilities you have in place, so they know how to avoid or bypass countermeasures.

Edward Snowden, the National Security Agency (NSA) contractor who stole information and provided it to the media, as well as likely to Russia and China, is an example of a malicious insider. According to the analysis of Ray Semko, who is a former US Army and Defense Intelligence Agency counterintelligence officer and had one of the most generous assessments of Snowden, Snowden was upset about not being offered the job he wanted at the NSA and wanted to retaliate in a way that was as damaging as possible. Snowden reportedly started downloading data as a contractor working for Dell, while stationed in Japan, and then took a new position working for Booz Allen, placing him in Hawaii where he was working for the NSA's Pacific hub, which gave him even more access to information.

Knowing his account had limitations, including him being a contractor and the potential network security monitoring, he solicited passwords from other contractors, as well as the NSA employees. He then used those accounts to gain further access to information and conceal his espionage-related activities.

Once the information was compromised, he provided it to reporters who effortlessly distributed the same. Additionally, as he fled first to China and then to Russia, and reportedly went to the Russian embassy while in China, it is likely that he provided the stolen materials to the Chinese and Russian intelligence agencies as well.

Although some people might describe Snowden otherwise, we ask people to consider that with all the materials leaked that contain classified materials just about every US ally, why was no information about China or Russia leaked? The NSA's top targets by far are Russia and China, and both these countries have the most extensive domestic surveillance efforts, which Snowden supporters pride themselves on highlighting that Snowden is protecting the civil liberties of people by disclosing the domestic surveillance efforts of their home countries. Yet the released documents contain nothing about the most prolific domestic surveillance efforts in the world.

Snowden knew exactly how to cause maximum harm to the NSA and the United States and its allied interests as a whole.

Criminal Hackers

The term, hacker, was initially coined to describe people who performed clever pranks, or otherwise bypassed system features so they could accomplish a task. With regard to computers, manuals were poor, if they actually existed. Computer users had to figure things out on their own. Since then, the term has been bastardized and the positive connotations have been lost. When the term is used now, it is almost solely used in reference to an unauthorized person attempting to compromise the security of a computer system for criminal purposes.

In this chapter, we will discuss criminal hackers, who want to illegally compromise the security of computer systems for a variety of purposes. This encompasses a wide range of attackers. Hackers vary greatly in skill level and intent. A very successful criminal hacker might not possess any significant level of technical talent. Criminal hackers can have a very base skill level; however, as many targets have insufficient countermeasures in place, it is easy for them, or any other party with criminal intent, to be successful.

Assisting this success is an infrastructure that provides technical and operational support to criminals. Chapter 7 describes this infrastructure in detail, but for now understand that criminals can outsource a great deal of their activities and do not need to be technologically advanced. Also understand that the level of an attacker's success is not an indication of his/her talent.

Criminals tend to stick to similar targets, tools, and techniques. For example, Albert Gonzalez was the mastermind behind a series of attacks against large retailers and credit card processors from 2005 to 2008, which resulted in the theft of possibly as much as 200 million credit card numbers. He and his accomplices targeted similar systems across all organizations. This team of hackers was extremely talented, but they generally used an established process.

The so far unnamed hacker who compromised the Target network to steal 110 million credit cards in 2012 demonstrated significant talent and versatility in bypassing several countermeasures and detection mechanisms, while understanding and exploiting multiple technologies. The attack still began with a basic phishing message.

If you assume that Gonzalez and the Target hacker were advanced, there are many hackers who are significantly less talented. Ironically, less sophisticated attackers can be more harmful, as they are less disciplined. They might accidentally cause damage. They tend to be immature, and do not have mature goals, such as financial gain. They might want to cause damage, as hacking is as much about the perception of power as it is about other goals.

When countermeasures are insufficient, it does not take any talent for a hacker to be successful. Clearly, though, hacking skills are on a continuum. Criminal hackers are typically opportunists. They scan for vulnerable victims; they look for the proverbial low hanging fruit.

Hackers may have a preference for certain types of computers. Like Gonzalez, they might have a preference for certain industries or types of victims.

Assuming hackers have criminal intent, they might want to steal information and money, commit extortion, collect bots, steal credit card numbers, and invade privacy, among countless other acts. When you consider threats to account for, you need to consider random hackers. They are pervasive and numerous. You, therefore, need to consider that if there is a vulnerability, it can be exploited by a random party with an unforeseen goal.

Minimally, this category of malicious threat should answer the all too common question, "Who would want to hack me?"

Hacktivists

Let us first be clear that a hacktivist is a criminal hacker, but a certain type of criminal hacker. The term hacktivist comes from combining hacker and activist. The implication is that these people are hacking for a political purpose. To a certain extent, this may be true. Generally, though, hacktivists are going to hack something; they just prefer to believe they are doing it for a noble cause, besides their own ego.

To explain, you do not assume the sailors of the Sea Shepherd, the ship that actively attempts to impede the activities of the Japanese whale hunters, would go out and find other ships to attack and impede, if the whalers stop hunting whales. On the other hand, it does appear that most hacktivists would be hacking or committing other computer attacks, if their cause went away.

Although we condemn computer crimes, we do admit our own hypocrisy in promoting and supporting the members of GhostSec or the Ghost Security Group, who are actively trying to counter the ISIS online recruiting and planning efforts. These people are skilled and have a noble intent.

GhostSec is an offshoot of Anonymous, which is known as more of a hacker collective. People have a fear for Anonymous because of their reputation; however, the reality is that they are a very random group of hackers. There is what might be considered an organizer that selects targets and puts out official videos; however, there is little organization and coordination. Beyond that, people associate themselves with Anonymous by launching attacks against the named targets. They might report their successes back to the coordinating sites.

People who associate themselves with hacktivist groups, assuming that they would otherwise be hacking, do so to gain significance and want to believe they are contributing to a higher cause. The cause may be irrelevant to them, as long as it gives them a sense of purpose. Although they could volunteer at a homeless shelter or help with a blood drive, they instead want to give a purpose to an activity they would otherwise be doing.

You can tell from the description of Anonymous that the people involved with hacktivism vary in skills and the results they can achieve. For example, in the Fall of 2015, Anonymous said they were going to target the ISIS social media accounts. They claimed that they disrupted 4,000 ISIS Twitter accounts. Reports later came out that many of the accounts were not associated with the ISIS, but with random Arabic speakers, and even accounts used by intelligence operatives attempting to infiltrate the ISIS activities. Although it was great for Anonymous public perception, the results might have countered the intended goals.

Hacktivists are especially dangerous, as their activities intend to cause harm, and usually intend to inflict the maximum possible damage. Sometimes the damage intends to shut down the victim. Sometimes they want to steal information and spread the information to embarrass the victim.

Some organizations are more likely to be victims of hacktivism than others; however, given the random membership of hacktivist groups, any organization is a potential victim. For the purpose of determining your risk profile, it is important to consider whether hacktivists are a likely threat that you need in determining your countermeasures.

Organized Criminal Gangs

Organized criminal gangs are a significant concern for a variety of organizations. When you consider that organized criminal gangs, which include the stereotypic mafia, Chinese triads, Japanese yakuza, Eastern European mafia, and drug cartels, want to make as much money as possible, you can assume that they will turn their attention to any profitable criminal venture. This includes computer-based crimes, which can have a very high payback for little investment.

Organized criminals have been involved with hacking efforts, because it made it easier to launder money. They needed to know how to move their money around as efficiently as possible without being tracked. Although criminal gangs are rather conservative and like any organized business, they prefer to expand only when the risk justifies expanding beyond their comfort zone. When it was clear computer crime would be a steady and reliable source of profit, they expanded their computer expertise. They can afford to hire and train already skilled hackers.

Typical activities of organized criminal gangs in cyberspace would essentially be an expansion of their physical crimes. Clearly, they want to facilitate money laundering. They also expanded their activities into reliable and low risk methods of stealing money. Credit card thefts and fraud can be attributed to organized criminal gangs.

There was at least one case where thousands of credit cards were hit with a small, but fraudulent, monthly charge. Although the monthly charge was less than $10, the total amount stolen quickly became millions of dollars. Additionally, the individual charges are so low that few people would choose to question the charges, and the banks are not likely to investigate the charges either.

Extortion is also a potential source of revenue, as well as enforcement. By hacking a company to create damage or by launching a distributed denial of service (DDOS) attack, organized criminals can extort money or other behaviors out of a potential victim.

Clearly, there are many gangs that can commit extortion, credit card thefts, money laundering, etc. Again, the Albert Gonzalez gang could be perceived as an organized criminal enterprise. However, what distinguishes true organized criminal gangs from groups of hackers is the criminal infrastructure at their disposal, and the scope of their efforts. The scope of traditional organized criminal gangs' efforts is hundreds of millions, if not billions, of dollars a year. Although a computer-based crime gang will generally be composed of a tight group of people, organized criminal gangs have unlimited resources at their disposal and can bring in as many people as they choose to accomplish their criminal goals.

Nation-State Actors

Nation-state actors are sovereign nations. They have their own political agendas, but for the purpose of this book, they represent a threat to certain organizations to further their political goals. They also have unlimited resources for all practical purposes. Different nation-states will pose different risks to the value you possess. However, like all threats, they generally have their preferred targets and methods, and therefore, you can be proactive in optimizing your risk as effectively as possible.

It is important to note that although political goals may come and go, as of this writing, the world political situation is relatively stable and the discussion that follows has remained consistent for more than a decade. Technology may change, but political goals from a worldwide nation-state perspective will not quickly change. The discussion is drawn from research and significantly from remarks by General Michael Hayden, former director of both the NSA and the CIA.

Russia, China, and the United States

Russia, China, and the United States have highly advanced computer exploitation programs. Generally, if they intend to target you, you must assume that they will gain the desired access. Their programs are well funded and employ some of the most talented computer experts on the planet. Their results are all impressive, and when you compare the results of anyone of these countries to those of the most noted hackers in the world, they make those supposed computer geniuses look like amateurs.

We must also note that although this book is primarily intended for people responsible for implementing cybersecurity programs, all these countries have extensive espionage efforts that go well beyond computer espionage. They all resort to human intelligence, signal intelligence, imagery intelligence, trash intelligence, open source intelligence, etc. They all have extensive collection efforts that are well organized, coordinated, and focused. Cyberespionage and attack are all a part of their overall military and political strategy.

The other threat actors will generally limit their attack strategies to targeting computers, but these nation-states will employ computer attacks as only one piece of the overall strategy.

The United States is clearly the leader when it comes to Computer Network Attack (CNA) and Computer Network Exploitation (CNE). They have incredible skills and resources. The successes of the US cyberoperations are not well known, and that is ironically a testament to their successes. One of the key goals of any sort of espionage and computer operations is that your victims should not know that they were compromised. The leaks by Snowden identified that the NSA has some incredible CNE successes that were previously unknown.

The NSA has also been credited with playing a key role on the development of the Stuxnet virus, which targeted Iran's nuclear research and production capabilities. Stuxnet set back the Iranian nuclear efforts by 2 years. Kaspersky, the Russian security software company, released a research report that identifies an attack organization it named as the Equation Group, which is assumed to be the NSA's Tailored Access Operations (TAO) group. According to the report, the Equation Group created a malware infrastructure that is impossible to detect and remove. It was reportedly in the wild for 14 years, before it was even discovered. Assuming there is any veracity to the report, the Equation Group's efforts are an amazing achievement in CNE.

Something important to note is that Snowden's leaks also demonstrated that the NSA shares information learned through CNE with other governments. It appears that the NSA is responsible for some of the most critical terrorist intelligence distributed throughout the world. It was also widely reported that when France wanted to retaliate against ISIS for the Paris attacks, it used US intelligence to determine targets to bomb. It is for reasons like this that although some countries might feign outrage over US espionage efforts, there will not be any significant repercussions from those countries that receive valuable intelligence gained through US CNE.

Although the United States does not target countries or companies for commercial purposes, it does not mean it they will not target seemingly commercial organizations. The US government does not target an organization to steal information for the commercial benefit of a US company, but it will target companies if it believes there is a legitimate national security purpose. For example, if it is believed that a company is supplying Iran with nuclear technology, it would be targeted. The US government will inform a US company, if it believes a foreign country or company is targeting the company. The United States will also attempt to compromise computer networks of legitimate foreign intelligence targets.

Regarding methods used by US CNE, you can assume that they use malware that might target an organization through phishing or other social engineering methods. The Stuxnet virus was apparently distributed through a US asset who dropped USB drives in areas where Iranian scientists might randomly pick it up. The Equation Group malware shows that malware might be embedded in equipment even before it arrives at your facility. They have zero-day exploits available, which are software exploits that are not known to the public and cannot be readily mitigated. If you are a valuable target, you may be physically infiltrated to have malware planted on your network.

China is extremely pervasive in its CNE as well. It is also more egregious and less concerned about being caught. China has three major sources of CNE operators: the People's Liberation Army (PLA) has many units devoted to CNE and CNA, the Communist Party likewise has its own CNE capabilities, and there are also universities and loose hacker groups that commit CNE. China formally denies it has any CNE or CNA capabilities. However, many significant attacks, including the Office of Personnel Management hack, in which a database containing information involved in background checks for tens of millions of US government employees was hacked, have been specifically attributed to China without reservation.

China targets a great deal of information for military and commercial purposes. China has been attributed for infiltrating US government contractors for a variety of purposes. It is no coincidence that the latest Chinese fighter aircraft, the J-31 and J-20, are near identical to the US F-35 and F-22 fighters. Although they appear physically identical, you need to have a wide variety of classified specifications and software to allow the physical similarity to be operational.

In 2009, the Wall Street Journal reported that China infiltrated the US power grid. It can be expected that they also successfully infiltrated other portions of the critical infrastructure. China considers this as preparation of the battlefield. Should there ever be a war between China and the United States, taking down the US power grid would be a strategic success.

Chinese assets are attributed to hacking just about every major US company. It can be expected that they targeted every major government and company throughout the world. It is in their natural interest to do so.

As China has a great deal of resources, it implements the "grains of sand" approach to intelligence collection and CNE. This means that it will comb through each proverbial grain of sand to determine if there is value. It will target as many organizations as possible to gather information.

China uses a variety of attack methods to compromise computer networks. The most traditional method involves using insiders. They will either intentionally place a Chinese operative inside an organization or recruit an insider to help compromise the organization. Chinese intelligence operatives target people of Chinese descent, or especially those in the country on a visa. They will prey on their love for the Chinese heritage or their loyalty to the Chinese homeland. They will then coach such people through executing espionage-related activities.

There is also physical exploitation when the targets have assets in areas under Chinese control. Given how pervasive the Chinese espionage activities are, it is common practice for business travelers going to China to take a clean system with them, with minimal data, that they will then destroy on their return. Also it can be expected that companies that have facilities in China will have those facilities physically compromised.

In one case, a Fortune 50 chief information security officer (CISO) called to tell us that he had a "story" he wanted to share. He relayed an incident during which his corporate network went down and only the Chinese facility was able to communicate with the headquarters. He contacted the person in charge of the Chinese network operations center and asked why they thought they still had connectivity. The response was, "It must be the backup router that the Chinese government installed for us." Of course the immediate response was, "What backup router?" The company had the router immediately removed, but it was a clear sign that they did not have control of their company networks inside China.

Any organization with facilities in China has to assume that those facilities are potentially hostile.

China obviously has extensive CNE and CNA capabilities as well. There is a very formal collections management process, where there is a very specific targeting and exploitation. It has a collections management team that develops targeting lists to identify targets, as well as the desired information. The requirements are then passed onto an infiltration team, which is responsible for establishing a foothold in the target organization. Once the infiltration has been established, the relevant information is passed to the data exfiltration team. This team is responsible for identifying and gathering as much information as possible.

During the course of the CNE, the Chinese assets will typically gain access to the network through spear phishing messages. Once they have access, they will then compromise a variety of systems and distribute malware throughout the network. The malware will be highly complex. In some cases, to further the success of the breach, they may even make improvements to the reliability of the network. They will establish data exfiltration servers, which serve the purpose of temporarily storing data inside the target's network until it is ready for a mass transfer.

Although there may be signs of a network compromise, you typically will need advanced tools to detect the attack.

Russia has likewise accomplished major attacks against countries and companies throughout the world. Like China, Russia has been attributed to infiltrating the power grid, defense contractors, and military assets, among just about every other organization that might strategically benefit the Russian military, political, and domestic interests. In 2015, Russia was attributed with compromising an email server of the US Joint Chiefs of Staff.

Russia has been attributed with CNE attacks since at least 2001. Much like the United States, it is more careful about its attacks. It uses many of the methods that the United States does.

One important note about Russia is that it uses Russian cybercriminals as a resource. For example, before the Russian invasion of Georgia in 2008, there was a DDOS attack against critical Georgian resources. These attacks had a significant impact on the Georgian government's ability to react and repel the invasion. The DDOS attack was not from official Russian systems, but from botnets used by supposedly independent Russian cybercriminals. The Russian government calls the DDOS attack, "A coincidence," but the likelihood of that is near zero. The implication is that the Russian government periodically calls upon and therefore protects and supports these criminals to a certain extent.

Iran and North Korea

Iran and North Korea both have very significant resources and skills. They clearly do not have the physical reach that the United States, China, and Russia do, but they do have incredible technical talent and resources.

Although the difference in resources is notable, the reason these countries are set apart from the previous three countries is that they are more likely to be destructive than any of the other countries. They will act out of anger.

The 2014 attack against Sony was an example of North Korea exhibiting immature and destructive behaviors in response to Sony distributing a movie that was unfavorable to the North Korean government and leader. In addition to the Sony attack, North Korea has been attributed to launching the Dark Seoul attack, which destroyed computers throughout banks in South Korea, the United States, and Canada.

North Korea apparently receives support in the form of training and resources from China. Its attackers do have skills that are substantial.

In December 2015, the Wall Street Journal reported that Iran infiltrated the control system of a dam in Rye Brook, New York. It could have caused catastrophic damage, if the systems were actually exploited. Iran is normally similar to Russia and China with regard to its capabilities and intent. However, Iran deserves special attention in that it technically has little to lose and has already exhibited a propensity for being destructive.

More than 100 attacks, primarily targeting the United States and Israeli assets, have been attributed to Iran. The most destructive attack by Iran was in 2012, when Iran launched an attack against Saudi Aramco, the Saudi Arabian oil and gas company. It essentially destroyed the computer infrastructure of the organization, causing irreparable harm.

What makes these countries especially dangerous is that they have little to lose at the moment. Cyberattacks are essentially asymmetrical warfare, which takes little resources and there is unlikely to be a retaliatory attack. North Korea has little to lose, as it does not have any significant computer infrastructure to target for retaliation. Iran similarly has a limited computer infrastructure.

The 2015 international nuclear deal with Iran does give Iran something to lose, and therefore makes it more predictable and significantly less likely to cause intentional damage. Without the political motivations, Iran would likewise be willing to be as destructive as North Korea.

Iran is potentially a concern, as it attempts to influence other countries in the region. For example, there was an attack against Saudi assets by Yemeni assets that could be tied back to Iran. It is possible that Iran might continue to use Yemen or other sympathetic countries as agents.

Again, these countries can be potent adversaries because they have more than basic skills that target poor security programs, and they have little to lose. This makes them extremely dangerous.

France, Germany, Israel, the United Kingdom, and Other First-World Countries

France, Germany, Israel, the United Kingdom, and many other countries have substantial CNE and CNA ability. Israel and the United Kingdom clearly have even more ability than the other countries. These countries are also more active with regard to their CNE and CNA for national security efforts.

Israel has a tremendous intelligence collection effort, and also is more likely to execute attacks against countries and other entities that are hostile to Israeli national security. It also has been reported to be engaged in economic espionage to support Israeli companies. It is a sign that Israel has some of the most robust and innovative cybersecurity companies in the world, as the companies are frequently founded by people who worked with Israeli military Computer Network Operations (CNO) units.

The UK CNE and CNA efforts were also prominent in the documents leaked by Snowden. It has very robust capabilities. It has not been well reported as to whether or not the UK CNE efforts have commercial espionage as a primary goal, but it clearly has a robust national security effort. There is a great deal of cooperation with the US CNE and CNA groups. Therefore, its methods are likely to be similar as well, if not as well-resourced and as effective.

Countries such as France and Germany likewise have robust CNE and CNA capabilities. However, they do not devote the resources to these efforts that the previously mentioned countries do. There are significant efforts to assist national security efforts; however, they also invest significant resources to carry on commercial CNE, with the goal of helping their domestic companies. To a large extent, these countries rely on the information from the United States and have extensive efforts to share information to mutual benefit.

What is notable is that in the words of Pierre Marion, the former director of the French Direction Générale de la Sécurité Extérieure (DGSE), the French foreign intelligence agency, "Everybody spies on everybody." He is essentially implying that we are all adversaries.

The implication is that if you are involved with a foreign country, or might be competing against a foreign-owned company, you may be targeted by that organization. Once the author, Ira Winkler, was supporting a US company that had its intellectual property targeted by a French company. Specifically, the US company was informed by a European subcontractor that representatives of the French company approached them and offered to pay for all the intellectual property of the American company in their possession. During that assignment, Ira took a weekend vacation to Paris and found himself to be under surveillance during that trip. It is also likely that the European companies will be targeted by CNE, if they refused the offer.

All first-world countries have a CNE effort in place. These efforts are clearly more economical and fruitful than the traditional espionage efforts. These efforts are all likely to pursue in identifying zero-day vulnerabilities. The Snowden leaks confirmed that just about every first-world country has domestic surveillance efforts, as well as significant CNE efforts. These are not only appropriate for satisfying national interests, but also extremely cost-effective.

Other Countries

Just about all countries can be assumed to have some level of CNE and CNA efforts. Typically, they might be used for both internal and external security efforts. Clearly, they are not going to be a significant threat to you or your organization, unless you have direct dealings with the countries or their companies. The level of resources invested in the efforts will vary greatly.

Terrorists

Terrorists are left for last in the discussion, because this is where they belong for the average reader. There is a great deal of hype about terrorists, and at the time of this writing, they do not represent a significant threat. There are many definitions of terrorism, but the working definition we will use for this book is, "The creation of fear, uncertainty and doubt to achieve a political goal."

This is a broad definition, but it is appropriate. As you can see, there is no actual creation of death or destruction necessarily involved. The mere implication that there may be a potential death can create fear and uncertainty and cause people to change their way of life.

When there was a broad power outage in the New York region in 2005, the immediate fear was that 50,000,000 people lost power, because of a terrorist attack. The news media went through every permutation of the implications of the event being tied to terrorism. When it was disclosed that the power outage was caused by a fallen tree, the news media and public lost interest.

It can, therefore, be implied that even a trivial computer attack can result in a great deal of fear, uncertainty, and doubt, as the news media and politicians will readily go through every permutation about the potential for future attacks. The actual damage can, however, be insignificant.

When you look at the capability of terrorists and specifically the ISIS operations, computers might be a relatively easy target, but they do not have the impact of physical attacks. Although we do not intend to downplay any deaths, the San Bernardino terrorist attack caused 14 deaths. This is actually a relatively small number when compared to the other deaths that occurred that day. However, it clearly created large-scale panic and action. On a daily basis, there are computer attacks, and it is hard to imagine that a computer being hacked will have anywhere near the impact of a single death.

Clearly, ISIS has demonstrated that it has computer literate people who actively support their cause. So far, most of those resources have been put into online recruiting and fund-raising. ISIS knows how to move large amounts of money and use various elements of the Internet to distribute propaganda, communicate with each other, and plan attacks, among other supporting activities.

Although their skill level varies greatly, and they do not currently represent a significant hacking threat, the so-called Cyber Caliphate of ISIS has had a couple of notable successes. In January 2015, it was able to access the US Central Command's Twitter and YouTube accounts. Although naive people questioned the security of military computers, the reality was that this was specifically an attack on Twitter and YouTube and was likely accomplished by guessing the passwords of the accounts, or perhaps through a simple phishing attack. Either way, this attack was more of an embarrassment than anything else.

In April 2015, people claiming to be affiliated with the Cyber Caliphate were able to compromise the computing assets of the TV5Monde, a French TV network. The hackers were able to stop the network from broadcasting, as well as take control of the network's website and social media accounts. Although this sounds like a major hack, and the effects were major, it is no coincidence that the attack occurred soon after TV5Monde accidentally broadcast their passwords during an in-studio TV interview. Behind the interview subject, there was a wall with different account passwords displayed. This is just bad security.

There are random reports that ISIS has attempted to infiltrate critical infrastructural elements and has so far been unsuccessful. It is likely that it will attempt to hack whatever it can as just another element of launching any form of terrorism it can.

Clearly ISIS is a potential threat. If it is successful in launching an attack, the intent will possibly be to cause damage. However, depending on the nature of the organization hacked, it could also be for financial gain to create a new source of funding for its operations.

With regard to attack methods, it will likely use traditional hacker methods. It has sufficient resources to hire mercenary computer hackers to support its goals, but as of this writing, it has not apparently done so for the purpose of creating actual terrorism.

THREAT SUMMARY

This chapter has clearly provided a great deal of information that can inspire people to think that they are facing many unstoppable enemies who are beyond their control. As stated earlier, this chapter intends to provide you with information that will allow you to best determine your risk profile to enable you to make rational decisions to optimize your risk.

The key issue to remember is that the described threats are not within your control. This information is to improve your ability to determine the vulnerabilities that are most likely to be exploited. You can then be proactive in mitigating those vulnerabilities. Should you ever find yourself being the victim of an attack, you can determine how to respond and where to look for other targets of the attack, among other aspects of response. As Sun Tzu says, "If you know the enemy and know yourself, you need not fear the results of a hundred battles."

CHAPTER 7

Adversary Infrastructure

We previously identified the nature of the threat; however, many organizations will need a deeper understanding of the resources the threat will employ to compromise them. Depending on the threat, they may use their own resources, or they could bring in an entire criminal ecosystem. This ecosystem is available on demand and can provide a criminal, who has minimal technical expertise, with world-class talent.

For this chapter, we specifically use the term adversary. The reason is that threats can be malignant or malicious threats and an adversary is specifically a malicious threat with the intent of Computer Network Attack (CNA) or Computer Network Exploitation (CNE). To exercise proaction, you need to fully understand what resources are available to target you by a given threat. Again, some threats rely solely on their own skills and tools. However, the more capable threats make use of a criminal ecosystem that makes them significantly more potent than they would otherwise be, creating significantly more risk to your organization.

Although it is impossible to list every threat, this chapter identifies the computer criminal ecosystem. This ecosystem allows individuals to specialize in a specific criminal function.

In many ways, the person who will actually target you can be considered a general contractor. When you renovate a house, a general contractor will run the project. The contractor will bring in plumbers, electricians, roofers, etc.; will buy the carpets, kitchen fixtures, etc.; and will do the work, but will rely on suppliers and specialized laborers to complete the projects.

Consider the threat who actually commits the crime to be the general contractor for the crime. The remainder of this chapter discusses the resources available to the threat to commit the crime.

Advanced Persistent Security. http://dx.doi.org/10.1016/B978-0-12-809316-0.00007-5

HIGHLY SOPHISTICATED ADVERSARY INFRASTRUCTURE

When you consider the types of adversaries that you face, the most potent are nation-states, organized crime gangs, drug cartels, and potentially some of the more sophisticated computer crime gangs. These organizations have a great deal of money, have a large number of people, and can create their own exploitation infrastructure. They do not have to rely on anonymous resources from the dark web, but have created their own highly refined exploitation ecosystem. These entities are who you would consider an advanced persistent threat (APT).

This does not mean that they will rely solely on their own ecosystem. As previously described, Russia apparently enlisted Russian computer criminals to launch a distributed denial of service (DDOS) attack against Georgian assets to coincide with the Russian invasion of Georgia. China sometimes enlists, or at least encourages, independent Chinese hackers to cause general damage to another nation. An example of this occurred when the United States accidentally bombed the Chinese embassy in Serbia in 1999 and the Chinese patriots tried hacking random US-related systems.

It is also important to note that the level of sophistication of an adversary is not necessarily determined by the sophistication of the individual attacks used, but by the methodologies, effectiveness, and efficiency of the overall operations. APTs might begin an attack with an extremely simple exploit. However, once they are in, they proceed methodically, covertly, efficiently, and effectively.

This section identifies the infrastructure that these entities create and foster. It provides for highly effective attacks that are also very efficient. These organizations typically attempt to keep their CNE and preparation of the battlefield as surreptitious as possible. They also plan to make their CNA as devastating as possible. This infrastructure allows for hacking at will.

Research and Development

The more a threat understands technology, the more effective it will be at CNA and CNE. Highly sophisticated threats will maintain their own research and development (R&D) efforts to actively study technologies and find vulnerabilities in them. Once the vulnerabilities are discovered, they will develop attack tools to automate the exploitation of the vulnerabilities.

By constantly examining technologies, they systematize computer hacking. When new technologies begin to be used, or even when they are in development, researchers will begin to study the technologies to find vulnerabilities. Some nation-states might even attempt to embed vulnerabilities into products. Such was the case with Juniper Networks, as reported in December 2015 that a malicious party found a way to embed a malicious code in the software baseline. The US government banned the sale of Huawei products to its customers, as it was believed the Chinese government had backdoors installed in the products. Products from Checkpoint, an Israeli company, were also banned for sale to the US government customers, as Checkpoint would not allow a review of its software.

In the first case of its kind, it was documented that a Swiss cryptographic company, Crypto AG, provided the National Security Agency (NSA) with a backdoor in its products for more than three decades. The previously mentioned Equation Group reportedly intercepted products shipped to certain customers and embedded backdoors into the equipment's firmware. The Snowden leaks indicated that NSA was able to infiltrate email systems throughout the world. All these cases are just what has been discovered and publicized. It is highly likely that there are many more compromises of commercial products that have not been discovered and/or disclosed.

Although these are operational espionage efforts, the extent of these compromises indicated that there were tremendous R&D efforts in place. One of the documents that Snowden leaked was essentially a catalog of attack tools created by the NSA Tailored Access Operations (TAO) office and available to the intelligence community. The tools allowed for the interception of cell phone calls and automated computer hacking, among other tools that automated or initiated attacks. The R&D is conducted by on-staff security researchers, who are extremely skilled and well-resourced. The TAO is essentially NSA's team of security researchers. Other US intelligence agencies, as well as multiple organizations in most nation-states, and all other APTs maintain their own teams of security researchers.

APTs will also make use of the resources available to less skilled and resourced hackers. They will monitor the dark web, hacker forums, etc. for any information that may help with their attacks. Although random hackers may not have as much resources available to them, given their sheer numbers, it is likely that they will find new zero-day attacks. They might already have information that the APT is interested in collecting. Also as mentioned, APT actors might make use of random hackers and the general hacking infrastructure to obfuscate their own actions.

Collection Management

Collection management is a formal process and a key function in all major CNE and potentially CNA efforts. Collection management is the tasking and coordination of intelligence efforts. The collection management team receives requirements from some authority. The assumption is that the authority has some strategic goal that has been passed on to them.

If we are talking about the US intelligence efforts, the director of National Intelligence sets the collection tasking requirements. These requirements do not necessarily say, "Hack this country," but they are to the effect, we need to know information on a specific subject. These requirements are then delegated to the intelligence agencies that are most likely to be able to satisfy the need for the information. Assuming it involves some level of hacking, it is passed to the collection management team that then initiates the process. You can assume that the previous description of the tasking process applies to all APTs.

Once the collection manager has the requirements, he/she passes the targeting information to the breach team. The breach team establishes a foothold on the system and ideally hacks enough systems within the targeted organization to provide a firm foundation for collection efforts. It has to pass on the information to the collection team and/or back to the collection manager.

The collection manager then ensures that the collection team is aware of the collection requirements. The collection team then gets whatever data it can and passes it back to the collection manager. The collection manager then has to evaluate whether the requirements have been satisfied. Ideally the collection manager also determines if there has been any information discovered that was not expected, but valuable. If so, the collection manager passes that information back to the tasking elements, along with the information requested.

The collection management team will then be informed as to whether or not the requirements were actually satisfied.

Breach Team

An APT breach team will have a wide variety of hacking skills. Its job is to infiltrate the targeted organization to establish a foothold in the target and ideally create an infrastructure inside the target that allows for easy movement on the part of the collection team. It will likely have specialists for different technologies and can call on the specialists required to compromise the target.

The breach team will either have its own security researchers available or have ready access to its organization's security research group. This allows the breach team to rapidly exploit a target, and if they run into a problem or a new technology, it facilitates rapidly overcoming the issue.

When the breach team learns that there is a requirement, it will perform research and reconnaissance on the targeted organization. It will determine the technologies in place and the potential points of entry. This reconnaissance also includes reconnaissance of employees and others with access to the targeted organization. It will perform LinkedIn searches, among other searches, to determine who might be the most fruitful to spear phishing attacks. Once it identifies a person or other entry point, it will research the best way to target them.

The reconnaissance can be incredibly thorough and extensive. In the widely reported breach of the RSA Security company, in which the Chinese attackers infiltrated RSA Security to steal the source codes to their SecurID security product, the attackers identified people who worked in the human resources department and sent them a spear phishing email that appeared to come from Beyond.com, a company that deals with recruiting new employees. The attackers attached a spreadsheet that supposedly contained potential recruits, but actually contained a flash file that contained a zero-day vulnerability. When a single user clicked on the file, it gave the attackers the ability to install a backdoor program that they then used to compromise the rest of the network.

In other cases, the Chinese hackers targeted US defense contractors. They assumed that the contractors would be interested in the agenda for an upcoming conference specific to people in the defense industry. The message appeared to contain the updated agenda for the conference. The attachment was a PDF file containing a zero-day attack for PDF readers.

Clearly the breach team has to have a thorough understanding of the target's language, culture, and business environment. Although the quality of attacks varies, APTs typically have extensive resources ensuring the success of spear phishing messages, and are able to rapidly exploit the technologies.

After establishing a foothold inside the target organization, they will identify other systems that can be used to stage attacks by the collection team. This may involve dozens of other systems. They need to identify the protections in place and how to bypass them, as well as to perform a general mapping of the target's network. All the information is compiled and provided to the collection team.

It is also possible that the breach team will set up a network for long-term compromise. In this case, the breach team will install malware throughout the target network. The malware will establish a large distributed system that constantly detects if there are any modifications to the network. The breach team will also install malware on critical servers, such as email servers, and personal computers of key executives, so that it can constantly monitor the data and services on those systems.

Collection Team

The collection team will receive the requirements from the collection management team, as well as the information regarding the preparation of the target from the breach team. Although it might not need as much hacking knowledge as the breach team, it does need to understand the technologies in place, so that it can navigate the network quickly. It also needs to understand the languages in use.

The collection team will scour the network for the required information. It might have a broad collection requirement, which means that it should collect as much information as possible. To support its efforts, it will use a variety of search programs, scripts that allow for mass downloads of information, and tools that provide data transfer channels, among a variety of other utilities. When it finds information of potential interest, it will typically send the data to an exfiltration server. An exfiltration server is one of the compromised servers that is compromised for the specific intent of the temporary storage of data. The breach team will likely create a hidden directory on the intended exfiltration servers, which allows the collection team to capture as much information as possible without sending out constant streams of data, which could be more easily detected. Instead, the exfiltration servers will store the collected data until a point in time when data transfer is less likely to be detected, and it will be transmitted via a covert channel. A covert channel is a nontraditional communications path. For example, it is typical to send data via ftp or other file transfer and command protocols, but they are visible. If you have the appropriate skills or tools, you can modify other Internet protocols, such as the Domain Name System (DNS), to transmit data or commands. You can make a data file look like a video file and transfer sensitive data out in a way that appears to be otherwise insignificant.

As required, the collection team may attempt to clean up all signs of the breach after the collection has been completed. In many cases, the collected data might be rendered worthless if the compromise is detected. For example, if the United States learns of a secret communications mechanism between Chinese warships, and the Chinese learn about it, the Chinese may stop using that communications channel, preventing the United States from exploiting those communications in the future.

DEEP/DARK WEB

The deep web and dark web are the subjects of a great deal of mystery. They are constantly mentioned in news stories, movies, and TV crime series. *CSI: Cyber* and other hyped-up TV shows love to mention the deep and dark webs as immediately explaining how there is a criminal underbelly of the Internet that cannot be tracked. The reality is obviously less sensational.

Although there is no universal definition for the deep and dark webs, we will use the generally accepted definitions. The deep web is that portion of the Internet that is not searchable through the traditional search engines. There is typically no nefarious intent for the lack of searchability. Some content cannot be indexed by Google, Yahoo, Bing, or other search engines. For example, some websites require people to pay for content. Some Web pages are dynamic and might generate content from databases that are searched before the criteria for the search is provided. Some sites intend that they will be accessible through The Onion Router (Tor), which is discussed later, and some content may be intended to be hidden and be part of the dark web.

In case of adversaries that you will likely deal with, you need to understand that if you have information or services that are essentially on the deep web, whether you knew it or not, an adversary might target data that you believed was confidential. Many content companies lose their competitive edge if their information is compromised. An example of this is porn sites. Although the typical sites are part of the deep web, some less scrupulous site owners have attempted to pay hackers to steal information off the site. Piracy in the industry is a significant problem. Clearly there are other industries that have similar issues.

We want to be very clear that there are pornographic sites with illegal content, such as sites that contain child pornography. These sites would traditionally be in the dark web.

The dark web is that portion of the web that is intended to be anonymous. There are some legal uses for the dark web. Initially, the US intelligence agencies intended to create the dark web to facilitate covert communications, as well as to provide forums for dissidents in totalitarian regimes. Some groups also prefer to communicate anonymously. Some people want to offer services that are legal, but otherwise maintain their anonymity.

The dark web requires that people use specific software to access systems or communicate with each other. If the system wants to support anonymous web access, using the Tor browser might suffice. However, if there is a desire to exchange files or have personal exchanges, a person would need to use specific software.

The dark web can be considered an anonymous Internet with friend-to-friend communications functionality. It allows for private communications between parties known to each other, which is why the Islamic State of Iraq and Syria (ISIS) uses the dark net to communicate with potential recruits.

The dark web also facilitates online markets that are generally used by criminals. Silk Road is a notorious case of an online market for selling illegal drugs. As discussed later, there are markets for leasing botnets, fencing stolen credit card numbers, buying weapons, hiring criminals to perform illegal acts, laundering money, etc.

As previously mentioned, ISIS members use the dark web to communicate with each other and with potential recruits. They provide information to facilitate communications, coordinate potential terrorist attacks, and distribute training materials to launch cyberattacks.

Although law enforcement and intelligence agencies have had some success in infiltrating the dark net, criminals still consider the dark web a reasonably secure mechanism to support their actions.

What is important for a security professional to consider is that the dark web provides resources for people targeting your organization. These resources might be information and software to make their attacks more sophisticated, allowing a person with little technological know-how to launch attacks with much more skill. Malicious parties may also hire attackers to attack you on their behalf, or fence stolen information or other goods through the dark web. The dark web itself is not inherently dangerous to a potential victim, but the resources and capabilities that it provides a would-be adversary with are what that makes it dangerous to the victim.

TOR

Tor is both a software and a network that helps maintain anonymity on the Internet. The average user will interact with Tor through a Tor web browser. The web browser encrypts traffic that you send. It also connects to the Tor network, which randomizes how the web browser connects to the destination. Servers associated with the Tor network facilitate an anonymous connection between the sender and the recipient. The browser will connect to one server and that server transfers the connection to another server. There will be multiple server connections, with none of the intermediate servers knowing the sender and intended recipient.

Tor is a basic tool of Internet anonymity. It is not perfect, but it is reasonably effective for the intended purpose. The average user can use it to browse the traditional World Wide Web. Tor, or similar browsers, is required to use the dark web.

BITCOIN

Bitcoin is a digital asset and a payment system that is used as a form of Internet currency. It allows for anonymous payment from one person to another and is therefore a preferred payment method for criminal actions on the Internet. It is, however, important to note that many traditional businesses are beginning to accept bitcoins.

Bitcoins are unregulated and the value of a bitcoin can fluctuate significantly. However, the anonymity of the transaction makes it a preferred tool for criminal endeavors, especially by Internet-based criminals.

A stereotypic example of bitcoin usage is the use of paying ransoms to unlock ransomware, as will be discussed later. Criminals exchange bitcoins with each other as payments for services, information, extortion, or any other monetary use. If you want to know how to make your own transactions using bitcoins, the reader is referred to the Internet. For the purpose of this book, it is sufficient to understand that bitcoins have tangible value and are widely used throughout the adversary infrastructure.

BOTNETS

Botnets are essentially a set of Internet-based computers under a common controller. Although the term can include legitimate networks of computers, the overwhelming use of the term is for computers that have been hacked and under the control of criminal hackers.

The hacker can then use these computers to send out spams or launch DDOS attacks, where the bots of the botnet are commanded to direct large volumes of communication requests to a targeted system. The hacker may also use these bots for data collection, as they can install spyware on the computer to monitor keystrokes, to constantly collect data, to use the system to monitor its network, or as a launch point for other attacks, including the collection of other bots.

Botnets are typically formed through a variety of illicit means. A bot herder may have systems randomly scanning the Internet for systems with unpatched vulnerabilities that allow for remote hacking. If a vulnerable system is found, it is hacked and the botnet software installed. Phishing messages can also lure naive users into downloading malicious software that adds the system to a botnet.

Legitimate websites can be hacked, and visitors to such websites might unknowingly download the malicious software as well. This is a type of "watering hole" attack. In one case, a website operator was contacted by a criminal and offered a commission for every instance of botnet software installed on a computer, after visiting the site. The criminal did not blatantly state that the software installed was illicit, but luckily the website owner was smart enough to realize the real intent and informed the appropriate authorities. In some cases, hackers might set up fake websites just to attract visitors to be duped into downloading the malicious software.

In another demonstration of the criminal infrastructure, a bot herder will pay commission for bots herded into their botnet. This incentivizes random hackers to hack systems throughout the Internet to install the botnet software and claim their commission.

Given the pervasiveness of botnets, it can be expected that almost all companies, universities, and other organizations will have some of their systems herded into a botnet. If an organization does not monitor its systems and networks properly, it could be an unknowing complicit in attacking other organizations.

There are reportedly botnets with more than 1,000,000 bots. Although some bot herders might use the bots for their own malicious purposes, such as the North Korean and Iranian intelligence services, many bot herders will lease their botnet through the dark web. Criminals can lease botnets by the thousands for a fee. Criminals do not have to create their own botnet, as they can lease as much botnets as they need. Botnets are extremely versatile and can be used for a variety of illicit purposes.

RANSOMWARE

Ransomware is a growing form of computer crime that is hitting all types of organizations, including law enforcement. Ransomware is malicious software that once loaded on a victim system encrypts the hard drive and issues a warning that unless a ransom is paid within 24–48 hours, all the data will become unrecoverable. The software then tells the victim to typically send between $250 and $1,000 to the criminal within the allotted period, usually via bitcoin. When the ransom is paid, the criminal will send the victim an alphanumeric sequence to unlock the malware.

The victims typically infect themselves by clicking on a phishing message or downloading the ransomware from an infected or malicious website. The relatively short period allowed to pay the ransom is to discourage the victims from finding alternative methods of decrypting the system. Many victims find that they need more time to figure out how to use bitcoin. In some cases, victims have negotiated with the criminals for lower fees.

Ransomware programs are occasionally hacked by legitimate security experts, and people make a master code to decrypt the systems available, but more frequently, it is impossible to find a solution without paying the ransom. In October 2015, an FBI agent actually stated that victims should just pay the ransom by default, if their systems were locked by ransomware. In April 2015, it was reported that many police departments were forced to pay ransom to computer criminals.

Generally, the criminals do not specifically target a victim. They send out random phishing messages and infect as many sites on the Internet as possible. It is also possible that they pay a commission to any hacker who spreads their software. Ransomware is a growing problem as people tend to leave their systems insecure and behave insecurely on the Internet. As long as people allow untrusted software to be installed on their system and do not maintain a proper antimalware software, ransomware will continue to be a problem.

SECURITY RESEARCHERS

We have discussed security researchers in Chapter 5, but we want to specify that there are security researchers who are also part of the adversary/criminal infrastructure. These people will find zero-day exploits and sell them on the dark web. They might also perform criminal consulting on an as-needed basis.

As previously defined in the discussion of APTs, it is possible that APTs may hire some freelance security researchers on a project-by-project basis. This serves to hide their activities and reserves their exploits for critical occasions.

The exploits created by the security researchers would have different values depending on the technologies being exploited. Clearly there is the potential to make a great deal of money. For the purpose of this book, it is just important to note that this level of skill is available to anyone with enough money to buy it.

LEASED OR PURCHASED MALWARE

Zero-day exploits are an example of malware, but there are more examples of attack programs that criminals can purchase to better automate their attacks. The website, TheRealDeal, claims to specialize in the brokering of zero-day exploits in the dark web. Again, criminals do not have to be computer geniuses to execute complex attacks. They can purchase or lease software tools that automate the most complicated attacks possible.

BROKERAGE OR ESCROW OF DATA

Once criminals commit a data theft, they need to be able to profit from it. This requires fencing whatever was stolen. For example, when Target was hacked in 2012, the perpetrator needed a way to profit from the theft. He/she had to fence the credit card numbers. The credit card numbers were apparently distributed via a variety of carder sites that allowed people to specify the criteria for card numbers available for purchase. Criminals were then able to search for the cards that were locally sourced, so that they were less likely to be flagged for fraudulent use.

For example, a criminal in the Chicago region could purchase credit cards that were issued to victims in the Chicago region. This way it was less likely to be considered fraudulent than perhaps a card issued to someone in Arizona being used in Chicago.

Many of these sites claim to provide excellent customer service and guarantees. For example, if you purchase credit cards from some sites, they will substitute any credit cards that are not valid. They even rate the sellers of stolen data. Some of the more notable criminal marketplaces include ShadowCrew, Russian Business Network (RBN), Carders Market, and Silk Road.

There is a very robust marketplace to fence virtual goods. Although credit cards are clearly a major focus of online distribution, there are other sorts of information that can be of value; for example, bank account information can be useful, personally identifiable information (PII) can be sold for identity theft purposes, and corporate information can be sold to competitors. Healthcare information contains the same information as traditional financial information, but also facilitates medical insurance fraud. Accordingly, attacks against healthcare organization are on the rise.

Some people may ask why would criminals not exploit the stolen information themselves. The answer is twofold. First, a successful crime, such as the Target credit card theft, results in more data stolen than a single criminal can exploit. It is to the criminal's advantage to sell most of the cards, as he/she would never get to take advantage of all the cards. More importantly, it is not the criminal's specialty. The criminal infrastructure allowed the Target hackers to make sufficient money from the criminal aspects that they specialize in.

HACKERS FOR HIRE

Criminals without sufficient technical skill to accomplish their intended acts can hire the talent they need on the dark web. There are many online forums that allow people to scout for the required talent. Clearly it is difficult to ensure that you are dealing with a truly talented individual, as many hackers exaggerate their skills and accomplishments. There is also the risk that some people soliciting hackers may actually be undercover law enforcement agents.

Regarding the potential skill level of would-be hires, some hackers have a reputation. Some sites have a rating system. It is also common for criminal enterprises who recruit hackers to test their skills. If they can pass the tests, they will make formal offers.

Again, this is another example of criminals being able to make use of world-class talent without having the skills organically.

ENCRYPTED APPS

In the November 2015 Paris attacks by ISIS, a great deal of reporting was devoted to the terrorists' use of mobile apps, such as Telegram, to help plan the attacks. Telegram and WhatsApp, among other communications apps, offer encryption and other capabilities to allow for sharing of data that cannot be easily compromised by law enforcement.

Although ISIS is one concern, the reality is that your employees, both good and bad, are going to use mobile apps to your detriment. Adversaries will be able to coordinate their activities against you through easily available applications.

Although our goal is not to make you think that all technologies are against you, it is important to understand that there are some technologies that are apt to be used by your adversaries. You have to understand what they are, so that you can design your security programs most effectively.

SUMMARY

Although this chapter can make adversaries appear to have unlimited resources, and can make you think that all technologies will be used against you, the goal is to help you optimize your risk. You can only do so when you understand the true nature of the resources that may be put against you.

The reality for most readers is that you will only face a small portion of the resources identified here. When you understand the threats you are most likely to face, you can determine which resources your adversary is most likely to use against you. Then you can figure out what countermeasures are most appropriate to implement given your risk.

Protection

In order to engage in Computer Network Defense (CND), you need to establish a firm base of protection. When you initially define the countermeasures for your organization, it is clearly based on a best guess as to where you may experience loss. You are, however, not expected to get it perfectly right the first time, and you will never get it perfectly right.

You will be attacked through attack vectors that you never anticipated. Even if you anticipated them, you may not have adequately mitigated the vulnerabilities exploited or even chosen to mitigate those vulnerabilities at all. For this reason, you need to consider your protection a dynamic program. You need to be proactive.

This section defines the issues involved in creating a strong and proactive defense program by first implementing protection mechanisms. Later sections will address detection and reaction. Reaction will help you modify and enhance your protections, based on the attacks and losses that you experience, and again, attacks and losses are expected.

We will cover a wide variety of protection mechanisms, but although the list will be robust, it will in no way be complete. There are countless potential protection mechanisms, and although we intend to cover the more useful ones, we do not have room to cover all of them.

It is also important to note that we specifically use the term protection mechanisms and not countermeasures. The reason is that countermeasures can include detection and reaction mechanisms. So although all protection mechanisms are countermeasures, not all countermeasures are protection mechanisms.

CHAPTER 8

Governance

To have a strong security program, it has to be defined. The broad term for that definition is governance. Many organizations have poor governance and do not have a thorough plan in place that clearly defines what is to be protected, how it is to be protected, what resources to be applied, etc. For lack of a better definition, governance is the formalization of a risk management program.

There is no universal definition for governance, so we will use the following: security governance is the combined set of tools, personnel, and processes that provide for formalized risk management. It includes organizational structure, roles and responsibilities, metrics, processes, and oversight, as it specifically impacts the security program.

This seems like a very resource-intensive effort, and for good reason. However, you must consider that security governance essentially protects the value of your organization. Although you do not want the process to be overly burdensome, the security effort should not become a vulnerability itself. Unfortunately, too many programs have no formal governance in place and that too becomes a major vulnerability.

For this reason, all security programs must start with proper governance. The governance must define all relevant facets of protection, detection, and reaction.

Before continuing, it is important to define the critical documents that formalize a governance program. These documents are frequently confused, and the terminology is not well promoted within the industry. The four categories of documents are standards, policies, procedures, and guidelines.

A standard defines an acceptable or minimum level of quality and is frequently created by an outside party that has acknowledged legitimacy. Standards often prescribe quantifiable or explicit mandatory controls.

A policy is high-level statement describing an organization's position on the protection of information and assets across the business. It also defines business rules for consistent treatment of technology and information and on

83

Advanced Persistent Security. http://dx.doi.org/10.1016/B978-0-12-809316-0.00008-7

how compliance will be assured. This is essentially a formal mission statement on the organization as it relates to security, as well as how it intends for that mission to be accomplished.

Procedures are a series of detailed steps and instructions required to accomplish a specific outcome, and for the implementation of policies.

Guidelines are suggestions or guidance as to how to function in a given situation, recommending but not mandating specific controls. Best practices are an example of guidelines.

THE IMPORTANCE OF SECURITY POLICIES, STANDARDS, GUIDELINES, AND PROCEDURES

Proper definition of security governance of any organization can seem overwhelming, especially when organizations have more than 100 people. To do this, you need to start from the top down. By doing so, you start identifying what needs to be defined and then go on to define it.

Governance is formalized with a set of documents. Although we ourselves know that documents are frequently written to check a box and sit on shelves, any organization that is serious about implementing a proper security program should create these documents and ensure that the guidance is implemented and adhered to. Without this formalization, any security program is haphazard. Of course, there are some security programs without documented governance that provide extremely strong security. But this is rare and is completely dependent on the individuals involved. It would require a security manager who intuitively knows what should be in place and also has executive support to implement the program properly, especially including the proper budget.

As with any good business process, security governance should be able to be implemented properly with any individual in any position. Much like how you can walk into any McDonald's in the world and get a hamburger prepared the same way, no matter which person is cooking the hamburger, your security program should be consistent no matter who is in the chief information security officer (CISO), CEO, help desk, or any other position in the company.

Again, the appropriate documents, adhered to properly, should ensure that the security governance is implemented consistently.

STANDARDS

In many cases, what needs to be defined is specified in standards. Such standards can be required by the vendors whom you do business with, in areas of the world where you do business, by the laws and regulations, etc. These standards rarely define security down to the specific implementation, but provide high-level guidance for a more structured program.

Examples of common standards that impact security programs include the Health Insurance Portability and Accountability Act (HIPAA), the Payment Card Industry Data Security Standard (PCI DSS), and the ISO/IEC (International Organization for Standardization/International Electrotechnical Commission) 27001 Information Security Management System (ISO 27001).

When there are standards that are deemed applicable to an organization, this should serve as a start for security governance. All policies and procedures created should ideally incorporate the requirements defined by the relevant standards.

Sometimes, third parties create standards or other requirements. Examples of this are legislation and regulations. Insurance companies can also impose de facto standards. For example, in most facilities, guards perform rounds; this is not to ensure that there is no illicit behavior, but because fire insurance requires that someone ensures at regular intervals that there are no signs of a fire. With the growing proliferation of cyber insurance, it is likely that new de facto standards will be created to reduce the likelihood and severity of cyber incidents that would be eligible for coverage.

Technical Standards Versus Industry Standards

As the term standard is used in many venues, it is important to understand that in the technical world, the word can be used for nongovernance-related standards. Some standards are used to facilitate technical interoperability vice organizational governance. For example, the IEEE 802 standard series is used for networking interoperability.

Industry standards, such as the PCI DSS and the North American Electric Reliability Corporation Critical Infrastructure Protection (NERC CIP), provide a governance model that are used for implementing security at a programmatic level. Such industry standards pose requirements on the security programs, and failure to meet such standards can result in penalties.

A Warning About Relying on Compliance to Standards

Although standards are important and security programs must implement the requirements of the standards, they should just be considered a base. A program that meets the standards, in other words, achieves *compliance*, is not necessarily an adequate security program.

Compliance means that you meet the base requirements of a standard. Standards, for example, might state that you have a policy created. It does not mean that the policy is sufficient or adequately implemented. For example, there are typically vague requirements regarding security awareness. Such standards state to the effect that all employees should receive awareness training. There is no definition as to what is adequate awareness training, or more importantly, what is improved behavior. Typically, an organization will just provide an auditor with a report that says all employees completed a computer-based training (CBT) course. It does not mean that users became more aware as a result of the course and improved their behaviors.

For the purpose of this chapter, it is important to recognize that standards and other mandates are typically hard to define and are very political. Sometimes standards are defined by the organizations being governed, which implies there is bias in minimizing the burden imposed by the standards. When there is a government regulation, it has likely been subject to intense lobbying. There is typically a great deal of negotiation in getting to the final version of the standard or other mandate, and therefore, it has been weakened from its ideal form.

Benefits of Standards and Mandates

As we defined standards as having limitations, and essentially stated that being compliant does not mean you have adequate security, it does lead to the question as to how standards are useful. In short, in the absence of standards, there may be nothing. Although there are many organizations that do have extremely good security programs in the absence of standards, there are other organizations that have grossly inadequate programs.

For example, when the PCI DSS standard was first implemented, we spoke with a CISO of a well-known retailer, who was complaining about her troubles in implementing PCI at her organization. Her quote was, "Do you know how hard it is to encrypt credit card numbers on a mainframe?"

The implication was that there were hundreds of millions of credit card numbers being stored on the retailer's computers that were not encrypted. This is something that was no longer allowed after the implementation of the PCI DSS standard.

So in short, standards and mandates should not be considered sufficient and might not raise the bar for many organizations, but they at least establish a minimum bar for organizations to meet.

POLICIES

The most concise definition of a policy that we can come up with is the following: a security policy is a concise formal statement that outlines nondiscretionary governing principles and intentions to guide a security program.

It is a high-level statement as to what is important to protect and what resources, at a high level, should be allocated by the security program. Although a security policy can be very vague and can mean the organization values information, a better policy document will have a reasonable level of granularity. For example, it should include policies regarding user awareness, mobile devices, physical access, the definition of different types of data, data classification, server security, database security, etc. The more inclusive the granularity, the more likely there will be a strong security program.

It is also important to consider that the more policies you create, the more guidelines and procedures you will be required to create. This is actually very good, because it implies that you will end up with a very well-defined security program. It does not mean it will be implemented, but at least it can be well defined.

PROCEDURES

Procedures are best defined as step-by-step actions to implement a policy as required. A policy states that something must be done. A procedure states how it should be done. Procedures will go down the hands-on level of specificity.

There will likely be multiple procedures per policy. For example, there should be a policy that states to the effect that all computer systems should have a standard security configuration. To implement the policy, you will need procedures for each type of computer operating system in use. Some policies may require procedures that impact other procedures. For example, a procedure on how to construct a secure password would impact how to configure password rules for each procedure for each operating system in use.

Although policies should be considered living documents, and organizations should consider updating and adding to them as required, they should be written at such a level that modifications should be rare. However, given that procedures may be tied to specific technologies, they will likely have to be updated as there are changes in the technologies. For example, if there is a procedure that states how to secure an iPhone, every change to the iOS would at least require a review of that procedure.

GUIDELINES

Guidelines are recommended (nonmandatory) processes that support the implementation of policies. They are in many ways identical to procedures, except that they are not mandatory.

Why some guidance might be considered mandatory (a procedure) and not recommended (a guideline) is dependent on the organizational policies and the standards and mandates the organization is required to follow. For example, although the encryption of credit card data might be mandatory, because of the PCI DSS requirements, encryption of organizational process data, not covered by PCI or HIPAA, might be considered optional, and guidelines for implementing encryption would be required.

SUMMARY

Although other people or organizations may use different names for the same documents, the nature of the documents is consistent. What is most important is that they exist. As stated, there needs to be a formal definition of your security effort.

Clearly, as much of your security program as possible should be formalized and documented. It is a fairly labor-intensive effort, but it is also a front-loaded effort. Once the policies, procedures, and guidelines are written and approved, there is little question as to what should be implemented.

But again, the most important aspect of these documents is that they should be properly implemented. Many organizations spend a great deal of time, effort, and money, and just have the documents sit on a shelf to show to auditors once a year, so that they may be declared "compliant." If the documents, however, do not reflect the security program in practice, and major incidents will ensue.

To implement Advanced Persistent Security, you must have a formalized program in place, and that program begins by being documented. It must then be approved and supported by executive management to ensure that it can then be properly implemented. Without proper governance in place, you security program will be a random accident.

CHAPTER 9

Vulnerabilities to Address

When people think protection or security, fundamentally they assume the implementation of countermeasures to mitigate vulnerabilities. This is a protection program vice a security program. However, an understanding of potential vulnerabilities is also critical to detection and reaction strategies. To detect incidents, you have to be aware of the vulnerabilities that could be exploited. Reaction requires determining the exploited vulnerabilities, so that they can be mitigated and an attack in progress can be stopped and future incidents can be prevented.

In Chapter 4, we introduce the four basic categories of vulnerabilities: physical, technical, operational, and personnel. In this chapter, we intend to better detail vulnerabilities. Each category clearly contains many different vulnerabilities that are very diverse. They are joined by the root nature of the individual vulnerability.

As we work through the vulnerabilities, what is important is not necessarily the individual vulnerability, but the commonalities among them. For this reason, we do not intend to detail each and every potential vulnerability. Frankly, even if we did, the list would be incomplete and outdated quickly. We focus on addressing common and representative vulnerabilities. This should ideally make the reader rapidly identify vulnerabilities. In this way, you should be able to understand those vulnerabilities that need to be considered for mitigation. If you want a more detailed listing of vulnerabilities, you can refer to Ira's book, *Spies Among Us*.

Intelligence operatives and Special Forces soldiers go through training that essentially involves them learning to rapidly recognize vulnerabilities and knowing how to rapidly exploit them. In implementing Advanced Persistent Security, you are essentially preparing to take on adversaries who are attempting to rapidly recognize your vulnerabilities, so that they can exploit them. You, therefore, need to be able to recognize those vulnerabilities first, so that you can consciously decide whether they require mitigation.

As discussed in Section 4 of this book, you are attempting to get inside the observe, orient, decide, and act (OODA) loop of the attackers when you are

Advanced Persistent Security. http://dx.doi.org/10.1016/B978-0-12-809316-0.00009-9

reacting to an attack. To do so, you need to remove the vulnerabilities that they are exploiting. In other words, reacting to an ongoing attack, and preventing future attacks if an attack ceases for any reason, requires understanding the vulnerabilities to be identified and mitigated.

As you read through this chapter, seek to understand the root of the vulnerability. Frequently, a vulnerability is just a symptom of a larger problem. Most frequently, that larger problem is a process, or operational, problem where the other vulnerabilities only exist because there is a process that creates them. For example, when systems are configured insecurely, which is a common vulnerability, the vulnerability only exists because there is likely not an operational process in place that defines and ensures that there are secure system configurations.

Through this understanding, you can begin to proactively determine the required countermeasures, which are defined in Chapter 10.

A common question we get is, "Why are you separating countermeasures and vulnerabilities?" As stated in Chapter 4, you cannot always stop a vulnerability from existing. It is also possible that a vulnerability can be mitigated through multiple countermeasures. It is therefore useful to understand countermeasures and vulnerabilities separately.

OPERATIONAL VULNERABILITIES

As stated, most vulnerabilities result in one way or another from an operational vulnerability, so it is proper to start with them. Although operational vulnerabilities were previously introduced, to summarize the concern, an operational vulnerability involves the way information is handled, disclosed, maintained, deleted, collected, etc. In other words, operational vulnerabilities involve a weakness in the general use of information or how access to information is granted.

It is impossible to create a comprehensive list of all operational vulnerabilities, as they vary as much as organizational policies and procedures. Frequently these vulnerabilities come into fruition accidentally, or haphazardly, because people just implement their own procedures.

Poor Governance

There is a significant reason why we began Section 2 with a chapter on governance. Governance is a critical countermeasure, but the lack of proper governance is a root vulnerability that needs to be addressed. It can arguably be stated that poor governance is the root of all the other vulnerabilities that we state or imply throughout the chapter.

As stated in Chapter 8, good governance is the root to all repeatable, successful security programs. It establishes how information should be handled.

It establishes technical security controls. The lack of established governance creates a haphazard security program that is frequently insufficient.

We will not rehash Chapter 8 in its totality; however, for the purpose of vulnerabilities, just know that poor governance, which would include both the definition of all policies and procedures and potentially the poor implementation of what might otherwise be well-defined governance, can be considered the root of almost all other vulnerabilities.

Poor Awareness

User awareness is knowledge that leads to appropriate security behaviors. Knowledge itself is insufficient. Awareness requires that people behave in accordance with that knowledge. For example, just because people know that they should not write down their password, it does not mean that they will do so. Users cannot be considered to demonstrate strong awareness unless their behaviors are in accordance with policies.

Poor security awareness is consistently at the root of most major incidents. The Verizon Data Breach Investigations Report demonstrates the prevalence of user susceptibility to phishing and other attacks that specifically target humans. It can be argued that everyone who fell victim to any of the attacks has been exposed to some form of awareness training, yet they still fell victim. It is impossible to believe that anyone with Internet access is not aware of the concept of phishing. It is likewise inconceivable to believe that people were never instructed that they should not allow outsiders into facilities without appropriate permissions.

Clearly, people require knowledge of the threats, as well as of the actions they should take. However, the most important aspect is that the individual is motivated to take the appropriate actions. Although people will contend that the attackers can be extremely devious in their methods to trick them into taking an action that they should not otherwise take, good governance and the awareness of the governance should stop an individual from committing the offense. The reality is that most people do not fall for the tricks; however, all it takes is one offense to compromise all security.

Chapter 11 discusses awareness-related concerns in greater detail.

Information Release Procedures

Too frequently, organizations are their own worst enemy. Through policy, process, happenstance, accident, or carelessness, organizations leak information that their threats would spend virtually unlimited resources to collect. These leaks can take many forms.

From an espionage perspective, China sometimes sponsors conferences and similar events where it invites scientists leading research that is important to their efforts. It might invite the scientists to present their research and pushes them to include the more sensitive aspects of their work. Even if they do not, the Chinese intelligence services might invite the researchers out for social events, provide them with a lot of alcohol, and then will subtly drill them for the more sensitive aspects of their work.

How the organization deals with the media is also a vulnerability. To curry favor with the media, organizations sometimes provide more information than they should. They might provide information on background. Poor media relations policies can result in people inside organizations providing information to media outlets in attempts to be helpful.

Sometimes revenge can lead to major compromises of information. Such was the case with Valerie Plame. In this case, Plame's husband, Ambassador Joseph Wilson, was a critic of the Bush administration policies, and in retaliation, Richard Armitage, a deputy secretary of state provided a reporter with information that Plame was an undercover CIA operative. This resulted in a massive compromise of CIA covert operations. Intelligence agencies from around the world, where Plame was stationed and visited, could then identify front companies and potentially other undercover operatives and people providing information to Plame and others.

For example, if Plame worked for an organization, it was likely that the organization was a CIA front company. Other employees of that organization also potentially worked for the CIA. People that Plame met might be spying against their host government. Not only Plame, but everything she was associated with was compromised, with basic research by the host governments where Plame was stationed.

Organizations sometimes post too much information on their websites. Sometimes the information is not considered to be sensitive. Sometimes the communications department just posts information as a habit, without considering the strategic value. Other times, sensitive information is not properly filtered. For example, in one case a PDF file contained information that was redacted by placing black bars over the text. The people posting the information apparently did not realize that the redacted information can be viewed by looking at the source file.

There are countless other examples where sensitive information was leaked. What is important is that the inadvertent release of information is considered a vulnerability that is considered for mitigation.

Social Media Usage

With the growth of social media, information can be spread to millions of people almost instantaneously. Facebook, Twitter, Instagram, Snapchat,

YouTube, etc. all provide for information to be distributed worldwide, with little ability to control further dissemination. It can be an extremely powerful tool for the intended purpose. However, it can also provide for tremendous disclosures.

Frequently, the results are embarrassing. Sometimes the results can lead to much more serious consequences. Some people have been denied employment, because of behaviors highlighted on their social media accounts. Criminals have been identified after they post the crimes or the spoils of their crimes.

Employees sometimes post information that is sensitive to their employers. Sometimes the information is embarrassing to their employers.

In one case, a squadron of helicopters came under attack because a soldier posted pictures on Twitter of the arrival of the helicopters at a base in Iraq. The picture files contained the geolocation where the picture was taken, which was the position where the helicopters were stationed.

In more conventional settings, people posting vacation pictures on Facebook and other social networks informed criminals that homes were unoccupied and ripe for theft. Criminals would friend everyone they could in their local area and wait for them to indicate they were away from home for extended periods. People facilitate stalkers by posting their activities and locations.

The ability to send out information, without review, by any individual at will is a tremendous vulnerability that can compromise some of the most sensitive information in an organization in seconds. This vulnerability must be addressed by security programs.

Carelessness Conversations

Although in comparison to social media in-person conversations have limited ability to compromise information, they can still compromise a great deal of information. A compromise requires that the information be heard by a party that is interested in the information, and in some cases that can be coincidental.

Although we have had conversations in places where we thought nobody would know the people or incidents involved, we also travel a great deal and know people all over the world. We have had experiences, where we meet people who know us on random airplane flights, in airport clubs, at restaurants, and county fairs in the middle of nowhere. Some of these people might be familiar with some of our customer dealings, or with people whom we might mutually know. We should therefore be extremely careful about what we talk about within the earshot of anyone.

However, many people are not that sensitive to information. For example, we know a person who performs legal competitive intelligence work. He frequently goes to bars that are located near locations of companies that he is trying to collect information from. He just listens for people talking about sensitive information and sometimes tries to chat with random people who work for the targeted organization.

When organizations are highly targeted by international companies, it is not uncommon for restaurants, bars, and similar locations to be bugged in hopes that people might discuss sensitive information with their coworkers.

Everyone should consider where they take work-related calls and wonder if someone could be listening. When Ira worked for the NSA, there were very clear policies that work-related conversations were never to be held outside classified facilities, no matter what the circumstances were. Few organizations make any reference to where and when people should hold conversations. This is a major vulnerability that needs to be addressed.

Business Partnerships

During the course of business operations, it is almost inevitable for an organization to partner with other organizations. Some of these partnerships are very specific in their scope. Some require the exchange of no sensitive information. However, many partnerships require minimal to extensive sharing of information.

Sometimes there is a basic sharing of price lists and discount ranges. Sometimes there is extensive sharing of details about manufacturing capabilities, designs, and other highly prized elements of intellectual property. How such information is exchanged and released can be a critical vulnerability.

The most glaring example is the establishment of joint ventures with Chinese companies. US companies received special guidance from US intelligence and law enforcement agencies that they should treat such joint venture companies as potentially hostile elements. Even if they are close partnerships and consider the venture a part of their own organization, it is recommended that they treat the entity as a separate entity with regard to information exchange and network connectivity. It is assumed that China, and other foreign countries, would use joint venture networks as launch points for attacks against the main organization's network assets.

There are countless examples, but you need to consider any deal with another organization to be a potential vulnerability. Any negotiations and related implementation should consider the potential for these dealings to be a vulnerability and proactively account for that potential.

Technical Security Procedures

As stated in Chapter 5, there are only two ways to hack computers: taking advantage of the vulnerabilities built into the software and taking advantage of how an otherwise secure computer is configured or maintained. At first glance, they seem like technical vulnerabilities, and they essentially are.

However, how a computer is configured and maintained can be considered an operational vulnerability. Specifically, there should be a systems configuration guideline or procedure that states specifically how the systems should be configured. Several organizations provide recommendations for secure configurations, including NSA. Not implementing such guidelines is an operational vulnerability.

Although the average organization does not write its own software, and is not directly responsible for the presence of vulnerabilities written into a software, there should be an operational process for the installation of software patches to account for these vulnerabilities. It would, therefore, be an operational vulnerability if there is no process in place to patch systems in a timely manner.

Giving Out too Little Information

Although the title of this section might sound counterintuitive, giving out too little information can be a significant vulnerability. Not disclosing information relevant to a person's job can lead to mistakes and cause loss. Employees have to know how their responsibilities fit within the overall structure and function of the organization.

This issue is especially true when it comes to security-related functions. For example, when organizations do not disclose information about past or ongoing incidents, employees might not be aware or, as previously described, motivated to practice good security practices. People should be made aware that some of the people they deal with might have committed acts that led to significant loss.

The employees might not be aware that some of the practices that they currently exhibit created a loss and that there is a need to preserve information. If there is an ongoing incident, if they are not told what signs to look for, they might miss other aspects of the incident that could prevent further loss. For example, if they have dealt with a person who is suspected of theft, they might have information that could help the investigation or lead to evidence of a further compromise. If they are not aware of the potential incident, they cannot report the relevant information.

Although there is a potential need to limit dissemination of information about security-related incidents, the limited information facilitates continued loss. Admittedly, sometimes the distribution of information is limited for legal reasons. More frequently, it appears that distribution is limited because the organization does not want to suffer embarrassment.

PERSONNEL VULNERABILITIES

Personnel vulnerabilities deal with how to hire, manage, and separate people. Clearly there can be significant overlap with operational vulnerabilities. Admittedly it might not matter as to how you want to categorize a vulnerability, as long as you consider it within your security program. For simplicity purposes, we place vulnerabilities that deal with how personnel are managed into this category.

As a general note, although this category generally refers to people as employees, it is referring to anyone who is considered subordinate to your organization. This could be direct employees, contractors, temporary employees, vendors, and any other parties in a similar relationship. All such parties should be subject to the same security considerations, and if they are not, that itself is a vulnerability.

Poor Background Checks

There is a sentiment that everyone lies while applying for a job. Resumes are exaggerated or misleading. People lie about their skill sets and experience. Some people put down fake references. Others assume false identities. Some people go as far as to work with conspirators to answer phones supposedly faking legitimate companies, when answering a predetermined telephone number. Criminals go to varying lengths to hide their true intent and identity.

There is also the concern as to what might not be reported by an individual. People might not state that they have criminal records. They might not report jobs where they were dismissed for cause.

Poor or the lack of background checks can be a very significant vulnerability. Even if there is something that might be inconsequentially found, the fact that a potential employee attempts to conceal or mislead could itself be the cause for future concern.

Treating Employees Poorly

When you treat employees poorly, they will treat you poorly in return. When you pay them less than they deserve, they might attempt to make up for it in other ways, such as lying on their timecards or stealing from the organization.

Even if employees do not commit detrimental acts themselves, they might be less inclined to report customers or other employees for their transgressions. As discussed in Chapter 11, your employees are a critical part of your protection, detection, and reaction capability, and if you treat them poorly, they will be less likely to perform those responsibilities at the desired levels.

Although poorly treated employees tend to have lower productivity, the security-related concerns should also be considered.

Weak Management

Treating employees poorly is one example of poor management. Management can also be weak in that there is poor oversight of activities. Clearly there is a need to ensure that employees adhere to security governance. If management does not ensure such adherence, it is a vulnerability.

Another concern is inconsistent enforcement of governance. This can not only lead to security failures, but also create legal consequences. For example, if you punish one employee for a security violation, but previously did not punish other employees for similar violations, the punished employee can claim bias and sue the organization. Inconsistency in the implementation of security policies is a major vulnerability to an organization.

Poor Separation Procedures

How you separate an employee can lead to major security problems. Frequently, people are leaving for competing organizations. They might have planned their departure months in advance. They might be leaving under adverse circumstances. There are many scenarios. Whatever the scenario, the absence of well-thought-out and properly implemented procedures can be a very significant vulnerability.

When people separate, the absence of a step-by-step process to recover equipment, information, and other sensitive materials can lead to a significant loss of information. Ideally, an organization tracks when an employee is provided with laptop computers, cell phones, and portable storage media. There should be a process to recover such equipment.

In many organizations, failing to inform the IT department to deactivate the departing employee's computer access leads to major incidents. Even if departed employees do not attempt to access their account after they leave, it creates a zombie account that hackers can exploit later. In many cases, co-workers have attempted to access the accounts of departed employees to cover up illicit activities.

Failure to analyze employees' activities before their departure can miss critical thefts of information. There are many other issues that can be missed with the absence of specific guidance on the steps to be taken on an employee's departure.

Human Resources Being Isolated

Frequently, human resources (HR) actions are considered highly sensitive, and for good reason. However, it does not mean that HR should never interact with other departments. When HR does not inform IT, management, and other relevant departments that an adverse action might happen against an employee, those departments cannot attempt to proactively mitigate illicit actions on the part of the employee.

Sometimes there are legal and other concerns for doing so. But if security concerns are not accounted for, significant damage can occur because of poor HR policies and procedures.

PHYSICAL VULNERABILITIES

Although a good deal of attention is placed on technical vulnerabilities, because of the focus on external hackers, tremendous losses are caused by physical failings. As with all sections in this chapter, there is an almost infinite number of vulnerabilities that can be listed here. This is especially true for this section. We do not intend to be exhaustive but representative in our discussion.

Apathetic or Poorly Informed Guards

When you think about people who are supposed to be the most alert to security concerns, you think about the security guards. The truth is that they receive minimal training and are not well paid. They frequently do not know what to look for.

By performing penetration tests, we noticed that security guards perform their rounds not to look for security-related concerns, but because insurance requires the guards to look for potential fires. They do not record people working late. They do not look for other signs of security vulnerabilities, such as information left widely vulnerable on desks or meeting rooms.

This is a generalization, as we intend to highlight when an apparent security countermeasure is actually a vulnerability. We have also met some incredible security guards, who are extremely well trained. There are some guards who receive poor training and pay, but still do an exceptional job. However, those guards who are poorly trained or apathetic are a major vulnerability that needs to be addressed.

Poor Physical Access Controls

Locks may not work. Doors may not have locks. There might not be tracking as to who enters and leaves facilities. This can be to enter facilities or poorly secured areas within facilities.

When anyone can enter or leave facilities, or even when access is limited but not well monitored, it is a major vulnerability that facilitates unlimited compromises.

Windows are a vulnerability to consider. When we perform penetration tests, we sometimes wait until it gets dark, and then go to a neighboring office building to our target. Given the lighting, we can frequently see into our target's offices and meeting rooms, and capture information from white boards or otherwise left within view.

Shared Office Space

Although somewhat akin to poor physical access controls, it is not uncommon for organizations to lease or maintain shared spaces with other organizations. This situation happens when organizations want to save money, and they rent out some of their facilities to other parties. Unless incredibly strict controls are put in place, the other parties will inevitably have access to the hosting organization's offices.

Organizations may also randomly lease space that shares facilities with other parties. Although these other parties might not necessarily represent a direct threat themselves, if these parties do not properly protect their facilities, another party can compromise your neighbor to get to you.

In one case, we performed a security assessment of a warehouse facility and found that facility to have subleased space to a museum open to the public. There was only a hallway door that separated the organizations, and it turned out that the door was not locked and the alarm did not work. In other cases, shared staircases allowed anyone to enter what should have been a secured facility.

Physical Location

Even if a facility is secure, the surrounding location can present other vulnerabilities. A facility could be in a crime-ridden neighborhood. This presents threats to vehicles and employees who have to travel through the neighborhood to get to the facility.

Sometimes there are environmental concerns. Facilities can be located in flood zones. They could be in areas that experience frequent hurricanes or other weather-related events. This can create service interruptions, if not the outright destruction of the facilities.

Admittedly, the physical location can add to security, such as placing a facility in a good neighborhood, on a secured facility, or next to a police station. However, it is important to review all facilities within your control to examine if the location itself presents vulnerabilities that need to be accounted for.

Garbage

How your organization disposes of garbage, which may include information considered to be no longer useful, can be a very significant vulnerability. People might think that a marked up document is worthless, but it could have information that is otherwise valuable.

There are military units devoted to TRASHINT, which is literally Trash Intelligence. They specialize in going through deserted facilities to find sensitive information that has been left behind. We know people who worked executive protection for the US government, and they relayed stories how when they traveled with a government official, someone was assigned to go through any area where the executive was located to ensure that no information was left behind, even including the bathroom.

It is not uncommon for hackers to go through the trash of their targets to find information that could help them perform social engineering attacks, or sometimes even find actual passwords.

Open Storage

Within facilities, information might not be properly secured. There is the assumption that everyone within an organization is trustworthy. Clearly this is not the case. Even if everyone is actually trustworthy, there are frequently cases where information should have limited distribution. Additionally, there may be visitors or interlopers who should not see all materials.

Whenever information is not secured, it is vulnerable to anyone with access to the facility, either legitimately or illegitimately. People can leave information vulnerable in desk areas, meeting rooms, common areas, etc.

Printers and Copy Machines

Copy machines present special vulnerabilities from a physical perspective. Information can be left vulnerable, if people transmit files to those devices. People frequently leave information behind accidentally. Anyone walking by can pick up this information.

Despite their stated functions, these devices are actually special purpose computers. Not only is there the physical consideration of printed documents, but also these devices have hard drives that can be stolen or left in the device when the device is sold or retired. This means that someone can potentially recover all the information that was ever printed or copied from the devices.

Electronic Media

Storage devices are frequently poorly controlled. USB drives are frequently lost. It is even easy to lose track of larger hard drives and storage tapes. Even small storage devices can contain the information for millions of people. Electronic media is required for the storage and transportation of information, but how these devices are used and allocated is critical.

It is also important to consider that laptop computers, cell phones, and similar devices are also forms of electronic media. Although many people may say that the media is embedded within the device, it can be argued that the only value to the device is the information it stores. The equipment can be easily replaced, but the information is the more devastating loss. Laptops and cell phones are frequently lost and stolen and present a major vulnerability.

Lack of Inventory Tracking

As stated, laptops, cell phones, and similar equipment are electronic media. They are also valuable pieces of equipment. Companies frequently lose track of such equipment. Although there is clearly the potential to lose this equipment, it is also frequently taken when employees leave the organization. When there is no tracking, it is impossible to know when information is lost or stolen. You cannot withhold paychecks if a person does not return equipment. Fundamentally, you may not know when the devices were lost or stolen.

BYOD Policies

Although this may be considered an operational vulnerability, many companies implement a bring your own device (BYOD) program that has employees use their personal devices for work-related purposes. This is especially common for cell phones.

BYOD saves organizations money. They do not have to provide their employees with phones, and depending on the size of the organization, it can save them millions of dollars a year. The problem is that when a person uses the device for business purposes, it means that the organization can lose control of the information it contains. Additionally, when a person leaves the organization, the device goes with them, and there is strong potential for the information to be carried away. Depending on the strength of the BYOD policy, the organization might have very limited ability to control the information on the device, or even ask to know what information is on the device.

TECHNICAL VULNERABILITIES

There are many books on identifying technical vulnerabilities, and we recommend that you find books on the technologies that you use. We therefore identify a few of the vulnerabilities that are common to all technologies.

Software Bugs and Configuration Errors

There are two root vulnerabilities to hack a computer: vulnerabilities built into the software and vulnerabilities in how a computer is configured or maintained. This theory of computer hacking is not specific to computer hacking, but to any device that functions with software. This includes just about any modern device such as network gear, printers, copy machines, cars, cell phones, and the growing Internet of things.

Besides the computers, or the equipment themselves, all applications loaded on those devices are subject to vulnerabilities. This includes common software such as word processors and spreadsheets, as well as less common software such as industrial control software. Sometimes an obscure software on systems, which people may not even be aware is on the system, is attacked to compromise the underlying system or other applications.

If there is any software, you should assume the device can be hacked. The potential for such vulnerabilities should be considered. Although most people primarily think of software written by vendors, they also need to consider the software that they develop themselves. Custom applications, such as web applications, are frequently riddled with vulnerabilities.

Poor Password Management

Passwords that are easy to guess have compromised computers, because there were accounts on computers. This vulnerability is common and continues to exist. This is just one form of password vulnerability.

With the regular compromise of passwords, another common password vulnerability is the reuse of passwords on multiple accounts. So if a person's password is compromised on a minor account, and then the person reuses the password for their Facebook account, the Facebook account is potentially vulnerable.

Another ironic issue that comes up is that even if you change passwords and if you reuse the password on the same account later, the account becomes vulnerable again.

A growing irony is that password strength is frequently irrelevant. Although some attackers may target a specific individual, and may resort to password guessing, passwords are typically compromised through other means. These means include phishing attacks, theft of password files, keystroke monitors, and other malware. So how you create and manage your own passwords can be a greater vulnerability than even having a password of "password."

Wireless Networks

Although all networks are subject to monitoring, public wireless networks present extra vulnerabilities, especially given their wide acceptance. Many wireless networks do not implement basic security measures. Sometimes hackers set up fake networks to impersonate real networks.

Wireless networks can be configured securely, but it is too easy to configure them insecurely. All the data transmitted on that network then becomes subject to compromise.

Data in Transit

As wireless networks demonstrate, data can be compromised during transmission. If you send an email message, submit data to or receive data from a website, or communicate with any system, the data can go through a dozen or more systems. Any system can potentially store and read the data. There is also the potential for a malicious party to tap the networks, so the data can be compromised at any point over thousands of miles.

Network Configurations

The design and implementation of a network can create vulnerabilities that should not exist. Although an attacker might be able to find an access point to a network, it does not mean that the attacker should get access to every system on the network.

The term, flat network, means that there is no network segmentation or hierarchy. If you can access one system on the network, you can access all of them. The absence of access controls, network segmentation, and similar configuration principles can leave a network much more vulnerable than it is.

Additionally, it is not uncommon to lose track of a network design and for individual departments to add devices to a network. Some locations acquire their own Internet connections, without the knowledge or approval of the appropriate IT staff. This is known as Shadow IT.

Shadow IT systems are not only unknown, but also frequently poorly maintained and are therefore extremely vulnerable.

Sometimes IT organizations lose control of their network configuration during mergers and acquisitions. When an organization acquires another entity, they traditionally connect the new organization directly to their network. Unless there is a knowledgeable IT staff with the authority to isolate the new network until the network can be brought up to security standards, the IT department will lose control of the network configuration by default.

SUMMARY

This chapter outlined some of the more notable vulnerabilities that might exist within your organization. It is, however, just a starting point. To create a strong security program and implement Advanced Persistent Security, you need to be able to recognize the vulnerabilities on your network, so that you can make a rational risk-based decision on whether and how to mitigate the vulnerabilities.

As you go through the following chapters, you can decide which mitigation strategies would be appropriate for your organization given the vulnerabilities. Clearly, we imply mitigation strategies during our discussion of the vulnerabilities. There are, however, many more mitigation strategies to consider.

CHAPTER 10

Countermeasures

As our risk management discussion defines, countermeasures are what you have ultimate control of when managing your risk. Countermeasures can provide protection, detection, and/or reaction capabilities. For editorial purposes, we provide this discussion in the Protection section as we want to discuss countermeasures as early in the book as reasonable. A large portion of countermeasures also focus on protection, so it is appropriate.

This chapter is broken into operational, personnel, physical, and technical countermeasures. We expect that readers will be most familiar and interested in technical countermeasures. To implement Advanced Persistent Security, you need to implement a holistic set of countermeasures, so we ensure that we provide adequate coverage of all categories.

This discussion is not intended to be exhaustive. We therefore highlight broad categories of countermeasures, as opposed to specific solutions or products. Regarding technical countermeasures, we provide a sampling of such countermeasures, but recommend that you research the technologies you have or need and then determine the appropriate technical countermeasures to implement. Section 5 discusses this in detail.

It must also be noted that some countermeasures cannot be perfectly categorized. For example, certain operational countermeasures could easily be considered personnel countermeasures. The categorization is not as important as the fact that the appropriate countermeasures be understood and implemented as your environment requires. The categorization may only matter to your organization, if there is a clear delineation of responsibility that requires that specific departments have specific security responsibilities.

OPERATIONAL COUNTERMEASURES

Operational countermeasures involve implementing processes that mitigate vulnerabilities. These processes can involve protection, detection, or reaction. All departments within an organization should be responsible for implementing

105

Advanced Persistent Security. http://dx.doi.org/10.1016/B978-0-12-809316-0.00010-5

operational countermeasures. Essentially, where there is sensitive information or processes, operational countermeasures should be implemented.

As previously stated, it can be argued that all countermeasures rely on operational countermeasures. Even technical countermeasures require that there be established governance to implement them consistently. Governance is by definition an operational countermeasure.

For the purpose of this discussion, we highlight those countermeasures that are a process and are not more appropriate to be categorized as physical, technical, or personnel countermeasures.

Governance

We devoted an entire chapter to this subject, and for good reason. A security program will be an accident without proper governance. Every aspect of your security program should be a process that is defined and repeatable. This includes exactly how information is handled. It also includes how technology is maintained.

We include this section here only for completeness, because the subject is thoroughly discussed in Chapter 8; however, as governance is an operational countermeasure, we also want to stress its importance. Without established governance, the strength of an organization's security program is random, as it would depend completely on highly skilled people being able to get the resources and cooperation they need from the entire organization, and especially their management. As we are sure all readers can assume, that level of cooperation and skill is not very likely to exist.

Security Awareness

Security awareness is also defined in Chapter 11. We do, however, want to ensure that it is recognized as an operational countermeasure. The fact that we have devoted a separate chapter to it should demonstrate its importance.

Security awareness is about creating and strengthening proper behaviors. It is not about providing people with training, which is by definition a fixed body of knowledge. You want to instill awareness, and training is only a method to inform people about the desired behaviors. For example, there is a difference between people being told what is a good password and people actually creating a good password.

Fundamentally, awareness should promote the procedures and guidelines as defined by your own governance. It should not be dependent on the random content in an off-the-shelf vendor video.

As simulated phishing attacks have become commonplace in awareness programs, it should be noted that they have highly variable effectiveness rates.

However, even if they were completely effective at wiping out phishing susceptibility, remember that phishing awareness is just one element of dozens that a good security awareness programs should cover.

Although awareness is generally associated with protection, proper awareness training should cover detection and reaction as well.

Technical Training

The proper use of technology might be considered a part of awareness training, but we want to clearly state that all employees should be trained in the proper use of relevant technologies. Where this book is concerned, it is important to especially define proper security procedures in the use and maintenance of common technologies.

People should be informed about how to ensure updates are applied as specified by governance. They should be familiar with ensuring that their mobile devices have the latest updates and security patches installed. Although the organization should manage technology as best as possible, every user should be aware of its proper use and maintenance with regard to all relevant aspects of protection, detection, and reaction.

Rewards/Gamification

A good security awareness program should provide incentives, a.k.a. rewards, to users exhibiting proper behaviors. We, however, want to specifically highlight rewards as something all organizations should consider. When an employee does something that saves the organization substantial resources, such as detecting and reporting a potential attack, the employee should be rewarded and his/her actions, including the reward, should be made known to all people within the organization. This not only highlights the importance of good security behaviors, but also encourages all people to perform similar actions.

Gamification is thoroughly covered in Chapter 11. Here, we want to stress that gamification is not creating a game for people to play, but a reward structure for performing the desired security behaviors. Although gamification programs are not appropriate for all organizations, it is a concept for security programs to consider.

Social Media Controls

Social media can be a security nightmare. It allows information to be spread around the world to millions of people in seconds. There are no filters, and even when the content is supposedly deleted, the reality is that it can never be truly deleted.

Individuals have caused themselves great harm by posting information that is embarrassing or otherwise harmful. For example, in July 2016, the 2015 Playboy

Playmate of the Year, Dani Mathers, took a picture of a naked woman in a health club shower and posted it on Snapchat, while criticizing the woman's body. Mathers was fired from a broadcasting job and faced potential criminal charges.

Such gaffes are not limited to private individuals. In 2012, Netflix CEO, Reed Hastings, faced a Securities and Exchange Commission (SEC) investigation and potential criminal charges for tweeting out information about Netflix user statistics. Although this is the most notable case affecting corporate leaks, there are frequent cases of sensitive information accidentally making its way to social media.

We assume that readers of this book are well aware of the combination of ease of use and damage that social networks, such as Facebook, Twitter, and Snapchat, can create. To account for such vulnerabilities, organizations must develop specific policies and processes regarding what is allowed to be posted on social media and how it is to be posted.

Generally, there should also be a process to remind employees of their responsibilities to protect information from social media. Although we realize that it is extremely sensitive to tell employees what they can and cannot do on social networks, organizations have both the right and the responsibility to define how information owned by the organization is expected to be treated and protected.

Internet and Social Media Monitoring

More established organizations have social media monitoring teams, or employ services that perform this function. It is important to search social networks and the Internet as a whole for brand references, as well as keywords and terms associated with the brands.

Some organizations have teams that try to actively engage with dissatisfied customers, as they want to appear to be responsive to customer concerns. An effective use of such teams can significantly improve brand loyalty. Likewise, when customers have issues with organizations, posting them on Twitter or Facebook can be the most effective way to have a situation corrected.

Sometimes organizations can have information removed from social media. Alternatively, they may provide formal responses that might mitigate the impression in the minds of other potential customers. Even if nothing can be done to remove information from the Internet, or provide any mitigating responses, it is better to at least know that a situation of potential loss exists, so that it might be possibly mitigated by other means.

Information Release Policies

Information can be released through means other than directly through the Internet. Marketing and communications departments release information by advertising and to the media. Employees sometimes give presentations at professional and academic conferences, and their presentations can cause the release of sensitive information.

An example of a negative release by an employee occurred when Andrew Pole, a statistician who worked for Target, detailed how Target uses customers' data to determine their buying habits and the resulting distribution of coupons based on a customer's buying habits. Pole explained how Target developed a pregnancy prediction score based on the products that customers buy. Although valuable to the company, consumers became upset to learn the extent that Target monitors and tracks customer purchases.

To prevent the release of information that should be protected, because it is either proprietary or otherwise harmful, organizations should establish clear procedures for the release of any information outside the organization. There must be a review process that is clearly defined to lay out the criteria for the release of information, as well as the review process itself.

Regardless of whether sensitive information is to be shared within or outside an organization, there must also be procedures for verifying the identity of the recipients. For example, people can pretend to be a legitimate party and ask to have information sent to them. Although it is impossible to predict all possible circumstances, when potentially sensitive information is to be shared with another party, the party's identity must be verified before sending it to them, or otherwise releasing the information at their request.

Data Classification

Not all data has the same level of sensitivity. Additionally, some data should only be visible to a limited population. For this reason, there must be established data classification policies, and those policies must be known.

The relevant governance must state specifically what classifies data into different categories, how that data is to be treated and protected, who has access to the classified data, and any other information relevant to that data. People must also be aware of their responsibilities for the classified data they come into contact with.

In some circumstances, data classification is required by standards and regulations. If so, those should be considered with the creation of the appropriate governance documents. Also the legal, compliance, and other teams should be intimately involved in this effort, especially for enforcement and auditing.

Conflict of Interest Guidelines

Addressing conflicts of interest could be considered a personnel countermeasure, but it frequently goes beyond that to include vendors, clients, and other parties as well. The creation of conflict of interest guidelines must be a priority.

Conflict of interest guidelines address not only competitors, but also what might be considered unjust enrichment for people within your organization. For example, if a person has a relative who works with a vendor, that person can be perceived as favoring that vendor. People can also potentially use information they learn about the organization, or even the vendors and clients, to make investment decisions, so the appropriate rules must be created for these issues as well.

Every organization has its own concerns regarding potential conflicts of interest. A detailed analysis should be performed to determine what are the potential conflicts of interest to allow for the appropriate procedures and guidelines to be developed.

All relevant parties should be informed that they need to let the appropriate people know when to expect a conflict of interest. This allows the organization to track the potential concerns and determine the appropriate course of action.

Data Retention Policies

Data availability is a fundamental tenet of security. Ensuring that the data remains available and is not deleted is critical to proper operations. Additionally, there are frequently legal requirements for data retention. If the organization becomes involved in a lawsuit, there may be additional and stringent retention requirements placed on the organization.

At the same time, the storage of unnecessary data can become a security vulnerability, because data that should have been long deleted, and pose a security threat if released, can be a security vulnerability. Even if it is not ever disclosed, there are additional costs associated with the storage and management of large volumes of data.

Data retention procedures and guidelines must be created to ensure that data is available to all people who need it and to adhere to all legal and regulatory requirements. At the same time, the retention policies should ensure that unnecessary data is deleted.

Business Continuity and Disaster Recovery Procedures Created and Tested

As problems are inevitable, disaster recovery should be anticipated. As many scenarios as possible should be included in disaster recovery and business continuity policies. Based on the scenarios, detailed disaster recovery and business continuity procedures should be created.

These procedures should include not only technical recovery, but also legal, public relations, and client concerns. The response team should be multidisciplinary.

The creation of procedures is important, but it is very rare that they will be perfect from the start. To the extent possible, all disaster recovery and business continuity procedures should be tested in as real circumstances as possible. You need to understand whether the procedures are complete and if they work in real circumstances, and make adjustments as required. In case of inevitable incidents, your procedures should be reviewed after the fact to ensure that they functioned properly and to see what improvements should be made.

PERSONNEL COUNTERMEASURES

Personnel countermeasures are those actions that you take to address the vulnerabilities resulting from people within your control. Although you would assume that the human resources (HR) department is responsible for implementing these countermeasures, they require the involvement of IT, physical security, and all levels of management as well.

Much like the other categories of countermeasures, it is hard to strictly classify them. Clearly, these countermeasures involve implementing procedures specific to hiring and firing, but they can also involve the handling of information and other processes.

Many of these countermeasures will require the involvement of the legal team and also enforcement by people and all the departments in the organization. Many of these countermeasures might be considered sensitive, whereas some may be considered common sense. As the joke goes, common sense can be very rare. For these reasons, the likely readers of this book will not be able to implement this set of countermeasures on their own. It is, however, important that people understand these potential countermeasures and are hopefully at a point where they can initiate their implementation, or at least recommend them to the appropriate people. However, from our experience, the absence of these countermeasures is likely to cause significant loss.

Consistent Enforcement

Before you initiate any other personnel security policy, you must intend to implement policies consistently. Inconsistent enforcement can lead to significant problems from legal and operational perspectives.

For example, if one employee violates policies and sends sensitive documents out of the organization and you do not punish that employee, then another employee can claim bias when punished for doing something similar. If people see other people getting away with an unauthorized act, they are more likely to commit the same act.

Consistent enforcement prevents people from questioning whether a policy is a policy. It will both serve as a consistent motivation for people to adhere to well-thought-out policies and provide a concern that if they do not adhere to the policies, they will be punished.

Treat Employees Well

Some employees will behave maliciously no matter how you treat them, but employees who are treated well will more likely treat your organization well in return. They will adhere to policies. They will feel a sense of pride and ownership in the organization. They will defend the organization as best they can. As discussed in Chapter 11, your employees should be on the front line of your security effort, and you should avoid doing anything to discourage their good will.

Treating employees well is not always possible. However, organizations should consider all possible methods for improving employee morale. There are many ways to do that without incurring costs, and you should have working groups to determine how morale can be improved.

Even when adverse actions are being considered, such as layoffs, they should be performed in such a way that causes as little ill feelings as possible. Even when an employee is not being laid off, the remaining employees witness how you treat others.

Perform Background Checks

Background checks are the staple of security programs. In some industries, they are required. Background checks should verify criminal records, identity, claimed skills and experience, and any other issues deemed relevant.

Nondisclosure Agreements/Confidentiality Agreements

In most organizations, employees are exposed to information that is sensitive to the organization. All relevant people should be required to sign a nondisclosure agreement (NDA) or a confidentiality agreement. Although this may not stop all disclosures, it does provide for some recourse and is likely to somewhat discourage people who may consider violating the intent of the agreement.

Some organizations may want to consider implementing noncompete agreements as well. These agreements legally prevent employees from leaving your organization and working for a competitor. The concern satisfied by such an agreement is that the person has knowledge that would benefit a competing organization. These agreements can be hard to enforce and should therefore be reserved for key personnel or for those who are reasonably well paid. There has to be a legitimate cause and compensation for impacting a person's potential professional mobility.

Prepublication Reviews

Prepublication reviews require current and former employees to submit anything that is intended to be released outside the organization for a review. This facilitates the unintentional release of information. Provide employees with a point of contact who can quickly review materials to ensure that there is no information that can cause damage to the organization, if it is released.

Prepublication reviews are standard in classified environments. They should also be considered for all environments where there is sensitive and proprietary information.

Employee Hotlines

As employees should be properly trained to look for security-related concerns, they also need an established mechanism to report those concerns. Employee hotlines offer a single reporting source. Frequently, organizations have some sort of reporting mechanism already in place. There are ethics hotlines and help desks that already have trained staff to answer calls from people requiring assistance. Their function can be expanded to handle additional responsibility.

Crisis Hotlines

Most people tend to be well intentioned and honest. However, everyone can go through highly stressful situations. Some people have addiction problems. These situations always create a loss of productivity and can potentially cause security-related concerns. Crisis hotlines provide a resource for employees who feel overwhelmed or otherwise need support. HR is in a unique position to offer this type of support, and it can provide an employee with support before the situation creates a significant impact on the organization.

Coordination Among Departments

As identified in Chapter 9, departments not working together can let security problems unnecessarily fester. When HR works with IT, physical security, and other departments, security matters can be coordinated. These include proactively preparing for policy changes, personnel who are under investigation for security concerns, etc.

Regular meetings are not required, but there should be established governance that details which personnel actions require coordination with other departments. This requires establishing the appropriate lines of communications.

Employee Categorization/Role-Based Access

People are brought into an organization for specific functions. Although small and new organizations might not have as stringent of a role definition as a more established organization, there are usually expected information needs.

As appropriate, organizations should establish access controls specific to job functions. This can include access to different facilities, as well as data access.

Ideally, access is well defined based on job function, department, etc. IT, physical security, and other departments can assign the appropriate data access and physical access to facilities, before the individual's arrival.

Reviewing Visitors

To the extent possible, all visitors should be cleared by the security team, before their arrival. There should be approval of the sponsor and the meeting purpose. In some organizations, such as defense facilities, banks, and pharmaceutical companies, there are clear reasons to do so. The scope of the review depends on the nature of the organization. Minimally, all visitors should have an internal sponsor and should be tracked. Ideally, they should also be escorted throughout their visit.

Applying Policies to All People With Access

Although this section used the word employee to describe individuals, the intent is for everything described in this section to apply to anyone with access to your organization's facilities, data, and other resources. This applies to contractors, vendors, and customers. Although different contractual relationships may limit the extent to which you can place requirements on certain individuals and organizations, it is critical that you do not establish a de facto backdoor by allowing certain groups of people to bypass security countermeasures.

For example, housekeeping services are frequently outsourced. The cleaning staff frequently have unfettered access to all facilities, while the facilities are otherwise unoccupied. Even though these people might be hired by an outside contractor, it is especially critical to ensure that they go through the same level of security clearances as direct employees.

Coordinating Terminations

Terminations, even under amicable circumstances, can be extremely problematic. Although issues such as health care and retirement benefits are well addressed, computer access, physical access, company-issued equipment, and similar concerns are not frequently accounted for. These require coordination with other departments, as previously described as a required countermeasure, as well as forethought and planning throughout a person's tenure in an organization.

For example, you need to track equipment requisition throughout an employee's tenure to know which equipment you need to collect upon their termination. You need to track their computer and document access as well.

Before completing a termination, the HR team should ensure that all relevant departments complete their responsibilities within the termination process.

PHYSICAL COUNTERMEASURES

Physical countermeasures are those countermeasures that mitigate loss to assets, information, facilities, personnel, etc., from a physical perspective. It implies that adversaries are denied opportunities to physically compromise assets, valid employees do not cause inadvert or purposeful harm, and that those assets are not susceptible to accidental damage.

Arguably, physical countermeasures are the easiest to understand and implement. It is much easier to understand physical harm and damage prevention than to understand other, more esoteric countermeasures. It therefore makes it easier to justify these countermeasures, as the need is clear.

There is sometimes a Pollyanna belief that there is no threat. Sometimes, there is an attitude that too much physical security discourages an open and trusting environment. While security can stifle certain functions, it seems more common that organizations opt for less physical security than is appropriate. So as you read through this section, it is important to choose and implement those physical countermeasures that appropriately reduce risk.

While other countermeasures typically have difficulty being justified from a cost perspective, physical countermeasures have difficulty being justified from a cultural perspective. While we clearly believe adhering to culture is a critical aspect of all security programs, we believe that in many cases culture needs to accept that physical security requires improvement and adjust accordingly.

Perimeter Security

Every organization should strive to ensure that only authorized people can enter their facilities. To accomplish this, the first step is to create a perimeter that can be reasonably secured. This includes the traditional mechanisms, which include locks on doors, fences around controllable grounds, controlled access areas for garages, gates, etc., window locks, among other security staples.

Clearly, there is an infrastructure that goes along with this. You need to ensure that locks are locked, windows are closed, visitors are contained, etc. Many organizations spend immense amounts of money on implementing and maintaining perimeter security tools, yet they do not properly make use of the resources they acquire.

Access Badges

Badges provide a quick ability to determine if a person is authorized to be in a facility, and potentially what level of access that person has. Visitors should be issued badges, with an indication that they are visitors and if an escort is required. While most organizations do not have badges that differentiate people with different levels of access, it is something to consider. Minimally, badges can indicate if a person is a regular employee or a contractor, should access for contractors be limited for legal or contractual purposes.

Badges can also be of the type with embedded chips that are used to unlock doors, track access, and sometimes also function to authenticate a person to computer systems. It must also be mentioned that badges are worthless, if people do not wear their badges and question those who do not. As Chapter 11 describes in detail, this is an aspect of security culture.

Use Available Locks

Locks are ubiquitous throughout an organization. Desks, closets, file cabinets, doors, gates, computer docks, and other storage and access resources tend to have locks by default. The problem is that they are frequently not used.

Documents, computers, keys, storage devices, badges, and anything else that has value can be locked up. Minimally, people with offices can lock their doors. People who do not have offices can put sensitive information in their desk and lock their desk. File cabinets should be locked. Sadly, many organizations do not make proper use of the security resources that are freely available. The use of these tools should be promoted and enforced.

Properly Train Guards

Security guards are common in many facilities. Generally, these people are well meaning and have good intentions. Unfortunately, they rarely receive sufficient training or guidance. That training and guidance should reflect what is in policies and procedures, so that their job is well defined and in conjunction with overall organization processes.

In the process of performing penetration tests, we noticed that guards frequently do not question people who are in facilities after hours. While we previously mentioned that guards perform rounds for insurance purposes, they should also record the names of people who are working afterhours. While the late night work can be innocent, anyone who is in the facilities for nefarious purposes will be discouraged. Malicious actors frequently work late hours, so that they can go through materials they would normally not have access to. Security teams can then look into why the person was there late and if there is a consistent pattern of working late. If there is a legitimate reason, then the person's manager can be impressed with their employee. If not, it is an indication that there might be a greater concern.

Looking for late night workers is just one example. Properly verifying visitors, knowing how to react to people in limited access facilities, understanding when something appears to be abnormal while performing rounds, looking for sensitive information and resources left vulnerable, and especially how to react to potentially concerning cases are examples of other types of training.

Sometimes, you might want the guards to be more cautious. For example, in the process of performing a penetration test, we drove around facilities after-hours just to get a feel for the grounds and to see if we could see into windows when it was dark outside. A very alert guard saw our car and came running out of the building to stop us. While we recommended that the guard be rewarded for his diligence, we also recommended that the guard be told never to do that again, as he put himself in danger by leaving a safe facility to stop and unknown number of strangers, with unknown intent, in a deserted parking lot. There are also potential concerns regarding guards overreacting.

Clean Desk Policies

When desks are unattended, people should know to lock up materials, so they are not left vulnerable to anyone who can access the desk. In a world of cubicles, there is little privacy to begin with. When work areas are unattended, it becomes that much more critical to lock up materials and to secure computers. The expression, clean desk, applies to the entire work area and would include locking file cabinets and drawers.

It also includes ensuring that any white boards do not have sensitive materials left on them. You should also verify that decorations of walls are not sensitive materials. For example, it is not uncommon for engineers to leave engineering diagrams on walls for ready access and decorative purposes.

Trash should also not be left out, if it contains information that should be shredded.

To support clean desk policies, supervisors should perform walkthroughs of areas to look for potential violations. Guards should also be trained to look for any potential violations as well.

Copy Machine/Printer Controls

Copy machines and printers represent a significant risk. People accidentally leave original materials on the machine. People send information to the printer, which may sit there for extended periods of time and might even be completely forgotten. There must be policies and practices to periodically check copy machines and printers to verify that materials are not left vulnerable.

There are some printers that allow for materials to be sent to them, and then a code must be entered into the printer for the documents to actually print. That prevents the documents from sitting unattended for periods of time. Another issue to consider is that as printers and copy machines are computers, with storage equipment, they must be treated like computers. They require proper patching and also require the appropriate destruction processes. For example, hard drives should be removed from printers and copy machines, before getting rid of the machine.

Shredder Availability

Given the fact that sensitive information is frequently in printed form, shredders should be widely available to destroy documents when they are no longer needed. If a person deals with a great deal of documents, it may be justified to give them a dedicated shredder. Ideally, there should be one for every team. Minimally, there should be one near every copy machine and printer.

There are shredding services that make bins available. People place documents and other materials to be destroyed inside the bins, and periodically the service collects the materials in the bins for destruction. This is a viable option, and good where large volumes of information need to be destroyed on a frequent basis.

Log Equipment Removal

While it is admittedly difficult to track equipment, there should be a procedure for logging removal of equipment from facilities. Ideally, you also log equipment entry, so that you know if someone claims it is their personal computer, for example, upon removal, there was a corresponding computer brought into the facility. While it can be argued that bad actors will try to sneak equipment out, having a tracking program will create a process that discourages removal of equipment, and can help distinguish bad actors from accidental loss of equipment, which is inevitable.

Alarms That are Monitored

Any controlled entry point should be alarmed. While that is frequently the case, alarms are frequently not enabled. When they are enabled, if an alarm goes off, it is possible that there is not a proper response.

While it is understandable that you want an alarm to stop, after the door is closed again, there needs to be an investigation as to why the door was opened. There is frequently video coverage of entry points, so that should be examined when available.

Screen Locks

Every common computer operating system has a screen lock function, where a screensaver comes on after a certain period of inactivity. This protects against unauthorized users accessing the computer when it is unattended, assuming it is a password protected screensaver; specifically, a password has to be entered for the screen and computer to be unlocked. While some people perceive the function to be annoying, if the time period when the screen lock is activated isn't too short, it is valuable and should be implemented. Generally, the screen-saver feature should activate after 3—5 min of inactivity, which allows for a short window of exposure if someone leaves the computer unattended.

Laptop Computer Locks

As it is extremely easy to steal an unattended laptop computer, physical locking mechanisms should be provided. There is a small oval hole on the side of most laptop computers, which is used as a point for a cable lock to be attached to the laptop. Organizations should provide cable locks with every laptop computer issued.

Another potential lock are laptop docking stations. Many brands of laptops designed for corporate users have features that allow them to connect to a dock-ing station that provides resources equal to that of a traditional desktop com-puter, such as a monitor, keyboard, and mouse. Should you have a docking station, they frequently providing a locking feature that locks the laptop into the docking station.

Document Library

When an organization has valuable documents, there should be some types of central document storage capability created. For physical documents, a docu-ment library should be created, where the documents have to be requested and access logged. This assists with investigations, if it is determined that an in-sider compromised the information at a later point.

If a library feature is implemented online, access controls should be imple-mented and all accesses logged.

Whether the library is physical or online, accesses should be reviewed regularly. If someone is accessing excessive amounts of information, or if they are access-ing information that they would not normally have need to access, an investi-gation should be performed.

Privacy Filters

Privacy filters go over displays and block people from side angles from seeing what is on the display. This helps limit the accidental exposure of information to un-authorized people within an organization and especially on laptops and other devices, when they are used in public places. Privacy filters should be placed on all laptop computers when they are issued by your organization. There are also privacy filters for cellphones, and they should be considered for use as well.

Awareness in Noncontrolled Areas

The use of privacy filters is one aspect of protecting information on a computer monitor, while it is being accessed in uncontrolled areas. Additionally, people must consider voice conversations, reviewing hardcopy documents, and any other use of sensitive information while outside organizational facilities.

People need to exercise proper behaviors that do not disclose information, in any form, to unauthorized people, purposefully or accidentally. The proper behaviors are promoted through awareness campaigns, but they must be constantly reinforced, and any violations should be reported and dealt with.

Location Choice
When choosing locations for facilities, meetings, and any other business purpose, your organization needs to consider all physical risks. This includes the traditional physical risks, such as flooding, hurricanes, snowstorms, etc. You must also consider the resilience of the infrastructure, as you do not want to locate in areas with poor reliability for electricity and other power sources, roads that cannot get employees and supplies in and out of the area, etc.

Likewise, you also need to consider how your facilities make you more accessible to potential threats. We have seen companies that share facilities with their competitors. You also need to consider if foreign locations present risks that are not worth the return. Some locations are in crime-ridden areas. Some locations might be placed in areas where bribery is considered a standard business practice. The choice of your physical locations must consider all potential vulnerabilities, as well as all potential threats.

Uninterruptible Power Supplies and other Physical Precautions
Uninterruptible power supplies (UPS) are a critical countermeasure. Power can go out for many reasons and the result can be a loss of any work not recently saved, as well as a complete loss of data should there be a disk crash that causes physical damage to the disk drives. UPS can be for entire facilities, as well as for individual computers. Laptops have a built in battery, which functions as a UPS. Buildings can have backup generators.

There is also a need to put fire suppression and other physical protections in place to stop fires, flooding, explosions, etc. There may also be a need to put in protection from electronic eavesdropping, if that is a reasonable concern.

TECHNICAL COUNTERMEASURES

We assume that most readers focus on technical countermeasures as part of their daily responsibilities. While the other categories of countermeasures are relatively static, technical countermeasures can be somewhat dynamic. We should be specific to what we mean by dynamic.

There are categories of countermeasures. For example, while there might be many ways to implement multifactor authentication, such as with hardware tokens, texting to cell phones, etc., it is a single broad category. As technology advances, categories of countermeasures can come and go. As of the time of this writing, behavioral analytics is beginning to become a mainstream category of countermeasures. As we discuss in Chapter 5, the fundamental ways to hack a computer are static, but the individual implementations change as the specific technologies change. Likewise, many categories of countermeasures are fundamental and static, but some categories of countermeasures will appear and evolve over time.

As we write this section, we will stick to categories of countermeasures. Again, it will still not be a comprehensive list and intends to cover the most notable categories of countermeasures to consider. The goal for the discussion is to highlight the potential uses of the countermeasure and to help you decide if it is a relevant category of countermeasure for you to implement in your organization. Should you decide that you have a potential use for the countermeasure, we recommend that you perform further investigation to determine the available features that are most relevant to you, so that you can choose the products or solutions (as applicable) that best fit your needs.

SANS Top 20

We recommend that you review the SANS Critical Security Controls, frequently referred to as the SANS Top 20. These are categories of countermeasures as well. They are well researched and established, and their goal is to identify the controls, that if properly implemented, would stop most, if not all attacks. If we would just refer you to that resource, we would satisfy our mission of identifying a reasonable set of countermeasures. However, we also want to be more granular in our recommendations. Additionally, while we believe that the SANS Top 20 is an excellent resource and there are some references to detection and reaction, it is primarily a set of protections. We therefore want to enhance it with additional countermeasures focused on detection and reaction.

Anti-malware Software

Anti-virus, anti-spam, and related malware prevention software are a fundamental requirement in any environment. Anti-malware software should be placed on all end user systems. While viruses are typically associated with Windows systems, there is plenty of malware-targeting Macs, so all end user systems should have anti-malware software.

Depending upon a server's operating system, anti-malware software should be considered for the server. Since the spread of malware is largely through spam and targeted e-mails with attachments, it is important to ensure that antimalware is integrated into your mail server and clients. However, malware can also be spread through malicious websites. Additionally, there are worms, which spread themselves and infiltrate systems through system ports.

While the anti-malware software should do periodic scans, it should be memory resident to actively prevent the installation of malware.

As many people learn the hard way, having anti-malware software on a system is important, but it has to constantly receive updates for the latest malware signatures. This means that licenses must be kept current, and automatic updates are enabled. We do realize that there have been periodic updates that create problems, however the risk is too great not to enable the auto-updates.

As implied, most anti-malware software is signature based; in other words, it looks for specific types of software. Some anti-malware software however looks at the behaviors of software programs and monitors if the software exhibits malicious behavior. Clearly, it is better to stop known malicious software, but you have to continue looking for malicious software that is not previously known.

Whitelisting

While anti-malware software focuses on looking for known signatures and can be supplemented with software that looks for malicious behaviors, for many systems it is better to only allow required software to execute. Whitelisting functionality requires that you specify the programs that are allowed to execute. Any software that is not specified will not be allowed to execute.

This functionality significantly limits the versatility of a given computer, and in a large environment, it can be burdensome to maintain. However for some critical systems, such as industrial control systems or point of sale (POS) systems, that have a very limited purpose, and the compromise of which can cause significant harm, whitelisting can be appropriate. For example, a large portion of the Target hack would have been stopped, if malware was not able to execute on the Target POS systems.

Firewalls

Firewalls are a perimeter security device that limits the ingress and egress of data and connections, primarily based on the network services. That is an oversimplification of the functionality, however for the purposes of this chapter, it is sufficient. Firewalls can be very useful in easing the security burden on individual systems.

While firewalls are associated with isolating an internal network from an external network, frequently the Internet, it should also be considered for isolating segments within an internal network. If an adversary gets into a network, they will use trusted systems to compromise other parts of the network. It also prevents malicious insiders from exploiting systems outside of their immediate access.

Intrusion Detection/Prevention Systems

Intrusion detection systems (IDS) and intrusion prevention systems (IPS) are generally being combined into a single functional system. Generally, they intend to monitor network traffic to detect and block traffic that could be associated with malicious actions. Frequently, the functionality is integrated with a firewall. As with firewalls, the technology should be considered for deployment at network perimeters, as well as within a network at appropriate network choke points.

Backups

The one inevitability of security is that something will go wrong. This especially includes the loss or destruction of data. Disks can crash. Data can be destroyed by ransomware. USB drives can be misplaced. Malicious insiders can delete or alter data. While you can never prevent all potential situations, backups provide a reaction capability to mitigate the loss of data.

If you have hot sites and real-time backups, there is the possibility that no data can be lost. This can be expensive. Automatic, periodic syncing of mobile devices can also prevent significant data loss. However, a process of manual, periodic backups might not save 100% of all data, but it does reduce the amount of loss.

While we are not endorsing certain services in the continuous data protection category, such as Carbonite, iDrive, Google Drive, and others, they provide automatic backups over the Internet. They can be a valuable service to consider.

Secure Configurations

For a system to be secure, it should be secured with a default configuration that is implemented with security in mind. Organizations should have security configurations that when a new system is delivered and installed, the configuration of the system is predefined to be secure by default. The configuration should define the services the computer runs, the default user permissions, file sharing, versions, standard applications with the appropriate settings, etc.

When an administrator installs or delivers a new system, that system should be essentially identical to all other systems of the same type in use within the organization. Not only does this provide strong security, it also eases administration and maintenance. Vendors and industry associations typically provide guidance for securely configuring applications and operating systems.

Automated Software Patching

As software vulnerabilities are discovered regularly, and ideally vendors release patches, it is critical to install those patches as soon after they become available as possible. Both Mac and Windows PCs provide an automated patching capability, as long as you allow it do so. The average person should allow that capability to run as designed. Organizational administrators might want to first test the patches to ensure that they do not cause any negative effects. It is possible that some updates might cause other software not to work. However, if an organization cannot perform the testing in an efficient manner, it is safer to enable automatic updates.

As previously mentioned, automatic updates should be enabled for anti-malware software. Operating systems are regularly updated. Applications are frequently updated. Given the common usage of the products, Microsoft Office, and Adobe Flash and Reader applications should be updated as rapidly as possible given the fact that attackers rapidly create and use exploits of those software products. But generally, unless you believe that you have extensive knowledge in the area, you should enable automatic updates of all software.

Vulnerability Scanners

Vulnerability scanners scan systems for known vulnerabilities. They look for outdated components of operating systems and applications that are known to have security vulnerabilities. In other words, they look for software versions that have known bugs. Depending upon the access of the vulnerability scanner, it can also potentially find configuration errors, such as improper file sharing and similar issues.

There are network-based vulnerability scanners that scan systems that sit on a network. They can detect the vulnerabilities that are exploitable by network-based attacks. There are managed services available, such as Qualys and Tenable, that perform regular scanning. There are also vulnerability scanners that run on individual systems and can do an extra level of scanning to find vulnerabilities that can be exploited by someone with system accesses.

There are some tools that look for changes in systems and critical system files, which can indicate a system compromise. For example, Tripwire detects if monitored files change and alert the administrators of a potential compromise. While most vulnerability scanners are a form of protection, to the extent they detect modification of system files, they can be considered a detection tool.

Behavioral Analytics

Behavioral analytic tools are a form of detection that looks for unusual activities. They can either look for that activity by looking at actions on an individual system or look at network traffic for unusual patterns. These tools are either programmed to look for known patterns of unusual activities, or study activity to determine what is normal activity, and then report activities that fit outside the norm.

Depending upon the nature of the tool, it can look for user actions, such as excessive file accesses, activities at unusual times, etc. Some tools look for unusual network traffic that might indicate the presence of attack tools used by advanced persistent threat (APT) actors. Whatever the target, these tools can be useful in finding activities that would otherwise be missed.

Data Leak Prevention

Data leak prevention (DLP) software looks for potentially sensitive data being sent outside the organization. These tools can be used on individual systems to look for data that is being sent intentionally or unintentionally by a user to unauthorized parties. There are also network-based DLP tools that sit on mail servers or network egress points and watch for data that are being sent over the network.

The tools allow organizations to set criteria for what data should be stopped from exiting the organization and what to alert the appropriate staff about. They can identify certain types of data, such as personally identifiable information (PII), or look for key phrases that are tied to sensitive project data.

In some cases, the egress is due to malicious software planted by APTs. Sometimes employees send out this data, before they quit so they have it available when they leave the company. In one case we know of, a well-meaning employee sent customer data to his personal account, so that he could do some extra work at home, which would have benefited the company. No matter what the reason, these tools can stop information from leaving the company, where there would be no control of the information.

Web Content Filters/Application Firewalls

Web content filters can be considered a form of DLP to some extent. They intend to prevent users from sending out sensitive data to other websites, while also filtering out potentially harmful or malicious data or information from a website. They can also prevent access to sites that have content that might be deemed objectionable, unnecessary, or harmful. For example, it is common for organizations to prevent connections to pornographic websites and web torrents. Many organizations ban social media sites on work computers. We have worked with several organizations that also ban access to hacker websites, as they do not want malicious tools downloaded onto their network.

There are also more broad application firewalls that filter out other types of data and attacks. They can prevent malicious software from getting to an organization's website. These tools should be considered for any organization with more than a trivial Internet presence.

Wireless and Remote Security

With more employees using mobile devices, more employees connect to wireless networks that are outside the control of the organization. Hackers can spoof a legitimate access point. Even if there are legitimate access points, data can be sent in the clear, and then become accessible to anyone else who has access to the networks.

When possible, organizations should distribute virtual private network (VPN) software that sets up a secure and encrypted connection directly to a trusted network. In the absence of a VPN, individuals have to attempt to ensure that they are using legitimate networks. They then should ensure that they use encrypted connections through their web browsers and hope that the end-to-end encryption is enabled. There should also be a purposeful attempt to reduce the amount and type of data that are accessed remotely.

When traveling to known hostile areas, it is recommended that you take a new system with minimum amounts of data and use it for purely tactical purposes. When network access is used, there is a conscious attempt to access as little data as possible. The system should then be "scrubbed" and no longer used upon return to a trusted area.

Mobile Device Management

Mobile device management (MDM) software provides security tools to cell phones, tablets, laptop computers, and related equipment. It allows organizations to control certain functions related to system configuration, data storage, and data access. MDM software can enforce software updates, look for malware, and perform other basic security functions.

MDM software also provides for control of the data on the devices. It can remotely delete data, if the employee leaves the organization or loses the device. It can potentially selectively delete e-mails on the device, reset the passcode, and perform other data and system administration functions.

MDM software can be deployed as part of a bring your own device strategy, where organizations let employees use their own devices for work-related purposes. Employees have to agree that they will allow the MDM software to run on their mobile devices for the benefit that they can have a more efficient work situation. It is a standard practice at many organizations.

Multifactor Authentication

Multifactor authentication basically means that you use more than a password to authenticate yourself to a computer system. There is a general rule that authentication can involve what you know, what you have, and what you are. Multifactor authentication frequently means you are using at least two of those methods.

What you know is a piece of knowledge, like a password. It can also be the answer to the hopefully more challenging authentication questions that ask for what is supposed to be more obscure information, such as your mother's maiden name, favorite movie, etc. While not perfect, it does make it significantly more difficult for an attacker to compromise an account. An example of it not being perfect is when the IRS Get Transcript function, previously discussed in this book, was compromised due to criminals being able to access information off of a person's credit report.

What you have can be token-based authentication, such as a SecurID card, or other access card that provides a one-time password, it can be a software token on a computer, and it is frequently your mobile device, where organizations send you a text with a one-time passcode that has to be entered to access the account. The assumption is that you need to be in possession of the account holder's cell phone to compromise the account. This is much more difficult to compromise than compromising a person's password. Google Authenticator provides a passcode on a mobile device, so that the person does not actually require cellular access and the passcode cannot be compromised in transmission.

What you are usually involved biometric authentication. Retina scans, fingerprint readers, hand geometry scanners, and similar tools provide a layer of authentication, and are much more difficult to compromise. Due to the perceived invasiveness, as well as the difficulty to collect the information, while it may be the strongest form of authentication, it is currently the least used. The common exception is the fingerprint reader on iPhones and other mobile devices that can be used to unlock the device, as well as for activating mobile payment systems.

Like all other security tools, no method of multifactor of authentication will be perfect; however, it is exponentially more secure than traditional password mechanisms and may allow for reducing password complexity, as the password is not used as the final tool of authentication.

Single Sign-On

Single Sign-On (SSO) facilitates a user-moving seamlessly across a network to access required systems and files. There can be many individual systems on a network that require authentication, and having a user be required to have individual accounts for each and every system can be extremely burdensome. SSO tools allow a user to log on once, and the SSO then authenticates the user to all required systems on the network as necessary.

It can save a great deal of administration effort, as well as frustration for the user, who may otherwise be required to create and maintain dozens of passwords. It does however require that the authentication to the SSO tool be accurate and secure. It also provides for a single point of failure. However, the assumption is that if you are using SSO, you are aware of this issue and implement stringent authentication, which would include multifactor authentication, heavy monitoring of activity, access from specific domains, etc.

Software Testing

As Chapter 5 describes, one of the two ways to hack computers is to take advantage of problems built into the software, i.e., software bugs. While it is not practical for most organizations to attempt to test commercial software for vulnerabilities, when an organization develops, or contracts the development of, custom software, there should be stringent testing of the software for potential vulnerabilities.

To make the testing a repeatable process, proper governance should include software design principles and identify basic testing protocols. Test programs can implement white and black box testing procedures. The former implies you know the structure of the code and can go through purposeful test cases. The latter means that you do not care about the structure of the code, but you intend to extensively search for bugs based upon general practices and functionality.

Another option is fuzz testing, or fuzzing, where you attempt to metaphorically beat the software up with all types of good and bad data. To perform fuzz testing, you need to use tools, which can be found commercially or for free. With fuzz testing, it is not uncommon to find errors rapidly, but as you fix the initial bugs, there becomes a more extended time between the identification of bugs.

Clearly, the amount of testing depends upon the value of the data at risk or product. Websites that provide PII and other critical information or services should go through very extensive testing. The most notable software testing programs, as of the time of this writing, involve testing of automobiles. The potential loss involved with a successful hack of the related software speaks for itself.

Encryption

Encryption is a fundamental element of data protection. While we assume that most readers of this book are familiar with the concept of encryption, encryption involves making data inaccessible through the scrambling of the data. Entities that do not have the authorized key to decrypt the data cannot read it. For example, if you look at a file that is encrypted, you cannot tell what you are looking at as it appears to be just a random collection of bits. Web browsers can encrypt data before transmission. Hard drives can be encrypted by default. Encryption is built into most storage devices. Most standards require the encryption of sensitive information.

The type of encryption tool and/or algorithm you employ depends on the technology that will use the encryption and the type of data you intend to protect. If you are transmitting military grade secrets, you need military grade encryption. If you are storing your own private data, and do not have nation-state actors likely targeting you, you can use generic commercially available tools and websites for the purpose.

From our experience with NSA, encryption does not have to be perfect, but sufficient. There will never be such a thing as perfect encryption. Given enough time and resources, it is expected that all encryption can be cracked. The best analogy is that encryption is like a safe; it has to be secure for as long as necessary. For example, if someone intends to rob a bank, a bank safe will never be impenetrable. It just has to keep the bad guys out long enough for the police to arrive.

Similarly, while you want to encrypt credit card numbers, you need to understand the level of effort that criminals would put into compromising the credit cards, and if it is a single credit card in transmission, or a storage device containing hundreds of millions of credit cards. When the military is determining how much to spend on encryption, they consider the longevity of the information and how long the encryption will be in use. For example, a military communications satellite that might be in use for more than a decade has to have encryption that will not only repel current cryptanalytic attacks, but also can repel exponentially more powerful cryptanalytic attacks that are likely to be discovered in the next decade. Then they have to anticipate the possibility that the satellite might be required to be functional for perhaps another decade, if it is not replaced as currently anticipated. That is clearly a different level of encryption required than if you wanted to make a single purchase on Amazon.com.

Audit Logs

Whenever we were called in to investigate an incident, we typically find that the logs have more than sufficient information to have proactively detected the attack before damage was done, if someone would have properly examined the logs. Likewise, when we perform penetration tests, we examine the audit logs that we can access and find potentially illicit activities that would have been easily discovered, if the audit logs were examined.

Most systems have the capability of creating audit logs, and they should be enabled to do so. They are potentially the greatest detection tool available. While the review of audit logs can be the bane of an admin's existence, if they really want to know what is going on those systems and the network as a whole, it should be considered a fundamental responsibility.

Security Information and Event Management Systems

Security information and event management (SIEM) systems assist in simplifying the review of audit logs, while elevating potential concerns as quickly as possible. SIEMs are best described as log aggregators that add intelligence to the analysis of the incoming records. By having a centralized ability to review relevant events for indicators of potential incidents, you can have a more consistent review of the information. Additionally, with the use of a SIEM, you can more likely ensure consistency of the analysis and response to indications of potential incidents. With a centralized function, you are, relying on people who are hopefully properly trained to review the data and make decisions, vice many diverse administrators, who may or may not have the appropriate training on knowing what to look for.

Managed Services

While it might be more of an operational issue to outsource critical security functions, we place managed services in the technical countermeasures section as it involves the administration of technical tools. While many people consider outsourcing of critical functions to be a mistake, it is a legitimate consideration when you do not want to devote the appropriate staff to performing the function of maintaining and analyzing key technical systems. Managed services should ensure that firewalls, IDS and IPS, SIEMs, vulnerability scanning, and other critical security functions are properly performed and the systems maintained. Frequently, they can offer a higher level of service at a lower cost than organizations can provide for themselves.

Clearly, there are drawbacks to outsourcing critical security functions. However if an appropriate level of service can be provided at a reasonable cost, and there are difficulties providing similar levels of service internally, managed service providers are a resource to consider.

SUMMARY

We want to reiterate that this chapter was neither comprehensive nor detailed enough to create a comprehensive security program. Again, we intend to provide you with background information to begin your own research in determining the countermeasures that are appropriate for your own protection, detection, and reaction programs. There are books devoted to many of the countermeasures that we cover with two paragraphs.

You should have however made mental or physical notes to determine how the countermeasures can fit within your security program, and how to prioritize those countermeasures. At that point, you can then determine whether or not a given countermeasure is worthy of further research.

CHAPTER 11

Security Culture

A security culture is the consolidated behaviors of individuals within an organization, and as anything that deals with humans, it can be a very tricky thing. It can simultaneously be a vulnerability and a threat, but it can also be a countermeasure. Although security culture will be formally defined shortly, to introduce the concept think of a security culture as how your organization behaves as a whole with regard to security. Does everyone wear a badge as they enter the facility? Do people talk about work in public spaces? Do people frequently browse Facebook at work? At a high level, that is your security culture.

A weak security culture is clearly a vulnerability, as people will behave in a way that constantly places your information, computers, and organization at risk. Regular behaviors will provide many threats with the ability to exploit the organization. If you consider your culture an entity, then it can be considered a threat. In other words, the organization itself is its biggest threat.

At the same time, a strong security culture is a strong and robust set of countermeasures. A strong culture provides protection in that people will take proactive actions that reduce the likelihood of loss. They will notice when things do not look right and detect attacks or losses in progress, or at least after the fact so that some efforts to deal with the loss can be implemented. People will react appropriately and report incidents to the appropriate people. They will choose not to click on a phishing message. They will not divulge their passwords and will report the attempted compromise. They will close doors that are left ajar.

As many studies highlight, such as the Verizon Data Breach Investigations Report, more than 90% of advanced attacks began with phishing and other social engineering attacks, implying that a strong security culture should definitely be a priority.

A strong security culture impacts protection, detection, and reaction. Although this chapter is in Section 2 that is primarily about protection, we will discuss some elements of detection and reaction. There will be further discussion of issues related to security culture in other sections as well.

Advanced Persistent Security. http://dx.doi.org/10.1016/B978-0-12-809316-0.00011-7

Clearly you need to implement a strong technology infrastructure; however, it can be argued that your technology infrastructure is dependent on having a strong security culture that requires and implements the strong technology infrastructure. To a large extent, this is very true. After all, a strong technology infrastructure requires a proper budget. It requires hiring the appropriate people, who know how to implement the technology. This requires money and effort as well. It requires management support to approve the security team's efforts, which may require some downtime and/or create inconvenience to the organization. A security team cannot operate in a vacuum and effectively implement a strong security infrastructure.

As we go through this discussion, it is critical to understand that a strong security culture means that the entire organization behaves in a way that acts, promotes, and supports strong security behaviors.

WHAT IS SECURITY CULTURE?

To provide a complete answer to this question, we searched the Internet for the best definition of security culture. The top definition is the following:

> A security culture is a set of customs shared by a community whose members may engage in illegal or sensitive activities, the practice of which minimizes the risks of such activities being subverted, or targeted for sabotage.

We have problems with this definition. It specifically implies that it only applies to communities that engage in illegal or sensitive activities. We believe that all organizations have a security culture. Although it can be argued that all organizations engage in sensitive activities, the need to specify illegal or sensitive activities would therefore be wrong. But for the purpose of this book, and we sincerely hope for your organization, it is required that all organizations should have a security culture.

We first define culture as the result of consistent behaviors within an organization. For example, at the National Security Agency (NSA), everyone wears a badge and anyone not wearing a badge is accosted by coworkers, and even strangers who pass them might stop them and try to contact security. In at least one case, guards had a person sprawled out on the floor, with their hands on top of their head, because there was no badge on the person. People do not talk about work-related issues outside work. Work-related documents are not allowed to leave the building, and belongings are searched on the way out of the buildings. There are many other consistent behaviors practiced by employees that create the NSA security culture.

Although it can be argued that the NSA engages in sensitive activities, the same behaviors, or lack thereof, are practiced in all organizations. Many organizations issue badges; however, your security culture would be represented by whether or not people wear the badges. Do employees regularly discuss work matters outside the work facility? Although the information might not be classified, it might still involve information that should be protected.

Individuals practicing bad behaviors that resulted in a compromise are to blame for it, but it is almost always the security culture of the organization that created, or allowed, such behavior that resulted in the compromise. So the culture of the organization is itself a threat and, depending upon how you want to define it, a vulnerability.

At the same time, a security culture that encourages countermeasures, such as wearing badges and not discussing sensitive information in unsafe areas is itself a countermeasure. This again is why security culture is defined in the chapters discussing threat, vulnerability, or countermeasure, but it is itself a chapter.

FORMING A SECURITY CULTURE

As a security culture is the combined behavior of the individuals of an organization, creating a strong security culture relies on creating consistent behaviors. To create behaviors, you have to create awareness of the desired behaviors. This implies the importance of a good security awareness program.

The Importance of Security Policies, Standards, Guidelines and Procedures

Organizational security behaviors should be defined for everyone in an organization. Employees, contractors, and everyone else comprising the organization should have acceptable behaviors defined in writing. You should not have people determine their own behaviors. More importantly, people's behaviors should be well considered and defined by the appropriate people with the appropriate skills. There should be no question as to the appropriate behaviors for people to enact.

It is crucial for those behaviors to be defined and supported from top management down. We discussed the importance of governance in Chapter 8, which implies that there are well-defined policies, guidelines, and procedures specifically related to security behaviors and awareness. These documents should define and specify the behaviors expected of employees, so there is no doubt as to what is required from employees, contractors, and other people responsible for the organization.

For example, if people are supposed to report a phishing message, it should be documented, ideally with how to report the message. Employee behavior should not be left to chance. You cannot expect people to behave appropriately when appropriate behavior is not defined and properly promoted.

Creating Security Awareness

There are three elements to a good awareness program: awareness of the problem, knowledge about how to solve the problem, and motivation to enact the solution. There is a fallacy that if you tell people what to do, they will do it. People need motivation to do the right thing.

For example, people should create strong passwords. People need to know that if they do not have a strong password, someone can guess their password. People need to care that this can happen. They then need to know what constitutes a strong password. However, many people know they should have a strong password, and usually have an idea as to what makes a strong password, but they frequently will not implement a strong password. The reason for this varies. Some people do not want hard-to-remember passwords. Some people discount all security recommendations, as they believe they are not important enough to be a target. A lack of motivation leads people to practice weak security habits, even when they know about the potential problems.

Frequently, security professionals believe you need to scare people to get them to practice good security. The potentially negative consequences of poor security practices should be discussed, and people need to be provided with information about what good security practices mean to them. A large part of motivation, at least in the workplace, should be that people should behave in a certain way, as that is what their job function requires. They should also be made aware that there are consequences for not fulfilling this aspect of their job.

We would contend that information about what the problem is almost irrelevant. Generally, a behavior should be practiced because it is in practice. Assuming a good governance is in place, there should be a clear expectation as to how people should behave with regard to regular functions, and those expectations embed good security practices.

Department of How

When people think of an organization's security department, they usually dread having to deal with it. They think of security as an impediment and/or as people who only show up when they do something wrong. In short, they look at the security department as "the department of no."

Although security awareness is just a function within the overall security department, it is in many ways the face of the security team. It is best when people look at the security team as an enabler that supports functions, and not as an impediment. For that reason, it is best if awareness focuses on highlighting the proper way to do things, and not on what they cannot do. In other words, security should be perceived as "the department of how."

To provide an extreme example, one of our friends is the chief information security officer (CISO) of a Fortune 30 company. He told us that during a meeting with his CEO, the CEO announced that he wanted to allow employees to bring in their mobile devices and connect them to the company network, so that the company did not have to buy devices. The CISO replied that it would be a security nightmare and that they should not do that. The CEO replied that in 2 weeks, he expects the CISO to return with a plan on how to safely add personal devices to the network or in 3 weeks there would be a new CISO.

According to more traditional examples, security policies should be clear and specific. Policies for calls to the help desk to request password changes or for similar issues should be well defined, and specific procedures should be identified for authenticating a user. You neither need go into the litany of potential reasons why attackers might call nor, even worse, give specific case-by-case examples of what not to do. You need to clearly state what to do, and if there is some bizarre circumstance, there should be elevation procedures that are equally well defined.

When you tell people what not to do in different cases, you are leaving out all the potential circumstances that you did not warn people about. You need to have repeatable processes that account for any circumstance that may arise.

Similarly, security teams should be involved in any major effort to ensure that security can be built into the effort proactively, and not bolted on after the fact. By being a cooperative part of a project, there will be no last-minute problems and any security feature can be incorporated into the effort as inexpensively and unobtrusively as possible.

The technical team should be provided with instructions on how to perform their normal functions securely, which may include administration, code development, and audits, and the security procedures are incorporated as a natural step within the overall process. End users should be provided with instructions on how to perform their functions with security embedded within the functions as appropriate.

In the ideal world, security teams should present themselves as a resource to the employee base. Not only should they provide information about how to behave safely at work, but they provide information and support to allow people to security themselves and their families outside of work. Such information can include how to protect a home network, how to protect your identity, and other information that is personally useful. Not only does this provide a favorable view of the security team, it also promotes safe behaviors outside of work, which will also create stronger security behaviors on the job.

FIGURE 11.1

The ABCs of behavior.

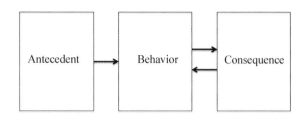

THE ABCs OF BEHAVIOR

As described, behavior is influenced by information and consequences of past behaviors. To simplify it, providing a person with information is considered an antecedent of behavior. An antecedent is considered to be 20% effective, whereas consequences are considered to be 80% effective. For this reason, you can see why awareness efforts that focus on consequences, such as gamification, are considered more effective.

Fig. 11.1 implies that antecedents can create or influence behavior and behaviors in turn create consequences. It is important to understand that although providing information may or may not influence or create behavior, there is always a consequence of behavior, even if there is no apparent consequence. Consequences then feedback into influencing and/or creating behaviors, as demonstrated by the following example.

It is important to consider that the lack of an apparent consequence should be considered a consequence itself. For example, if a server tells you that a plate is hot and you grab it and find it not to be hot, there is no consequence; however, it reinforces your grabbing of a potentially hot plate in the future. A consequence can be positive, negative, or neutral.

In security, a neutral consequence is usually the equivalent of a positive consequence. A positive consequence would encourage the behavior to be continued in the future. There is typically a drive for the behavior in the first place, so if there is a neutral consequence, there is no reason to change or unlearn the behavior. It is therefore more likely to continue the behavior, even in the absence of a positive consequence.

A positive consequence does not mean that it generates the desired security behavior. For example, bypassing security procedures could result in accomplishing a task faster. This reinforces bypassing the security procedures in the case in question, as well as in other circumstances. A negative consequence, such as downloading a virus because procedures were not followed, increases the likeliness of practicing better security behaviors in the future.

When you implement gamification or other awareness programs, you need to strive to create positive consequences for the desired behaviors. Although we generally do not encourage being quick to punish employees, as appropriate, you should devise negative consequences for undesired behaviors, especially those that put the organization at serious risk. Similarly, you need to attempt to eliminate positive consequences for undesirable behaviors, and especially eliminate negative consequences for desired behaviors.

For example, it is critical that people feel comfortable about reporting incidents. All too frequently, people believe that if they report a potential incident, they are scrutinized and could be punished for being the source of the incident; this must end. Although there are some people who do commit bad acts, when acts are accidental, people must feel comfortable to report the acts so that the damages can be contained and mitigated.

Peer Pressure

Perhaps the most effective way to create a security culture is to have everyone behave appropriately. Peer pressure is very powerful. For example, if everyone wears a badge inside the organization, any new person will feel obliged to likewise wear a badge. Similarly, if a new employee walks into an organization and starts wearing a badge, but everyone else is not, the new employee too will stop wearing the badge. Going against peer pressure creates negative consequences, whereas adhering to peer pressure generates positive consequences.

As consultants, we have to fit in. As security professionals, we try to set examples. However, when everyone we run into is not wearing a badge, we will almost always put the issued badges in our pockets, so as not to stand out.

At NSA, employees not wearing badges are teased by their coworkers or accosted by strangers when they are in public areas. It is part of the culture.

What is important to note is that the NSA security culture was implemented from the top down and is well enforced. The last person leaving a work area is responsible for inspecting the area for unsecured desks, unlocked file cabinets, and computers left turned on, among other potential security violations. They were required to correct the issue and report it to a supervisor. Additionally, random checks could be performed where security guards could open up rooms and inspect the area. If any violations were found, they were reported through the chain of command. This creates not only the motivation to adhere to security policies and procedures, but also peer pressure to adhere to security procedures.

Whether people realize it or not, peer pressure always exists. Much like with teenagers, peers strongly influence a wide variety of behaviors, which include choice of clothing, physical appearance, health habits, study habits, and attendance; work peers strongly influence behaviors, especially security-related behaviors.

It behooves organizations to create an environment where people do the right thing just because it is the right thing to do. This can be accomplished by creating punishments, as is done at NSA, or by creating incentives. When the entire organization instills good behaviors in an individual, there can be less reliance on focusing awareness training on individuals. Peer pressure is always present and can be the most effective tool in securing good behaviors.

Just be aware that it can also be the most effective tool in compromising security.

Gamification

We describe gamification as a tool that can potentially be used to create peer pressure. However, when people hear the term gamification, they assume it is a game, such as a software game. They believe that you play a game and learn from the game. This actually makes gamification a tool for a traditional awareness program.

Gamification, in the scientific definition, involves creating a reward structure that encourages the desired behaviors. In other words, it is designed to create positive consequences. Common examples of gamification include frequent flier programs and grocery store reward programs. With airline frequent flier programs, the desired behaviors include brand loyalty to the sponsoring airline and use of partner reward programs, such as credit cards, through which the airlines make additional income. With supermarket reward programs, customers get special discounts for groceries and gasoline in exchange for essentially allowing the store to track every purchase that they make. The store can then use that information to better market to the customer and sell the information to other parties.

To create a true gamification program, you need to understand the business drivers and the organizational culture. Business drivers combined with policy define the behaviors that you want to reward. Culture defines the rewards that will have the maximum impact.

Actions to be rewarded may include completing training, detecting potential incidents, reporting ongoing incidents, and assisting other employees in their security actions. You can reward an individual for a specific action, or potentially assign a different number of points for different actions. Should you choose the latter, you assign more points for more critical actions. You then set tiers that when people achieve different point levels, they receive increasingly greater rewards.

The rewards need to be relevant to the culture. For example, in Japan, a prestigious reward is to be recognized by the executive management. Some cultures might prefer money or extra vacation days. Lower levels of rewards might include T-shirts, certificates, and other gifts. In one case, we were involved with, we organized a contest between development teams to see which team developed the most secure software. They wanted the pride of being the best team.

Of course, you can reward people for specific actions, as well as have a tiered reward structure. You can also implement reward structures only for parts of an organization, such as development teams, as mentioned earlier. Generally, gamification tends to work best in white-collar environments.

ELEMENTS OF A SECURITY AWARENESS PROGRAM

As described earlier, the first link of generating a strong security culture is awareness. Even if a gamification program is in place that proactively creates the appropriate consequences, there is still a need for a traditional awareness program that pushes information throughout the organization. Although awareness programs seem to generally focus on mandatory computer-based training (CBT) and phishing simulations, they are limited only by creativity.

Phishing is clearly an important topic to address, given the fact that many attacks rely on phishing. However, phishing simulations do not eradicate phishing attacks, and you generally find that if 20 phishing messages are received by an organization, there will be at least one person who falls victim to the attack. Even if you completely eradicate phishing, that is, just a single attack vector, a good awareness program must assist people in protecting the organization, detecting attacks, and knowing how to respond to all attacks; not just phishing attacks.

With regard to CBT, it is a valuable tool in sharing information, but it cannot be considered the only communication tool used in a good awareness program. We have found that when people are required to take CBT, they frequently fast-forward through the training or share answers, so that people can minimize the time on the training. Additionally, different people have different learning styles and preferences, so you need to provide training in as many formats as reasonable.

Traditional awareness programs are very much like gamification programs. Business drivers, including policy, determine the content to be distributed, whereas the culture determines the communication tools used. Clearly, there should be as broad a base of information distributed as possible; however, it has to be presented in a coordinated way that is constantly reinforced.

Organization culture, including the population demographics, determines the optimal communication tools. Although traditional passive communication tools, such as posters, should be considered by default, sometimes they might not be appropriate. For example, in one New York investment bank, we were specifically told that posters would not be used because, "We're not putting a f*cking poster up next to a Picasso." In another organization, they did not want to use posters, but they did have monitors throughout the organization that allowed for rotating displays.

Organizations should also consider role-based awareness programs for different types of employees. For example, if you consider large retailers, they have at least four distinct categories of employees: executives, IT personnel, warehouse workers, and store associates. Each of these groups have different awareness needs, work environments, and communication styles. Such an organization should, therefore, consider implementing at least four different awareness programs.

Awareness topics to address include phishing, physical security, social engineering, mobile device security, password security, and intellectual property protection. Each of these topics should be broken down into subtopics. For example, physical security could include clean desks, perimeter security, handling visitors, what to do when you find USB drives, and more. Even when broken down, these are just the common topics. There can be compliance related topics, technology specific topics, situation related topics (such as travel security), among countless other topics.

Traditional communication tools include posters, videos, newsletters, blogs, Twitter feeds, table tents, desk drops, and checklists. More engaging tools include contests, displays, games, exhibit tables, lunch and learn presentations, bringing in outside speakers, and printing messages on coffee cups.

The discussion on the creation of awareness programs can fill several books. For additional information on the recommendations for and guidance on the structure of awareness programs, topics, and forms of communications, you can search the Internet for relevant content by the author, Ira Winkler, and Secure Mentem, Ira's company.

MANAGEMENT SUPPORT

No matter what the structure of your awareness program may be, it cannot be successful without management support. As with any discipline of security, awareness efforts, to include individual responsibility with regard to protection, detection, and reaction, must have the appropriate resources allocated to the program. Management must provide funding, allocate personnel, and ensure that people make time for the program, potentially taking time away from other obligations.

This type of management support also includes ensuring that security culture concerns are embedded within all organizational functions. Developers are not going to prioritize the security of their software without appropriate guidance. Guards will not perform their functions diligently, if it appears they are there only for demonstration purposes. Employees will not wear their badges, if nobody else wears theirs. Without adequate management support, the security culture will be weak by default.

SUMMARY

Security culture has a direct impact on all other areas of security. If people do not behave appropriately, no combination of technologies in the world will secure your organization and its assets. People will do a poor job of protecting information, if the security culture is weak. They will not know their responsibilities to protect information. They will not know how to protect information and computers, even if they want to.

Likewise, they will not know how to detect potential incidents, and even if they did, they will not know the appropriate response to the incident. Even if the response is to alert someone else, they will not know who that person is and how to contact them.

Many security programs do not properly engage the people within the organization, and the security programs will suffer unnecessary loss. It is, therefore, our strong recommendation that before you complete reading Section 2 of this book consider the type of security culture you have to work with. If it is a weak culture, you must stop and consider how you can quickly improve that culture. It will very likely be a more effective use of your resources, especially your time, to first determine how to strengthen your security culture, before improving technology.

CHAPTER 12

What Is Threat Intelligence?

Threat intelligence means a lot of things to a lot of people. Its origins, like many of the concepts in this book and in the security industry as a whole, are largely derived from our experience in military acts of identifying, understanding, anticipating, and thwarting the activities of adversaries to a given critical asset. As tools and technologies emerge and trend toward simultaneous innovation, automation, and commoditization, threat intelligence has taken on an air of being something that can be not only amassed, cultivated, and matured, but also purchased wholesale.

However, lest we fall victim to past mistakes regarding the reduction of valuable security elements and metrics to the lowest common denominator, where they inevitably lose fidelity to their core principles and functions, it is important to step back and consider what it means to truly consume and operationalize intelligence, beyond the misleading notion that intelligence is something innately measurable, finite, articulate, uniform, and rote enough to comply with a one-size-fits-all method of collection, implementation, and adoption.

At a high level, and for the sake of conversation, threat intelligence in cyber space refers to technology and operational disciplines that enable the collection, correlation, and analysis and the meaningful use of data on threats or threat actors to inform and adapt security defenses. Threat intelligence platforms and solutions continue to grow in their reach and capacity to collect and interpret information from a multitude of sources. Their receptiveness to interpretation and analytics that point defenders to threats and to mitigating actions that fit their respective environments, vulnerabilities, and available countermeasures is also on the increase.

By aggregating threat data from multiple sources, correlating and interpreting the data, and then porting it elsewhere into the environment for use by other systems and teams, threat intelligence seeks to identify and inform avenues for the mitigation through the implementation of countermeasures.

A true threat intelligence program stands apart from traditional security technologies and products in that it is an ecosystem that can be not only tuned, but also

143

Advanced Persistent Security. http://dx.doi.org/10.1016/B978-0-12-809316-0.00012-9

culled, programmed, and continually analyzed to suit the resources and threats with which they are working on a daily basis.

TYPES OF THREAT INTELLIGENCE

Threat intelligence comes in many forms. Some sources overlap and fall into or include multiple categories, and they frequently reference multiple sources of data, much of which will overlap. Some of these sources are highly academic. Some represent all-too-real-world occurrences, and some are the direct result of law enforcement investigations and takedowns that expose the inner workings of a given attack or vector. Some are corralled or created by idiots who are speculating wildly or are grossly out of touch with the practical application of any of the threats they purport to reference. The source and type of the intelligence you seek to integrate into your threat intelligence program is as important to its value as how or if you use it. It is therefore important to identify the type of intelligence that source represents as you determine what, if any, action to take with it. There are a number of accepted classifications of intelligence, but to set the stage, we will highlight those that are most commonly collected and consumed as part of an enterprise cybersecurity threat intelligence program.

External Intelligence

External intelligence, in a nutshell, is any information gathered and/or interpreted by sources outside your organization. Most commonly, external intelligence takes the form of feeds purchased or subscribed to and is based on data amassed by external analysts and organizations. These sources come from independent security researchers, product or service providers, and law enforcement agencies based on patterns uncovered in previous investigations. These sources often cross-reference and overlap with one another and are subject to constant change.

External intelligence may take into account threats that relate directly to your organization, industry, and attackers, or may speak to goings-on observed in the wild or at the malware level.

Institutional Intelligence

Institutional intelligence, also referred to as internal intelligence, refers simply to any data gathered about your institution, by your institution, and for your institution. The most basic and vast sources are typically your logs from things such as security information and event management (SIEM) systems and firewalls and user behavior analytics. Amusingly enough, low-level system and event logs are often thought of as the most pedestrian and uninteresting collection of data we gather and hoard as technology professionals. They would just as soon drive forks into their eyes as volunteer to work with and review them, but more often than not, when something goes horribly wrong, evidence is right there in our internal logs and can be leveraged to investigate or, if caught earlier, advance or bring about earlier defenses against an attack.

Institutional intelligence, at a more evolved and programmatic level, can include data points gathered from less rote sources, including people ("see something, say something" conversations and behavior monitoring), workflow and interteam operational processes, and incident response and investigations. A level of maturity is often required before these sources of institutional intelligence can be consumed, interpreted, and incorporated into something actionable and repeatable, but they are attainable, nonetheless. Institutional intelligence cannot be bought, and it remains one of the richest, most immediately available, and most relevant sources of usable information an organization can work into its appetite. Contrarily, it is one of the most under-appreciated forms of threat intelligence.

Open Source Intelligence
Information need not be secretive or esoteric to provide immense value. It may not always be easily found, but it does not have to be impossible to acquire in order to be precious. We sometimes get so wrapped up in the advancement of the adversary that we assume that anything we do as defenders has to be similarly cutting edge, cloak and dagger, and unknowable to the masses to be effective or worth spending time and money on.

Put in this context, we can recognize the folly of that mentality by comparing it to the number of breaches that gain a toehold through exploitation of basic security hygiene failures. Useful, relevant, and otherwise telling data is readily available in the things we read, hear, and see on the Internet every day. In the same way that the innumerable streams of information that we consume as natural observers of our environment, media, and other input streams serves to provide context for our view of our surroundings, circumstances, and conditions, open source intelligence (OSINT) serves to inform security practitioners of the threat and cybersecurity landscapes.

The intelligence community generally refers to this freely available information as OSINT. It includes sources such as:

- the Internet (websites, blogs, articles, vulnerability and common vulnerabilities and exposure (CVE) data, etc.)
- media and news outlets (broadcasts, newspapers, magazines, etc.)
- social media, chat room and forum musings, and conversational rants by other observers

- breach disclosures and corporate filings
- research and studies, presentations, and white papers
- geospatial information (map and satellite data)
- threat feeds supplied by vendors, service providers, and law enforcement for the purpose of information sharing
- the dark web (discussed in Chapter 7)

More than 80% of threat intelligence available is open source, so defenders must up their game when it comes to collecting and using it. Publicly available sources frequently offer a low-cost, high-value intelligence tool for analysts, if they know where (and where not) to look, and can be used to identify indicators, perform link analysis, and tune security operations.

There are a number of readily available threat feeds and exchanges that can be feasibly and meaningfully integrated into a threat intelligence program, whether as individual or aggregate feeds. Popular examples often work with accepted threat information sharing specifications, such as STIX/TAXII, to facilitate the automation and consumption of vetted threat data. Two favorites, AlienVault OTX and Hail A TAXII, both leverage STIX/TAXII, among other frameworks, to enable open collaboration and sharing of threat data among practitioners within the security and intelligence communities. They can be very helpful in founding or fueling an organization's threat intelligence program at the technical level.

Closed Source Intelligence

Converse to OSINT, closed source intelligence (CSINT) is information gathered from sources that are not freely available to the community at large. Although this may be broadly interpreted to include intelligence feeds that must simply be paid for to be acquired or accessed, the intelligence community typically distinguishes CSINT as being intelligence that requires a quiet and trusted partnership in order for the information to be shared.

Examples of this definition of CSINT might be data exchanged with law enforcement or government agencies as part or result of ongoing investigations or nation-state actor threats. Infragard is an example of a government partnership with industry, and information is only shared among vetted members. There are industry-specific information sharing and analysis centers (ISACs), where members share threat-related information among themselves. CSINT of this type may also include partnerships between developers and users that make use of the knowledge of code or systems that constitutes trade secrets. It is not to be shared as part of a broader vulnerability or threat disclosure, or in the case of critical infrastructure or systems that would cause greater vulnerability if made publicly known.

CSINT that is regarded as closed, because it requires a subscription or payments in some form may be widely available and feasible to consume. In general, though, CSINT will typically, not constitute more than a small fraction of a threat intelligence program, if any at all.

Human Intelligence

Human intelligence (HUMINT) is intelligence acquired from human sources. This can include the observation of human-to-human interactions. This data gathering exercise is frequently laborious to engage in and even harder to validate or make meaningful use of. However, more cursory and practical examples of HUMINT in the enterprise sector can be found in the reputation and brand protection exercises, where agents of an enterprise seek out mentions of corporate monikers appearing in the wild and monitor communications of employees for signs of disgruntled or reckless behavior that might lead to data leakage.

Some organizations may have a small team of researchers who patrol forums known for trading malware or sensitive data, such as credit card numbers, as a means to check what might be trending or affecting them. They may do this by posing as a criminal. However, generally speaking, the collection and validation of this kind of intelligence is best left to experts and specialists, who typically are law enforcement agencies and service providers in the business of infiltrating adversary communities and checking for or investigating evidence of wrongdoing. It is mostly not feasible to devote the capital resources or manpower to build a posse of personnel, who are well skilled and covert enough to penetrate these darker communities and, furthermore, identify actions that can be taken before assets are compromised. A looser interpretation of HUMINT is keeping an eye on your employees and their watercooler conversations or monitoring corporate chat vehicles.

THREAT INTELLIGENCE PLATFORMS

Threat intelligence platforms enable practitioners to confront the threats and adversaries directly, tuning and adapting their responses as an attack plays out and evolves. Many times, these things are recognizable. Countless analyses have demonstrated that although the threat actors may change or evolve, they frequently recycle effective attack methods, because they are effective. Even in many new cases for which no malware signature has been derived, the methods themselves are represented by patterns that persist even as the adversaries' tools and targets change. It is very important for an organization to have in place a flexible, cohesive means of collecting, aggregating, reporting, and sharing what would otherwise be an excruciating amount of disjointed detail that would drown operators in minutia and obscure patterns that emerge when incident data is viewed holistically.

At various stages of an attack, threat intelligence platforms may serve to identify the threat actor, detect the presence of a threat tool, stop the actions associated with a threat, disrupt the means or infrastructure being used to effect an attack, or just focus on turning the target network and systems into a live laboratory where the threat can be studied. Through threat intelligence, enterprises and researchers can identify the threat details that are the most useful and relevant to their own environment and risks.

When speaking of threat intelligence platforms, we include the tactical processes, tools, techniques, and technologies that are used to carry out the mission of the threat intelligence program. Although a mature threat intelligence program may include a number of layered or ancillary components, at its most fundamental, it should include detection, incident response, threat assessment, threat modeling, threat hunting, and life cycle learning. A well-oiled threat intelligence machine, in as automated a process as possible, throttles the intelligence and experience it gains directly back into explicit operational elements, namely, perimeter defenses [firewalls, intrusion detection system (IDS), etc.], SIEM systems, investigations, and training and awareness programs.

The primary function of a threat intelligence platform is to collect, organize, and interpret. It informs stakeholders and communities in order to respond to threats efficiently and effectively. These intelligence ecosystems enable practitioners to coordinate tactical and strategic activities with operations both inside and outside the security teams, extending the reach of actionable threat and security data to incident response, risk management, and nontechnical line of business owners. However, this is not its only benefit.

One of the greatest ironies of our industry is our hiding of secrets. As we discussed, adversaries do not function in this manner. They readily share tools, tactics, infrastructure, and financial resources to make their shared objectives more successful, while the security community expects to keep pace by putting a stranglehold on its methods, technologies, and failings. To discuss security breakdowns would be to provide a glimpse into failures and would subject us to judgment by our peers, customers, and enemies. Without a sincere and overnight shift in this line of thinking, information sharing will not occur even within an organization, and never in the greater security community. A threat intelligence program provides a neutral, unbiased lexicon and forum by which security teams can share threat information with one another, interoperate more effectively with compatriots and law enforcement, and avail themselves of the expertise of others to improve and coordinate advanced countermeasures.

There are several tools available to organizations. The Collaborative Research Into Threats (CRITs) is an open source tool for analysts engaged in threat defense. Soltra Edge, which is distributed by the Financial Services ISAC, provides a single platform to process many intelligence feeds, as well as providing a variety of analytic tools.

THREAT INTELLIGENCE PLATFORM CAPABILITIES

Threat intelligence platforms comprise several functional areas that actualize and embody an intelligence-driven security approach. Ideally, a mature platform enjoins these functions by automated workflows that streamline threat detection, management, analysis, and defensive processes and track it through to completion. However even a largely manual effort that is well established and documented will increase the efficacy of a security program by an order of magnitude. Threat intelligence platforms should provide the following foundational elements:

- Collection: Collects and aggregates multiple sources and formats of data, such as CSV (comma separated value) files, STIX (Structured Threat Information Expression), Custom XML/JSON, CVE (Common Vulnerabilities and Exposures), OpenIOC (indicators of compromise), device logs, and email. This is not your SIEM. Although SIEM systems can handle multiple threat-intelligence-related feeds, they are improperly instrumented for taking in and interpreting the unstructured formats of the free-form, text-heavy unstructured data that frequently characterize intelligence feeds. It is not uncommon to augment a threat intelligence platform with an SIEM, but it is not good to attempt to replace it with one.
- Correlation: Facilitates the automatic analysis and correlation of data so that an attack can be mapped out, linkage can occur, and countermeasures can be deployed. Human sanity checks and creativity should prevail and be involved in the evaluations of correlated data, but automation and machine learning are all that is required for this function to be met at even a basic level.
- Context: Provides enrichment and circumstantial details on given events, without which they remain arbitrary and without reporting patterns and linkage. Information is organized data. Intelligence organized information, with context. A threat intelligence platform should be able to take in and relate additional details garnered from other events and investigations to properly and intelligently make decisions and take action.
- Analysis: Evaluates and draws conclusions surrounding threat indicators. Analysis identifies the intricacies of relationships between events to deliver meaningful threat intelligence from the otherwise unrelated data in pivoting sets.

- Integration: Supports operational workflow and funnels threat intelligence data into security tools and products for action and life cycle maintenance. Platforms should gather and redistribute normalized, interpreted data to other operational tools such as SIEM systems and perimeter defense technologies, as well as other processes, including incident management, reporting, and/or ticketing systems.

- Action: Accelerates and manages the processing and validation of subsequent action and response, whether inside or outside an organization. Action in this context includes cooperative efforts within the security team and other lines of operations and business within an organization as well as between an organization and other contributing parties or stakeholders, such as regulatory bodies, law enforcement, or (ISACs), with whom the organization has sharing or response relationships.

SUMMARY

Threat intelligence provides an opportunity to understand the threats so that you can better prioritize countermeasures to prevent attacks. Additionally, the more you know about the threats, the better you are able to both detect and react to them. Understanding them allows you to anticipate their actions and optimize your defenses and reactions. We further discuss the application of threat intelligence in defining your security program in Section 5.

SECTION 3

Detection

We talk in this book about the importance of building a security program through balanced protection, detection, and reaction. In this section, we cover some of the principles associated with detection and how it does more than simply catch things that have gone wrong and slipped through the cracks, but rather helps shape, tune, and even systematically bolster your defensive position.

Examination of the foundations and applications of passive and active detection will help an organization determine where to best deploy technology and focus the eyes of security professionals. Detection solutions shed light on where countermeasures will be most necessary and impactful, as well as aid in redirection and containment of adversary activity to an area where it can be best controlled. Under ideal and mature circumstances, it can also be used to learn more about the nefarious actions.

CHAPTER 13

What Is Detection?

Despite the churn and innovation in prevention technologies, it is safe to say that many organizations' security programs depend on outdated methods that provide only marginal efficacy when it comes to prevention of compromise and data loss. Mostly security seems to focus on perimeter defense and intrusion prevention, but actually barring the adversary from access and entry is a losing battle. Statistics touting an intrusion success rate of over 90% is inversely proportional to the intrusion prevention rate. Even worse, this percentage is directly proportional to the number of times breached organizations have had evidence of these intrusions present, but undetected, in log data.

However, we sliced and diced the breach details and found out that what was once a doomsday scenario for enterprise defenders is now an almost daily occurrence. Enterprises are under attack, and the success of the attackers is increasing. The cost of prevention and containment is rising as an enterprise's success rates are falling, and the effectiveness of advanced persistent threats is increasing at a much faster pace than the effectiveness of solutions.

Defenders must consider security intelligence and behavioral analytics that go beyond traditional signature-based defenses and firewalls to disrupt attacks across the attack chain, from intrusion to exfiltration.

We are well past the point of needing to diversify our focus on what is traditionally regarded as the frontlines, i.e., prevention, and start honing detection skills as the first line of defense in a cyberwar. Breach detection focuses on identifying intrusions after they happen and mitigating the damage, in part by using big-data technologies and by reintroducing lessons learnt from unsuccessful security practices into both the monitoring and defensive streams.

PREVENTION IS INSUFFICIENT

Particularly in a small-to-midsize business space, a commonly held belief is that sufficient security comes in large part from being a little more difficult to access. If security is a balance of being less interesting than you are available, then with this mentality, applying controls effectively enough to show that

153

Advanced Persistent Security. http://dx.doi.org/10.1016/B978-0-12-809316-0.00013-0

you or your data are not the lowest hanging fruit in your field should drive the majority of the attackers to pursue an easier victim. Many of us have quipped in a casual conversation that outrunning a gator or bear, depending on where you grew up, required you only to run faster than the guy next to you. This philosophy has been alive in the security field as well, as we have sought to outmode our collective adversaries. Said out loud, however, defining your security strategy based on trying to keep your head down and shoring up your defenses just a little more than the next guy sounds naive and ridiculous and isn't the inspired battle cry you want to put before your board. Begging the postbreach forgiveness of your internal and external customers, because you relied on the poor security of your competitors is not a compelling verbal defense either.

In the past years, analysis of the breach space indicated that hackers were preying on the low-hanging fruit and effecting opportunistic easy breaches. In the majority of cases, adversaries used a shotgun blast approach to find targets and take hold in a "spray and pray" fashion. These attacks and attackers are still alive and well, and signature-based security solutions that aim at known malicious code patterns remain reasonably effective and even scale well. If one entity uncovers a new threat, a signature written for it can be distributed to others to protect them from such similar manifestations. Such practices have become the core of the security mainstream, and their use is considered to be basic security hygiene.

However, as organizations have grown more aggressive, innovative, and consistent in shoring up their security posture, attackers have also evolved. Every time we step up our game, so do our adversaries. Attacks today are more sophisticated and targeted than ever before. The use of generic one-size-fits-all malware is declining in percentage of successful attacks and is being gradually replaced by custom malware created just for a specific target rendering signature-based protections nearly useless.

As new providers innovate and deliver solutions intended to thwart these kinds of attacks, attackers face the explicit challenge of overcoming a specific defense, frequently purchasing all the same technologies and intrusion prevention systems being used by their targets and designed to disrupt their efforts. In highly targeted cases, attackers recreate the target environment almost identically, creating a training and testing ground that enables them to "train as they fight," a practice that the defender community would do well to keep in mind as it tries to build effective response programs.

LASTING DAMAGE FOLLOWS AFTER INITIAL COMPROMISE

Initial compromise and further intrusion takes minutes to a few hours, and rarely more than a couple of days. However, the real aim of the adversary and, therefore, the real damage to the target generally manifest well after the attacker circumnavigates and penetrates the initial defenses, in terms of both time and action. Action on the objective—the true goals of the attacker and the actual purpose of the intrusion—transpires often after a series of actions that almost provides the intrusion with access to the actual target of the attack. These actions could later be interpreted as leading and trailing indicators of compromise. If the methods used to gain initial or later access are not of the type for which signatures could be written in advance, then after-the-fact detection efforts are imperative in regaining control and preventing further or real damage.

Once an attacker has successfully penetrated a target, the protection strategy changes completely. We have long understood the importance of detection and prevention, but as the profile and regulation of the security industry has increased, it seems that much of the focus has shifted to building an impenetrable line of defense, rather than an adaptive and agile line of defense.

Consider a traditional castle. There are outer walls and inner walls. There are towers. There may be a moat with a drawbridge. Despite all of the protection put in place, they designed the castle expecting that the layers of protection will be compromised.

In addition to the built in protection, there was built in detection and reaction. The towers watched for areas that were breached, and the design allowed for rapid reinforcement of breached areas. Detection is integral to traditional security programs.

Much like with castles, once attackers breach the wall, mayhem ensues if there is not a rapid response. To minimize damage, a breach of the perimeter must be detected as soon as possible, and resources marshaled to repel attackers, before they further advance. Clearly, when we discuss information and computer systems, detection is much less obvious than watching for invading hoards, but it is still as important to rapidly detect the attackers and marshal the appropriate resources.

DETERMINE WHAT IS TO BE DETECTED

While this might seem obvious, it has to be said. There has to be a conscious effort to determine what to look for. Clearly, you need to look for signs of unauthorized access to information. You need to look for the perimeter being breached by an adversary. There are however more complicated issues to be detected.

In Chapter 17, we discuss the difference between events, incidents, and breaches. They are very specifically defined, and even within a category, there can be a range of importance. For example, an incident could be the accidental deletion of a relatively unimportant file for which a backup exists, or it could be North Korea destroying all files and leaking sensitive files on the Internet.

Events, incidents, and breaches need to be defined in advance, and indicators of compromise (IOCs) for each of these compromises need to be determined. Once you have the IOCs, you can begin to determine what needs to be detected.

IOCs require some contextual knowledge. In the case of the Internal Revenue Service (IRS) Get Transcript hack that we mention throughout the book, the IRS should have looked for not just legitimate access, but unusual patterns of access. For example, they should have noticed a spike in activity, as well as multiple accesses from the same IP address, as well as other indicators of a single user from overseas accessing many accounts.

DETERMINE WHERE TO LOOK

When you identify the IOCs to look for, you can look within your architecture and to your people and determine where to look for the IOCs. This is clearly complicated and requires a thorough understanding of your environment. Systems that store critical information are prime targets.

Truly sophisticated adversaries will target servers involved in infrastructure command and control (C2). C2 servers include email and messaging systems, executive computers, systems involved in controlling network access, and administration systems.

There are also network choke points where you can look for ingress and egress of attacks. The network perimeter is clearly a place to look, even though many people will claim there is no true perimeter. Despite the claimed disappearance of network perimeters, there are clearly perimeter devices that connect an organization to the Internet and other external networks. While it is true that there are likely more of those systems than most organizations know about, they are points to identify and monitor.

Given both the insider threat and the likelihood that your perimeter will be breached, you should also install detection capabilities at choke points within your network. Depending upon the resources available, you need to install detection capabilities between each department and each location. We of course assume that you do not have a flat network, and that there is appropriate segmentation that allows for such monitoring.

In an ideal environment, you should place detection tools where you can watch data egress and ingress. This is the most telling detection capability as you might be able to see a cause and effect.

ENABLE THE DETECTION CAPABILITIES THAT YOU HAVE

We talk about this throughout the book, but it is important to understand the detection capabilities that are built into most technologies. For example, most systems have logging capabilities. Sometimes those capabilities are not enabled. Additionally, even if logging is enabled, someone has to review the logs. We discuss this elsewhere, but we need to constantly stress that log files need to be reviewed.

There are detection capabilities built into most devices. User systems can log failed access attempts. Network devices can log failed connection attempts. While it is common for administrators to deactivate logging and detection capabilities, as they do not have the resources to examine the logs, while we do not necessarily support it, it is a least better that it is a conscious decision to deactivate detection than to not know that the capability exists.

For all systems, you need to examine what capabilities they have, and enable as many as you reasonably can.

HUMAN INTRUSION DETECTION SYSTEMS

Chapter 15 discusses this subject in detail, however we want to take this time to stress that everyone in your organization should be deputized as being part of the security team. All employees, contractors, vendors, and anyone else with regular access to your facilities and resources should know to be on the lookout for unusual activities, to know how to behave when they witness such activity, and to know how to report that activity.

SUMMARY

The remainder of this section covers other detection concepts at a level that is sufficient for people who are not responsible for implementing detection programs. The goal is to enable people to being to ask the right questions. Implementing a proper detection program is not something that can be covered in a section of a book.

We strongly recommend that if your job involves implementing detection programs that you look to experienced people and look to other books and resources. As we imply, a large portion of implementing a detection program is tied directly to the technologies in use, and you must be familiar with those technologies.

You may also want to consider acquire security information and event management (SIEM) tools to simplify the management of detection related information. Chapter 10 covers a variety of countermeasures, which includes some countermeasures that can be used for detection. The resources provided should at least have you begin to understand how these tools and processes fit within an overall security program that includes detection as an embedded process.

CHAPTER 14

Detection Deficit Disorder

There are a few iconic data breaches that keep providing fodder for media outlets, bloggers, doomsday preppers, and a host of other fearmongers. To prove a point, let us take a cursory look at a few of them that serve to humanize a programatic problem.

Target: Target has easily become the punching bag of the retail and data breach spheres. A criminal obtained network entry by sending a spear phishing message to an air conditioning vendor. They then subverted network defenses and went from the vendor network to the business network. They compromised a variety of critical systems throughout the network. Rogue exfiltration points were established. Approximately 110,000,000 data records were exfiltrated out of the network. They criminal went undetected.

Sony: Another favorite to point fingers at. In Sony's case, adversaries infiltrated by sending spear phishing messages to administrators, stood up exfiltration servers, throttled extraordinary amounts of media, which was ultimately meant to be shared, just not at that time, disclosed private emails and personally identifiable information of many Sony employees, from their environment and to top it off, deleted critical data from the network and destroyed critical systems. Again, the attackers went completely undetected until they wanted to announce their presence, first through extortion, then through the destruction of systems.

U.S. Internal Revenue Service (IRS): Let us not forget the IRS. In this case, practically innumerable attempts were made to thwart an authentication schema that leveraged taxpayers' credit reporting data, resulting in about $50 million in fraudulent tax returns being filed. All told, at least 700,000 tax records were compromised, and the attack was undetected while all of the data was compromised.

While we are clearly concerned about the fact that protection failed in the cases cited, the worse fact is that the attacks were not detected. In all of the cases, the attacks were not detected until other entities reported the attacks and/or the

Advanced Persistent Security. http://dx.doi.org/10.1016/B978-0-12-809316-0.00014-2

damage was already done. The failure to detect the attacks was much more devastating than the actual failure in protection.

We are back to a core theme again: protection programs have to be allowed to fail; specifically protection will fail, but your security program doesn't fail until the attacker achieves their outcome. The given has to be accepted to be built on to become a strategy. Regardless of the amount of work and capital resource that has gone into their design, development, and deployment, it is ridiculous to assume that your defenses will never experience an unexpected or undesirable condition or outcome.

If any single security solution were impenetrable, we would not have created terms such as layered defenses, defense in depth, and compensating controls to pervade our culture and drive how we instrument security architecture. If a security team were infallible, we would not be so driven by compliance budget, nor staff up our internal audit teams to answer the question, "Who's watching the watchers?" In the enterprise world, there exists a reasonable expectation of failure at a tactical technical and personnel level, and a system of checks and balances is instituted to counter things that may go awry or fall through the cracks. Why should security at a philosophic strategic and programmatic level be any different?

It is critical to note that most data breaches and incidents are discovered not by the compromised organization, but by third parties. The 2016 Verizon Data Breach Investigations Report (DBIR) finds that 80% of breaches are initially detected by third parties. Similar studies by McAfee find that pecentage to not only be consistent, but increasing over the last decade. In other words, third parties notice the results of the attacks, before the victims, and the situation continues to get worse.

As mentioned earlier, whether you are speaking strategically about a security program or tactically about a specific attack, security itself is a combination of protection, detection, and reaction. To be effective, security programs need to embrace and leverage all three processes equally. So many organizations have what would be described primarily as protection programs and not security programs, because they look at detection as a fail-safe approach, not as an additional intelligence, and as a lens into how their other controls can be leveraged and optimized.

WHAT IS ADD?

The security industry gets its fair share of mileage out of references to attention deficit disorder (ADD). As practitioners, we have ADD, claim to have it, joke about having it, and joke about selectively hiring for it. Most of us cannot or will not argue that its characteristic multitasking and juggling, and hair-on-fire tendencies are almost bred for technologic spheres and roles. It is commonly believed that our pop culture disorder du jour is rooted in a marked and often debilitating inability to focus, because of high levels of distractibility. However, this flair for chasing the bright and shiny is only a singular symptom. Furthermore, its label is actually a misnomer in and of itself.

ADD is actually a condition characterized by hyperattention, or the ability of the sufferer's attention to be so easily captured by and hyperfocused on anything and everything in his/her perception sphere. It is in this way that ADD very aptly resembles and parallels a condition and dysfunction of security information gathering and processing, or what we refer to as detection deficit disorder (DDD).

At an organic and visceral level, most people have a similar concept of attention. Attention is the capture of mindshare and mental cycles in a deliberate and practical form of one stream of thought versus others that compete for mental cycles. Attention suggests the focused and explicit opting out of some things to deal deliberately, judiciously, and mindfully with others. It is in stark contrast with its twin, the discordant, haphazard, and wayward inattentive state considered distraction.

For some, there is an important difference between attention and distraction, and this applies to individuals and organizations. When confronted with tasks that are mundane or tedious (such as reading this lengthy recap of what ADD actually is), as long as is something important to them, most people, or programs, can focus on the tasks at hand.

For the sake of those who are attention challenged, and for this book, let us just oversimplify ADD as referring to inattention that is not caused by apathy, but rather by paying too much attention to too much stuff, which equals distractability or becoming overwhelmed by the size and scatter of the data set.

WHAT IS DDD?

Security practitioners constantly bemoan the burden placed on a given event management or logging system and its analysts by mismanaged signal-to-noise ratios. Despite the complaints, we continue the pursuit of the gluttonous consumption of intelligence, gorging on feeds, and slurping log data in and out of binged upon appliances and console views. We collect more and more data and input it into dashboards in the simultaneous pursuit of data science and the art of threat intelligence. With an overload of security information and event management (SIEM) feeds and big data voodoo, we expect to divine some undefined predictive detail about our current state of security and to translate that into action to bring about mission and operational clarity for our next-generation security solutions.

Organizations that have their security acts together and fall higher up the security maturity food chain also suffer. For them, a more refined sample set and analytic process yields the same problem. Not too much noise, but rather too much signal, and they still cannot discern the necessary patterns or identify proper mount points for defense. The sheer volume of actionable data and interesting feeds is as burdensome as trying to get your arms around bad and cluttered data. Organizations have gone from looking for the idiomatic needle in a haystack to looking for it in a "needlestack."

This is exactly why people think attacks are sophisticated; because they want them to be. They are tuned in and ready for the next big thing to hit; therefore, everything should be the next big thing. We are dialed in and ready for everything to be advanced, to be persistent, and to be a credible threat and harbinger of a dynamic menace of an adversary. We expect the dimwittedness of our aging, fractured, or underfunded controls to be our Achilles' heel; not our inability to heed the warnings they are trying to give us. Unfortunately, this is as big a part of the problem as is improper basic security hygiene.

We are inclined to take security threats more seriously when they are perceived as highly sophisticated and cutting-edge. Mundanity is wearying, so deeper looks at security basics and routine activities are often back-burnered in favor of more bleeding edge controls and more interesting security problems than foundational detective controls. The irony is that the consequences of not paying attention to basic incidents, such as an outage or a breach, are imminent and severe enough that they should be far more interesting than an adversary or attacker who is unlikely to fully actualize.

The analogy we use in our talks is that the while movies that feature Medieval times focus on dragons as the enemy, the most devastating creatures of the times were the common rats, which spread the plague. While security professionals might sometimes fight a proverbial dragon, in the form of an actual advanced persistent threat, we are much more likely to be called upon to stop a common breach, virus incident, unauthorized access, etc.

DIAGNOSING DDD

Long story short, we have a problem. But more often than not, it is not a protection problem, but a detection problem. A detection problem may be a complicated one, so it is important to identify why your detection methods are failing, before you add more solutions. Security programs suffer inattention for a variety of reasons that center generally on an imbalance among signal, noise, resources, and visibility. This applies to architecture, staff, leadership, devices, groups, and individuals, all of which may become ineffective, if they are overwhelmed or improperly utilized. However, generally speaking, the causes for detection problems fall into three categories.

Too Much Information

This should be fairly self-explanatory and has been discussed earlier, as its theme is reoccurring. Suffice it to summarize this category of causation as untenable volumes of log and intelligence data being laid out before a practitioner or team, such that no patterns can be isolated or identified. We see shocking statistics each year on the number of breaches that should have been proactively detected by the data readily available in log files.

In the case of the Target breach, it has been widely reported that the security staff had been alerted about anomalous activity on affected systems and had multiple opportunities to engage and take a different course of action than that was chosen as part of investigation. The alerts received were evaluated at a cursory level, classified as lower priority, and then dismissed as noise. This oversight exemplifies the problem of having details available in logging and intelligence tools, but failing to act appropriately, because the volume of detail or the level of visibility. This coupled with too many competing interests results in missing or misclassifying incidents as events in favor of carrying out other job functions.

This is arguably the most common detection problem of all. It happens when the security staff has too many things to do. Forcing even a highly skilled team to monitor a mind-numbing deluge of alerts would quickly consume the attention of limited resources to the detriment of their other responsibilities will inevitably cause incidents to be missed. Optimization and tuning of the devices requires manpower to complete, so they do not happen until either an incident occurs or a compliance initiative requires it to occur.

Security is full of ironies. Ironically, as detection fails, the incident response and/or compliance assessment processes will often take the collective eye further off this ball in the short term. Even worse, the mind-numbing volume and compliance orientation of many of the alerts results in the absence of intuition, and this is why there are too many alerts to wade through in the first place. This hides the precious details of an incident that would tell the security team more about their security program than all the alerts combined. The exhausting nature of monitoring logs creates a churn and burn turnover rate in staff that ensures that you will lose your knowledge capital and expertise almost as soon as it is amassed. People with high-value talent will not want to stick around to waste themselves on the grunt work that made them talented.

It is of paramount importance to break this cycle and go from information to intelligence, which Chapter 12 discusses in detail.

Looking in All the Wrong Places

Devices and attackers alike have become more clever and are generally aware of their surroundings. In earlier days of perimeter hardening, firewalls and intrusion detection system (IDS) became the systems of record when it came to identifying intruders. As the perimeter "disappeared" and systems became more articulate in their ability to accept monitoring and reporting about their anomalous goings-on, we turned our attention to the endpoints. This ebb and flow and oscillating visibility have led many times to divestiture of logs that should be correlated, as well as relying heavily on one point of visibility over another.

In the Sony breach, a number of security controls were functioning as they should have been, leading to a false sense of (wait for it) security, such that the creation of exfiltration servers by the adversary on the Sony network was not detected. Furthermore, the spike in the amount of data leaving the network was so extraordinary that its escape is almost unfathomable. In this case, the intrusion was not nearly as cataclysmic as the extrusion of the proprietary media, which the company wanted to keep a secret until the target release date. If Sony's resources were allocated to monitor egress traffic and the creation of new network entities as carefully as they were monitoring for intrusion and endpoints, there would have been an opportunity to prevent the actual damage of exfiltration. There was also the failure to detect the compromise of critical file and communications servers. There was a failure to detect known malware installed on endpoints. If this was detected, or even if the data egress was detected, Sony could have looked for these action as well.

It is as important to balance resources as it is to obtain and conserve them. Detection programs often fail when too many technologies are acquired and not correlated, or when too much is invested in overlapping or redundant areas. Depth perception is achieved only when lenses is looking from and compensating for complementary vantage points and taking time and motion into account.

Not Looking at All

This is another category that suggests an internal logic of its own.

Whether it is resource consumption, ignorance, or being overwhelmed by the data set available, some security teams and organizations are simply not looking at all when it comes to critical points of visibility in their environments. Sometimes this results from the expectation that other active defenses are sufficient, and other times it is the recognition that a security team can only do so many things reasonably well. In the end, there are many cases where necessary visibility is either not being established or if established, not being used properly.

Taking the IRS breach as an example, the noteworthy failure is the failure of the authentication scheme, which purported to use data known only by the individual to satisfy multifactor authentication pursuits. Although this was a huge contributing factor to the breakdown in security, it overshadows the failure to detect that large numbers of these access attempts, successful and unsuccessful, were coming from the same IP addresses. Most of us encounter server-level controls that warn of too many attempts to execute on something transactional within a given period, using IP address data as the identifier. Had the IRS instituted some basic detective controls to catch the glaring red flag of numerous attempts to file returns from a single IP or range thereof, the opportunity to thwart the authentication process would have ended quickly.

Completely omitting vantage points from view is a guarantee that detail will be missed. Capturing data, but not looking at it, is just as bad as not capturing it at all. Log information alone is not detection, and controls only become detective if they are being actively culled and correlated for test and use cases that would indicate compromise.

TREATING DDD

Most detection programs fail because of a combination of the above-mentioned causes, or because too many eggs have been placed in one basket. To get a handle on your own DDD problem, you need to determine which of the mentioned causes is causing your problem. This involves asking yourself some tough, but basic, questions about your current security program.

> *What are you not doing?* Evaluate your detection program for missed detection opportunities.
> Working from the outside in, what is your organization currently not looking at as part of its detection lens? Are you actively monitoring perimeter devices, lateral movement between systems that use valid credentials but exhibit anomalous behavior, lateral movement between systems that use valid credentials and have high levels of access? What monitoring does not exist at the system level and the file level?
> Document the workflow of a transaction or external access attempt as it relates to sensitive data and systems, with the aim of identifying the existence of unmonitored points of attack. Then work your way back out, as would the data or intruder as it/they leave your environment. The outcome of this exercise sheds light on overt gaps and shapes acquisition

strategies for technology and staff. Repeat this to account for human interaction as you advance.

What are you doing? Evaluate your detection program for what you are currently doing, but not doing well, to uncover suboptimal detection practices.

The previous exercise should have left you with a list of what you have in place, as well, so take a look at it and consider activities and controls that are particularly cumbersome, clunky, or rote. Which ones are devoted to doing routine things routinely and managing the exceptions? What time and resource consumption do they create versus what they tell you about your environment? What can be automated and where is human intervention critical to avoid dismissal of an incident as an event, or missing its true scope? How much talent is present in the environment versus how much talent is required to derive salient information from the environment? The outcomes of this exercise will provide your growth path and should help shape your go-forward activities.

What are you doing well? Evaluate your detection program for what is genuinely working well to identify your detection strengths.

The elements you identify here should be the those that you are confident are beneficial, have reached a level of maturity you feel confident about, and fit your culture and resources. They can often be identified as areas you leverage in crisis or when another area is found to be deficient. For example, you may leverage a talented investigations team to run down anomalies where your ability to write signatures and rulesets is lacking. Another example is if you perceive a loss of control over systems security and detective controls thereupon, you may be relying on network devices to catch nefarious outbound activity coming from an enclave or data leakage protection (DLP) software in order to thwart leakage of sensitive data. This step not only tells where you are effective and what resources you have to react most effectively, but also tells you where you should be maintaining or reducing further investment in favor of growing other areas of your detection program.

What do you want to do well? Define desired detective capabilities and evaluate current detection program in terms of overall function to determine the next steps.

By this point, what is left should help you frame where you want to go from where you are. Breaking down your detection program in terms of what you want to do well versus what you want to do minimally, if at all, helps identify aging technologies, unnecessary resource consumption, and opportunities for partnership or outsourcing, as well as overall gaps, opportunities for improvement, and priorities for your security program as a whole.

SUMMARY

DDD is a much too common problem with most security programs. Arguably, when you assume that protection will inevitably fail, and you have to look for the most telltale signs of failure, there is a very broad task to accomplish.

It does not help that detection traditionally relies on reviewing voluminous log files, and new capabilities have varying levels of usefulness and accuracy. Additionally, there is a lack of people with the appropriate level of skill and experience to step in and address the problem.

By following the directions in this chapter, you can determine the root, or maybe roots, to your detection deficits. From that point, you can begin to address the problem, and create a comprehensive detection program that allows you to implement a comprehensive advanced persistent security program.

CHAPTER 15

The Human Intrusion Detection System

When we talk to organizations about the goals of their security awareness programs, one of the top outcomes should be that every person within their organization is a human intrusion detection system (IDS). Every user should be both able and expected to have the awareness to identify potential security issues, know how to report the issues, and then be expected to actually do it. While most security teams feel overwhelmed with everything they have to worry about, consider how much better it would feel if they believe that if there is a potential incident, that any person within the organization would be able to detect and report it, and potentially stop it.

In Chapter 11, we highlight the importance of creating a strong security culture, which fosters an environment where users are aware of their responsibilities to properly protect information and related assets, and also to detect and respond appropriately to potential incidents. While there is a fine line between protection and detection in some cases, it is important to reiterate each.

Consider that if a user choosing a good password would be considered Protection. When someone calls up a user and asks the user to divulge the password, while a user saying, "no," would be Protection, the user should also detect that there is something wrong with the request itself.

Put in other terms, Protection is when a user prevents malignant threats from compromising the organization, while Detection kicks in when a malicious threat is attempting to compromise the organization.

Users should also be able to detect when a malignant threat can be prevented from causing damage. For example, if they see an unsecured door, they should know to secure it. If they see documents unattended on a printer, they should know to secure the document and find the owner. In other words, Detection with regard to malignant threats is noticing when others failed to take appropriate actions, so they can mitigate the damage.

Advanced Persistent Security. http://dx.doi.org/10.1016/B978-0-12-809316-0.00015-4

PERFORM POSITIVE OUTREACH

One of the best things any security team can do is create a positive relationship with the organization as a whole. The better the relationship, the more likely people are to detect potential security incidents, and especially report those incidents.

When people feel a reasonable connection with the security staff, they will better engage with them. Anything that can be done to ensure that the security department does not just appear when there is a problem will improve the willingness of people to approach the security team when something goes wrong.

There are many ways to instill such goodwill. For the purposes of this section, we will focus on two primary methods: providing useful information and outreach. Regarding providing useful information, the security team should provide awareness information that helps individuals to secure their home, family and personal resources. This gives people the belief that the organization cares about them, and provides a useful benefit back to them as well. It helps to foster a sense of both belonging and responsibility to the well being of the organization.

When preparing security awareness programs for some organizations, we find that there are two type of organizations: those that want to provide information relevant to employees for personal and business purposes, and those that state all information provided should be specific to workplace security. We find that the organizations that state that they are interested in protecting information at home tend to have better overall security.

For example, just like safe drivers will drive as safely in company cars as they will in their personal automobiles, people who practice safe computing practices at home will likely have safer computing practices at work. Minimally consider that employees who fall victim to computer related incidents in their private lives will be distracted at work, and will need to spend time to clear up the resulting problems. So we always advise that organizations should reconsider any limitations on their awareness programs.

Topics that are specific to home use include how to protect children on the Internet, how to securely configure your home network, and protecting your cellphone. Clearly, any topic that appears not to have a work related aspect to it will be welcomed by individuals for what it is. Employees appreciate any information they can apply in their personal lives.

The type of resources to distribute can include newsletters, tip cards, handouts, and more creative materials. For example, you can provide mobile device security kits, which may include privacy shields, tip cards for securing mobile devices, and subscriptions to anti-malware software for mobile devices. Many companies also give away annual subscriptions to anti-malware subscriptions for personal computers and laptops. All of these materials demonstrate an interest in the individual's well being.

Additionally, the security team should hold events as a form of outreach. These events can be as traditional as booths in public areas to hand out information, holding contests, showing movies that could have a security related theme and bribing them to attend with popcorn, holding lunch and learn briefings for employees, providing briefings to different departments within the organization to highlight concerns specific to those departments, among any other creative endeavors. Remember, food always helps.

Any time you can engage with employees or other insiders, in a way that does not involve an incident or confrontation, makes those people more willing to seek you out when there is an incident. For this reason alone, the security department should encourage its staff to engage in non-work related committees and efforts, so that people have more opportunities to engage with the staff and have ready access to the security team. This is similar to the Police Athletic League, where police departments set up athletic opportunities for children, so that the children develop positive feelings toward police in general, but also get to know some police officers personally, so that they trust them and know they can go to them should they ever have a problem.

IF YOU SEE SOMETHING, SAY SOMETHING

The title of this section should be, "Making People Feel Comfortable Enough to Report Incidents". However, the Department of Homeland Security's *If You See Something, Say Something* campaign embodies that sentiment. It gives people the impression that it is their duty to report any questionable activities.

If people are not comfortable reporting potential incidents, then it doesn't matter whether or not they detect the incidents in the first place. It is critical to both empower people to report potential issues, as well as to make them feel comfortable enough to actual report the incidents. Otherwise, they will actively try to ignore potential issues.

People are naturally hesitant to report unusual circumstances and especially other people, who may be committing security violations. There are many reasons for this. In the first place, some people don't want to get involved. They are hesitant to stick out in any way, and prefer to keep to themselves. If something happens, and it might draw attention to themselves, these people will ignore the incident and hope it goes away.

There are also very few people who will readily report the potential transgressions of others. Even if you believe a person reporting an incident is not callously reporting a third party, and it might even be to the third party's benefit, there is a natural hesitance to report someone else to security. Bringing another person to the attention of the security department rarely has positive benefits for the person reported.

Some people may also fear retribution, should it become known that they reported a coworker. The retribution could be direct, if the reported individual wants to get even, or it could be ostracization by the entire organization for reporting the individual. No matter what the potential reason, you need to acknowledge and expect this type of hesitance.

Some people are self-conscious about potentially being wrong. They don't want to raise an alarm that proves to be wrong, and then they appear "stupid." For example, if a person sees another individual wandering around the facilities who they believe might not belong there, if they report it as an incident and it turns out the person actually belongs there, the reporter will be embarrassed. The reporter might also believe they look like the proverbial, boy who cried wolf.

A common concern for many people is that if they report an incident, they might be somewhat culpable for the incident. For example, if they saw something unusual, but thought about it for awhile before reporting it, they might believe that their lack of action allowed damage to be larger than it should have been.

In many cases, an individual might actually be responsible for damage, and they will create negative consequences for themselves. For example, if a person clicks on a phishing email and causes malware to be loaded, and realizes it after the fact, if they report the incident, they are highlighting how they caused damage to the organization. Similarly, they may have divulged their user credentials to an outside party.

In some cases, the user might have created a situation, where they are the only person who might know that an incident happened. For example, if a user loses a USB drive, it is extremely likely that the organization will not realize it. However, it would be critical for the organization to know that there is some risk to the information that was on the USB drive.

There are many situations where individuals are hesitant to report it. It is therefore critical to ensure that people feel as comfortable as possible to report incidents. This is admittedly not easy, but the security department should provide a feeling of safety, not dread.

KNOWING WHAT TO LOOK FOR

People need to be informed about what you want them to report. It is not as obvious as you would assume. While there are clear issues that stand out to most people, many issues are not as obvious to the average person. For example, doors that should be locked that are not locked. People should know to report individuals in unauthorized areas.

While it is not possible to identify every specific circumstance that should be reported, circumstances should be grouped and generalized to make things simple for people. While you can tell people, "If you see something, say something," it doesn't mean that they know what they should be seeing.

For example, in airports, people are told that they should look for unattended luggage. They should be on the alert for strangers that ask them to carry something onto an airplane. There is some specificity provided with the buzzwords. You need to provide similar guidance in the workplace.

In Chapter 8, we discuss governance and specifying appropriate behaviors. Ideally this information should serve as a base for helping people understand what they should be reporting.

IT'S BETTER TO BE SAFE THAN SORRY

When you promote, *If You See Something, Say Something*, you need to ensure that people understand that it is always preferred to report something, even if there are doubts that it is a concern, than not report it. Stories abound where after some major incident, coworkers or other witnesses invariably say, "I thought there was something unusual about that person," or, "I knew that would be a problem someday."

Whenever there is some type of outreach program, you need to ensure that the motto, "It's better to be safe than sorry," comes across strongly. There will always be a hesitance to report incidents for fear of being wrong, however there must be an instillation of the belief that the security team wants to hear about any suspicions, and will not belittle or punish anyone for being wrong.

Dealing With Ignorance

Around the time of this writing, there was an incident where a woman on an airplane reported the person next to her, because she thought he was writing cryptic comments in Arabic. The plane was delayed for 2 hours, while the airline investigated the man. It turns out that the man was mathematics professor at the University of Pennsylvania, and was solving mathematical equations. The professor was also Italian, and not Arab, as the woman reported.

Unfortunately, incidents like this are becoming common. There are clearly some people who are racist. At the same time, there are some reports that the people thought the San Bernardino terrorists were behaving suspiciously, before the attacks, but they did not report them for fear of being perceived as racist. This demonstrates the importance of reporting things, even when there could be the perception of racism, or just being silly.

The potential for people to vindictively report others cannot be discounted. In the workplace, some people report others for theft and other transgressions for revenge or to cover their own transgressions. While these cases are rare, they do happen. We fully realize that while we write that while people should be encouraged to freely report incidents without fear of retribution or penalty, we also state that, in some cases, reports may be without merit and potentially malicious. This is just a fact that must be accounted for.

The burden falls upon the security team to handle reported concerns properly, and with discretion. People will be people. There will be people who are just ignorant, such as the woman who cannot tell the difference between Arabic and mathematical equations. Frankly, even if the person was writing in Arabic, that is in no way an indication of a would be terrorist. Ignorance should not however mean that a plane should be significantly delayed on the basis of mathematical equations.

It falls to the security team to determine how to triage potential incidents. It is understandable that an airline would not just want to walk up to an individual and say, "We have a report that you might be a terrorist." There should be an expedited review process to determine the likely validity of concerns versus ignorance.

There must be established procedures to evaluate any reported incidents. The risk posture and the potential severity of the incident should drive the speed of the investigation.

ELIMINATE PUNISHMENTS WHEN REPORTING INCIDENTS

While this may not always be possible, when it is, the security team should try to avoid punishment for individuals when they report security related incidents. This should be a well-publicized policy.

As previously stated, many people are hesitant to report potential incidents, as they fear retribution. Even if there is culpability, amnesty should be provided if at all possible. There are clearly circumstances, such as outright criminal activity, where amnesty is not appropriate, however in general the organization being made aware of a potential security concern outweighs the need to punish wrongdoing. The policy should be that by default, amnesty is granted barring other concerns.

IMPLEMENT REWARDS FOR DETECTION

While it is unfortunately more important to eliminate punishments as much as possible, when people report potential incidents, it is even more desirable to reward people for reporting incidents. As people have detected potential incidents, and then properly reported them, they should be rewarded for these behaviors.

We discuss gamification in Chapter 11, as a method of rewarding desired security behaviors. By default, people reporting incidents should be thanked for their diligence. Ideally, there should be some trinket or material acknowledgment as well. This goes further than verbal thanks, and serves as a reminder of the appreciation of their detection. Depending upon the severity of the incident reported, cash rewards or gift cards should be considered.

Bug bounty programs are an example of gamification to reward people for finding and reporting problems with software. The US Department of Defense implemented the *Hack the Pentagon* campaign, which rewards people for finding bugs on Department of Defense assets. Many software and Internet companies, such as Google and Facebook, have implemented bug bounty programs. They allow people to report vulnerabilities without being accused of attempting to commit a crime.

When Ira worked at NSA, NSA had a suggestion program that provided financial rewards. He reported that there was a bar on top of the fence. The bar was above the barbed wire, which could allow a would be intruder to climb over the barbs. While Ira's recommendation to remove or lower the bar was valid, even he admits it was a relatively innocuous suggestion. However given the validity of the suggestion, Ira received a $100 cash award and pubic recognition.

Publicly Recognize Those Rewarded

The NSA example clearly demonstrates that not only does NSA reward desired behaviors, it publicizes those rewards. Additionally, such rewards are considered during promotion evaluations. That encourages other people to constantly look for security concerns.

Public acknowledgment shows that security does not just punish people, but again looks for ways to benefit everyone. The fact that such rewards can positively impact promotions adds long-term incentives for people to detect incidents, besides of generating tremendous goodwill.

KNOWING HOW TO REPORT THINGS

When people detect potential security related issues, they need to know how to report those issues. The reporting mechanisms should be as plentiful as possible. Generally, there should be internal email addresses that are well known and publicized. Email is readily available in most traditional office environments, and should be exploited.

Frequently, there is a security portal on organizational intranets that can be designed or enhanced to provide a capability for people to report potential incidents. Many organizations have IT or HR Help Desks that can be used to also receive security related reports. If there are already other security or emergency hotlines, you can refer people to them. The people working those reporting venues can then be instructed on how to handle the calls that you are concerned about.

There will always be a preferred mechanism for receiving reports. Wherever possible, that preferred mechanism should be promoted. For example, you can list preferred email addresses, websites, and/or telephone numbers on posters and newsletters that are regularly distributed throughout your organization.

Establish Anonymous Reporting Channels

As stated, there is a predisposition for some people not to get involved. Additionally, when potentially reporting other people, they do not want to be blamed by, or face being ostracized by, coworkers. There are many other reasons that people may not want to take credit for reporting incidents. For this reason, security teams should provide a mechanism for employees to anonymously report potential incidents.

Previously there were suggestion boxes that allowed people to write something on a piece of paper and drop it in a conveniently located box, which provided reasonable expectation of anonymity. Today, most security reporting mechanisms involve the Internet and provide for tracking. For example, sending an email to a general inbox would provide the sender's email.

If there is a webpage that allows people to enter a potential incident, most people understand that the location of the person submitting the report can be readily determined. It is possible for people to use the Internet with a reasonable expectation of privacy, however that requires specific expertise that most people do not have.

Currently, the way to report things with the greatest perception of anonymity is a telephone hotline. People can make a call from their own telephone, borrow a phone, or find a payphone.

Inside companies, there are frequently interoffice mail systems, and you can just address a letter to a department without providing the sender's information. This depends upon the distribution mechanisms inside the organization.

Clearly, you need to provide as many reporting mechanisms as possible. Also, you need to state that even if there is no anonymity provided by the reporting mechanism, the person's identity will be protected. There should be a clearly stated policy, with clearly stated procedures, as to how a person's identity will be protected throughout the investigation process, when reporting was not via anonymous means.

SUMMARY

If you have 1,000 people in your organization, you should have 1,000 intrusion detection systems. You can only expect this type of circumstance, if you properly nurture the people. You need to create an environment where people believe that their detection capabilities are expected and welcomed. People need to know what to report, and most importantly, how to report it.

When you consider the potential benefit of having everyone in your organization detecting issues of concern, it can justify significant resources to create such an environment. While it may not be an easy task to accomplish, it is worth the trouble if you can implement it effectively.

CHAPTER 16

Kill Chain Analysis

We espouse kill chain analysis a number of times earlier in this book. To a large extent, we want you to anticipate and adapt to adversary activity and attack. You therefore have to be able to reposition yourself to think and fight like your adversary. Reaction is a key strategic principle in an engaged defense. Your countermeasures and counteractions should be staged in such a manner that you cannot only adapt and recover ground, but also bring the battle on your own terms and engage your adversary at the most advantageous time and place possible. To identify these mount points and establish your own defender beachheads, it is helpful to consider how intrusions and exfiltrations universally occur, breaking them down into chunks where the adversary motivation is clearly defined and distinguishable and subsequently, where your operational goals change to deter, detect, deny, defeat, and defend.

Looking at an attack from this perspective is a different approach from the battle most of us have been conditioned to wage: defend. Nothing gets in. Perfect security is the mission; failure is not an option. If something untoward was granted entry, you have failed. But as we have discussed, this is not a feasible or effective way of building or running a security program. Your goals may be to prevent intrusion and your compliance objectives and metrics may well be a report card based on this measurement alone. However, your mission is ultimately to stop the adversary from achieving their goal. By and large, your adversary's success is not measured on a singular goal of intrusion, so it stands to reason that the mission of the attack is not so myopic either, and there are many opportunities for you to engage an active, adaptive mode of defense that pits your actions against what ultimately constitutes their success.

Breaking an attack into phases suggests that one is underway, but that is not the ball game; an intrusion in progress is not necessarily one that is successful, and each phase of the intrusion provides a point at which a defense can be mounted. In reality, staging your defenses in a similar fashion, as if they were a counterattack against the adversary activity, improves the odds that your mission of defense will ultimately be successful, and the adversary's mission of accomplishing the intended action on the intended objective will fail.

179

Advanced Persistent Security. http://dx.doi.org/10.1016/B978-0-12-809316-0.00016-6

WHY THE KILL CHAIN IS IN DETECTION

It is possible to put the kill chain discussion into any section, and many people would contend we should put it in the Protection section. We chose to put it in the Detection section as it seems more appropriate for kill chain application in practice.

We already assume that security programs will apply protection mechanisms as appropriate. When you examine the phases of the kill chain as follows, you see that you can examine where to apply detection mechanisms. For example, an attack begins by finding a target from the adversary's perspective. You need to try to determine if you have been "found," which is detecting early reconnaissance efforts. As the adversary steps through their attack, you need to understand where they are in the attack, so you can observe and react to the attack in progress.

So, while the phrase, kill chain, implies you are killing an attack, it actually looks at an attack from the attacker's perspective. If you can understand that perspective, and apply that perspective, you can determine which phase of the attack they are in, and know where to look to best detect when you are under attack.

WHAT IS A KILL CHAIN?

In military terminology, a kill chain is a phase-based model that classifies offensive activities based upon the stages of an attack and uses the deconstruction of the attack to prevent it. These stages are referred to as follows:

- find
- fix
- track
- target
- engage
- assess.

Ideally, the earlier in the kill chain that a defense can be engaged and an attack can be stopped, the better. When the attacker has less access, information, or ability, it is less likely that future attacks, following the same methods or patterns, will occur or take advantage of the same exploits or attempt the same actions on the objectives in the future.

Based on motives and objectives, the military kill chain model broke enemy activity into four primary phases:

- target identification
- force dispatch to target

- decision and order attack on the target
- destruction of target.

THE CYBER KILL CHAIN

Years later, Lockheed Martin expanded this concept to digital warfare and cybersecurity defenses as the Cyber Kill Chain. In this case, the phrase kill chain outlines the form, mechanics, and motives associated with an information security intrusion and is expressed as seven phases:

- reconnaissance
- weaponization
- delivery
- exploitation
- installation
- command and control
- actions on objectives.

The Cyber Kill Chain presents a means by which security events could be oriented and interpreted in contexts that focus on the attack and the attacker, as opposed to independent, isolated, or discrete data points and/or device-specific occurrences. This creates a common format and language for evaluating security events by association, motivation, and integration, where they could be aggregated and correlated according to objective and attack vector.

The kill chain's roots are military, its language is sexy, and it suggests an innate ability to counter an attack with surgical precision, which quickly made it a very popular and satisfying way to communicate about threats and countermeasures in the defender community. However, when confronted, practitioners in other lines of business, leadership positions, and program management capacities often confess a complete lack of understanding as to how the kill chain factors into the implementation of strong defenses, let alone into a defense strategy.

Reviewing each of the seven attack phases functionally, it becomes apparent how each event within an attack stream can be placed into a phase and assigned to one of the following discrete actions or objectives:

Reconnaissance—target research, identification, and selection. These activities can range from looking for choreographed scans of Internet-facing network assets to trawling through Internet-present networking sites, including benign publications such as marketing slicks, corporate contact information, social media blasts, and industry conference registrant lists.

Weaponization—devise and delivery of an exploit as an executable payload. This is often done remotely via an automated tool or piece of malware, but increasingly involves more common applications, files, images, and documents that can be attractive for a user to acquire and run.

Delivery—transmission or infection of the weaponized payload or the weapon to the targeted environment. Most commonly, these transmissions occur through e-mail attachments, infected websites, and removable storage media.

Exploitation—activation of the exploit payload. Exploitation usually targets a system or application vulnerability or manipulates the user into taking further action to ensure its spread and success.

Installation—installation and instantiation of functional code that enables remote access to a victim system and permits continual use and access to the adversary.

Command and control (C2)—establishment of outbound communications from a victim system for secure communications between victim and adversary systems. Compromised hosts typically beacon out and await further instruction or exploit when higher order interaction or data exchange is required. This is the hallmark of advanced persistent threat (APT) attacks and data exfiltration.

Actions on objectives—adversaries accomplish target objectives. These objectives range from additional and expanded undetected residence and lateral movement (also referred to as dwell time), within a target environment, to explicit exfiltration of data from the victim environment, to any level of unauthorized access in between. The scale and overall choreography of the attack will dictate the action on the objective for a given system or data element, and demonstrates the importance of considering the entirety of the adversary activity and motive in attempting to thwart adversary actions.

APPLYING THE CYBER KILL CHAIN TO DETECTION

When you understand the phases of an attack, you can begin to determine where and how an adversary will come at you. It allows you to anticipate where you can best see their activity.

For example, we have worked with companies that have been successfully attacked by a traditional APT, most likely Chinese hackers. In almost all occasions, the way the attacks were discovered was because their command and control activity was discovered. The early phases of the attack were completely missed, but things like malformed DNS packets and unusual use of other traditional network protocols were used as covert channels. This is why many of the latest intrusion detection tools, such as Darktrace and Securonix, are applying behavior analytics, which search for patterns of behavior to user actions and network traffic that are unusual.

The growing use of these tools is notable as it demonstrates the reality that attacks are not being detected until an attack is successful. These tools are ideally catching behaviors that indicate reconnaissance and other activities associated with earlier phases of the kill chain. Additionally, by applying threat intelligence and knowing the methods and operations of your likely adversaries, you may be able to tune your detection processes to search for behaviors typical of those adversaries.

APPLYING THE KILL CHAIN TO PROTECTION AND REACTION

Clearly, an understanding of kill chain principles can help determine protection and reaction countermeasures as well. As we state early in this chapter, when you anticipate reconnaissance as an action by all attackers, you can determine how to make reconnaissance more difficult. Similar measures can be taken in all phases of the kill chain.

With regard to reaction, once you detect an adversary, you can apply kill chain principles to determine where and how to stop the ongoing attack. You can go back earlier in the kill chain and end their method of entry into your organization. You can also identify their command and control systems and remove them, thereby stopping the attack in progress. This may also help you identify the compromised systems, and repair them. Alternatively, you can anticipate the next phase of the attack and put extra protections in place to stop the attack, before the adversary achieves their ultimate goal.

SUMMARY

Understanding the kill chain, as a concept, allows you to implement a more logical approach to implementing a detection program. When you can understand the methodic way a skilled adversary attacks you, you can determine the best places to detect their activity. This then leads to the determination of where to place detection mechanisms within your network and security program, and what mechanisms might be optimal for the environment.

While there may be an assumption that only advanced adversaries use a methodic approach to execute an attack, the fact is that all attackers use the same principles, whether they realize it or not. For example, a script kiddie, who just wants random access to an organization, would run random scans looking for openings into the organization. They might not call it reconnaissance, but the principle applies. They then attempt to gain a foothold in the organization, which is delivery. The process would continue. While skilled adversaries have specific processes to accomplish an attack, and likely document the process and have reviews of the attack in progress, unskilled attackers implement the processes intuitively. They will be less effective and more haphazard, but a process is there.

SECTION 4

Reaction

Reaction is what differentiates a traditional security program from a program that employs Advanced Persistent Security. More specifically, it is an appropriate reaction strategy that creates Advanced Persistent Security. It allows the program to adapt to attacks, incidents, and changing circumstances.

Implementing such a reaction strategy is clearly not simple. It takes a great deal of expertise from a technical and operational perspective to implement a reaction program effectively. It must be able to take the results of detection and then use that to triage the incident and determine the appropriate way to move forward to reduce potential loss, and further use the results to improve security.

We intend to provide a foundation for implementing an appropriate reaction strategy. We provide a strategic perspective for implementing incident response (IR), and follow up with providing a step-by-step strategy for IR. That step by step strategy cannot go into the details of implementing IR at a tactical level.

We would have to write a separate book to cover the information in sufficient detail, and for the moment, we recommend that if your specific job responsibility is to implement or participate in IR that you find such books.

Here we provide the depth appropriate to consider how to incorporate reaction into a comprehensive security program.

CHAPTER 17

Setting Reaction Strategy

Once again, there is no such thing as perfect security. Incidents happen. They just do. Even if you have Jedi-mastered all the concepts we have covered thus far on proaction, adaptation, risk management, and detection, you are still going to have to deal with incidents and, therefore, with response.

Why is this? Because defense itself is innately reactive. To defend is to respond to external forces, both operationally and philosophically. No matter what you have in place on the front end, your controls and defenders will be vastly outnumbered by the countless nasties trying to worm their myriad of ways into your environment. No amount of threat modelers, pentesters, or assessors poking and prodding at your environment will anticipate or eliminate the constant boring away that goes on when you are Internet connected, or have insiders with access to information. Period.

So, your security program should expect things to go wrong. You should be equally prepared for incident handling and response as you are for implementing defenses. When it comes to incident handling, prior planning is of paramount importance to achieve success. Being adaptive is defined by reaction.

The reality of the situation is that no matter how well our defenses are designed, instrumented, implemented, maintained, and operated, attacks are bound to make their way through them. Systems are designed to be accessed and are therefore doomed to be compromised. The sooner we as defenders accept this eventuality, the better-off we will be in terms of our abilities to not only respond, but to also anticipate and combat the adversary and future compromise. This means, quite simply, programming failure into our defense strategy and tuning our capacity for reaction.

This seems pretty logical, right? The problem is, as practitioners, we are measured in terms of success. Our objectives are defined in terms of desirable business outcomes and include action verbs such as protect, block, and eliminate. Our metrics are constructed to use things such as number of viruses caught and number of intrusion attempts prevented as a measure of technical

187

and programmatic efficacy. Our technologies are built and marketed to meet and report those needs.

As stated earlier, many organizations are in need of a drastic culture change. Arguably, in responding to demands for demonstrations of success, we are ignoring an extremely rich data set; specifically, what led to the failures in the security program. This would be more relevant than any market research or external threat data possibly. Like comment cards collected by restaurants to gather customer feedback on much-needed improvements, the more valuable feedback lies in evaluating places where the program failed in accomplishing its mission. We need to get more comfortable with the idea that more is to be learned about success from failure.

Training ourselves, our constituency, and our leadership to embrace such a culture shift can pose a real challenge. There is an appetite for change, process, formality, and risk in an environment, so a good chunk of that battle is getting on the same page with all parties at a strategic level.

EXECUTIVE SUPPORT

The need for executive support is one of the industry's most beaten dead horses, but it is as important here as anywhere else. This is especially true where success is defined by how you deal with failure. Additional staff and technology from other teams or outside parties may be required to respond. Law enforcement and the media may need to be engaged. Client trust may be at risk. Executive buy-in is an absolute must, given the serious and potentially longterm implications of any incident.

The speed with which an organization can identify, analyze, and respond to an incident determines the damage levied and resources required to resolve and recover from it. So getting executive leadership onboard with that understanding will increase the likelihood that funding and resources will be there when you need them. You can then operate with the confidence and autonomy necessary to bring about the best possible outcome. In the middle of a high-profile incident is probably the worst time for a security practitioner to be going toe to toe with executive leadership.

DEFINE YOUR TEAM

An incident response team is responsible for responding to security incidents end to end, from intake to investigation and resolution. Although other members of the security, technology, and leadership teams can be deputized and brought in on a case-by-case basis as needed, it is not advisable to respond to incidents with a posse formed ad hoc. Ideally, you will formalize and dedicate select members of your security staff to incident response, with the majority of their job functions being related to the management and investigations of incidents. When under attack, a dedicated team tends to function with greater efficiency, expertise, and mission clarity and resolves the incident with fewer conflicts of interest. This allows other players to maintain tighter alignment to their line of business responsibilities and facilitates continuity of operations.

Depending on the size and type of an organization, it is likely that you will not be able to maintain a team dedicated to incident response. You would then need to identify people to call in, when there is an incident, in advance. Whether or note there is a dedicated team to handle incidents, the make up of the team is critical.

Clearly, people from the security team will be key players on the response team. It is also important to include people from the broader IT team to ensure that there is knowledge of the network, as well as the ability to contact the administrators of systems throughout the organization. Given the varied nature of incidents, you have to anticipate that there may be operational, legal, personnel, public relations, among other issues to consider during formal responses. For this reason, you need to consider proactively having the incident response team having permanent members from other departments. Those departments may include, but are not limited to:

- Operations
- Legal
- Human resources
- Physical security
- Corporate communications
- Investor relations
- Media relations/public relations
- Accounting
- Any operational areas that may be impacted by a significant incident
- Representative of executive management

Definition of a team should include definition of a mission statement or charter that describes its purpose and commitments to the business. The mission statement allows the members and stakeholders to understand the objectives of the team, as well as develop expectations and success metrics as to how those objectives are to be achieved. A mission statement might include commitments that resemble those in use by the computer emergency response team (CERT):

  - provide a comprehensive view of attack methods, vulnerabilities, and the impact of attacks on information systems and networks; provide information on incidents and vulnerability trends and characteristics;

- build an infrastructure of increasingly competent security professionals who respond quickly to attacks on Internet-connected systems and are able to protect their systems against security compromises;
- provide methods to evaluate, improve, and maintain the security and survivability of network systems;
- work with vendors to improve the security of as-shipped products.

It is also important to include non-technical elements of a mission statement, as many incidents may not involve traditional hacking, and will very likely have impacts that go well beyond technology. For example, calls or phishing messages to attempt to have people transfer money are on the rise, and involve a compromise of process, not technology.

Many security teams enjoy a kind of cloak-and-dagger or cowboy culture within their organizations and levy their rapid response capabilities to avoid formalities such as charters and mission statements. However, this shooting from the hip may eventually cause you to shoot yourself in the foot, as your team may not wind up with the aforementioned necessary leadership support when they really need it. Without the clear and agreed-upon objectives and direction provided by a charter or mission statement, the incident response team may lack the authority and support necessary to function at all, let alone effectively.

DEFINE AN INCIDENT

Before responding to an incident can be done in earnest, it is probably a good idea to get on the same page as to what an incident is in the first place. Technology professionals tend to use three terms interchangeably: event, incident, and breach. It is not uncommon to find news articles label any successful intrusion as a breach. Even within the technical world, it is not uncommon for courseware to recommend that practitioners comb through logs in search of specific "incidents." Most security purists, however, will distinguish the three terms. This aids in the proper classification of security-related goings-on, as well as the subsequent response required for cohesive security incident management. Furthermore, when considering things such as legal ramifications and disclosure requirements, discipline around this terminology takes importance beyond semantics and feeds directly into proper incident response and investigation.

For the purpose of this book and in keeping with the most foundational definitions, we define the three terms.

Event: A recorded or observed change to the normal or anticipated behavior of a system, environment, object, process, component, or person. Examples of events range from changes to device policies, alerts generated by a monitoring system, or contents of populating system and event logs. An event is basically anything that may prove interesting when considered in the context of security.

Incident: An event that adversely affects the confidentiality, integrity, or availability of a given system, independent of whether the data thereby exposed was accessed or exfiltrated from the system or environment. Examples of security incidents include intrusion, phishing attempts, distributed denial of service (DDOS) attacks, user account compromise, and virus or malware proliferation. All incidents are events, but not all events are incidents.

Breach: The unauthorized disclosure of confidential, sensitive, or protected data that has been viewed, accessed, stolen, or removed from a system or environment by an unauthorized party or process. Examples of a breach range from the inadvertent mailing of consumer or health data via postal mail to another party in error to the exfiltration of data that occurs as part of an elaborate phishing scheme or unintended accesses to cardholder data kept on an organization's systems. All breaches are incidents, but not all incidents are breaches. Furthermore, in many cases, organizations are not required to report many security incidents, but they are required by law to follow particular procedures when a data breach has occurred, up to and including the interaction with governmental agencies and costly notification processes that inform the owners of the information compromised.

It is important to remember that events, incidents, and breaches are not limited to technical happenings, and an organization has to be able to readily identify and respond to them as well. These must be defined and considered as well. You will also need to define the types of security incidents for your organization. Examples of security incidents include

- disruption, denial of service, or destruction of key systems, services, or data,
- unauthorized attempts to access critical systems, facilities, or data,
- compromise or unauthorized use of a system or data,
- unauthorized changes to systems, applications, or data,
- loss or unintended disclosure of sensitive data,
- loss of access to critical systems or data,
- suspected security event or unexpected security-related event,
- violation of security policy, process, or procedure.

One of the important things to keep in mind about incident definition is that you are just as much excluding what is not an incident. This is not obvious for many programs and will proactively eliminate many concerns. This is especially important where there is still an environment a perception that success is measured by the lack of incidents.

CONTROLS SUCCESS VERSUS PROGRAM SUCCESS

Incidents can be a big mess. Part of the problem with information sharing on incident data and breach detail comes from the unwillingness of the security community to speak about things that have gone wrong in their practices. Although much of that stems from explicit and material concerns regarding increasing brand damage, liability, and overall exposure for the organization and its clients, the unwillingness to admit to having made a mistake or having missed something is also a barrier. The effort to identify fault and place blame is detrimental to take advantage of an opportunity to learn and improve.

We also have a terrible habit of further victimizing the victim. It does not take long for coverage of a very public breach to turn into a nasty blame game. We hear about how poorly the organization handled things and about the myriad people who were asleep at the wheel for it to have happened. It is not just mainstream media who delight at the prospect of sensationalizing the breach and droning on about the horrific state of security that demands answers. Fellow industry professionals cannot wait to commence with the lambasting and ranting about how woeful and loathsome their brethren at victim X were to have let something happen on their watch. It is horribly unproductive. We, the authors, admit that we highlight the failings of organizations to adequately protect themselves after incidents. In some cases, it is to highlight the importance of proper cyber hygiene. In other cases, it is to highlight grossly inaccurate statements put out by victims to deflect responsibility.

Considering this, it is not surprising that victims immediately brand any successful attack as being advanced. Unfortunately, the adversary community is far better at collaborating about work and how they can work together to improve their craft and achieve their desired and shared outcomes.

Just like controls do not define a security program, incidents do not either. As such, incidents should not be measured in terms of what controls failed. They should be defined based on the actions of the adversary and the ability to respond, rather than focusing entirely on what oversight allowed them to manifest in the first place. As is the case with the adversary community, information needs to be shared, both internally and externally, about what was successful in the accomplishment of an objective as well. This is especially true when the adversary was thwarted through nontraditional means or recovery was made possible after an initial failure.

The adage, "It's not what you did, it's what you did next," is applicable when speaking about incidents versus controls. Fine; a security control failed and an intrusion was successful. But what did you do to detect that, and how did you respond? What did you learn about your environment that you did not know without battle testing, and how have you improved your posture as a result? How are you using that failure in measuring and quantifying that improvement? Little will be accomplished if an organization's attitude is that the only way for a security program to be successful is for its reactive elements to be never taxed or used.

METRICS: A TALE OF TWO LENSES

Most security metrics in common use are misleading or not useful. Technical countermeasures might keep some level of metrics, such as anti-virus tools tracking the number of viruses detected and blocked and firewalls tracking the number of illicit connections blocked. When user actions are involved, it becomes obvious when a user falls victims to ransomeware, but nobody tracks how many times users do not activate ransomeware. When there is an incident or breach that becomes known, that is considered a failure, while the countless incidents that were avoided go unknown.

Information security, such as risk, is patently tough to quantify and therefore to measure in any meaningful manner. It is like proving the negative. "Prove to me you did not read this book." How do you prove you did not have an incident? So it seems we measure the observable positives; events the tools could detect as being blocked, or actual incidents causing obvious harm.

Information security is risk management. As such, if we assess risk correctly and apply the appropriate security controls accordingly, we can reduce the incidence and impact of security incidents. But what does calculating the number and severity of incidents really tell us? If the number and severity are reduced, is that an indicator of higher functioning security controls, a lower number of attacks, or an unknown number of attacks of significant sophistication? If the number and severity of incidents increase, is that an indicator of ineffective controls, an increased number of attacks, an unknown number of attacks of significant sophistication, or possibly just better detection capabilities added to your program?

As you evaluate your security program objectives, also evaluate your security program metrics and make every effort to ensure that they accurately represent the success of your program as a whole. An individual countermeasure might or might not stop what it intends to stop. Those metrics are easy to collect. Metrics that determine the number and scope of actual breaches are the ultimate measure of the success of your program. Ensure that honest metrics do not get confused with failures. Measure successes and failures against the "outcomes" you want to avoid, not just against the "events" you want to avoid. Lastly, communicate interpreted metrics, especially those regarding incident handling, and not numbers in a vacuum, to ensure that the success of your countermeasures does not control the success of your program.

SUMMARY

We stress throughout this book the importance of being able to be adaptive above all else. The elimination of risk is a futile pursuit. A remotely functional security program hinges on its ability to function in a crisis, meaning that the response to the crisis is preplanned. The program has to be able to withstand the very failure that it was designed to prevent, so there must exist actions that should already have been planned and put in place to address breaches that occur. In many situations, the correct implementation of the reaction strategy has an impact and importance well beyond the exploited vulnerabilities.

A comprehensive response must have a firm foundation. This includes extensive planning that accounts for as many potential incidents as possible. It should have the appropriate level of support from management and all required employees already approved and required. Once this base is established, actual responses can be executed properly.

CHAPTER 18

Incident Response and Investigations

INCIDENT RESPONSE IS COMPLICATED

Although the section title sounds both basic and obvious, it is critical to note. In writing this chapter and section of the book, we had a great deal of difficulty in determining the level of detail to include. We both have extensive experience in investigating incidents, small and massive, and we continue to learn ourselves. Although the majority of incidents are clearly basic, the adversaries are constantly tuning and improving their tactics.

This chapter could be a series of books, but in determining how much depth to provide, we chose to focus on high-level strategies in approaching the creation of an incident response (IR) program. Advanced Persistent Security is about creating a comprehensive security strategy that is adaptive and proactively accounts for incidents, and especially anticipates building those incidents into protection strategies.

Readers also need to be aware of the complexity of IR. Again, many incidents are straightforward. However, the potential complexities have to be built into your IR processes. An apparently basic phishing message may be from a nation-state actor trying to get a foothold in your organization for a massive attack. You need to account for preserving evidence, while not corrupting information. You need to establish a chain of custody. The person who appears to be a victim of a virus incident may have intentionally downloaded the virus to hide illicit actions. A witness might be afraid of being accused of being at fault for doing something wrong. You might kick the bad guy out of your system, but he might have installed backdoors anticipating your actions. A skilled adversary might launch one attack to divert your attention from other resources. Although these instances may be rare, you have to account for the possibility.

At the same time, you also need to ensure that you do not violate policies and laws. For example, you need to understand your internal infrastructure and know where your network ends and a vendor network begins. If potential evidence is on an employee's cell phone or personal computer account, you cannot run roughshod over their privacy or personal rights. If you make

Advanced Persistent Security. http://dx.doi.org/10.1016/B978-0-12-809316-0.00018-X

backups that contain protected information, those backups have to be protected per the respective regulations.

These are just examples of the issues to consider. Again, we provide this discussion, as you must be familiar with reaction as a fundamental element of a comprehensive security program. We strongly recommend you review other resources, such as the National Institute of Standards and Technology (NIST) Computer Security Incident Handling Guide when you begin to design or evaluate your IR program.

This chapter primarily addresses technical considerations. To a certain extent, this is true. However, the same principles apply to nontechnical responses. The reality, however, is that just as most attacks involve a combination of technical and nontechnical tactics, investigations will similarly involve both technical and nontechnical response efforts.

PROPER TRAINING

The previous section touched on how complicated an investigation can be. It is therefore that anyone involved with an IR is well trained to execute his or her responsibilities.

Technologists have to be very well versed in the technologies involved. In all likelihood, incidents will involve multiple technologies. It is very likely that responders will have to examine end user systems, multiple types of servers, routers, firewalls, and intrusion detection system/intrusion prevention system (IDS/IPS), among other systems. They will also need to be skilled with forensic tools and techniques. Even something as simple as knowing to take pictures of a work area and not to turn off systems being collected for evidence, so that the information in RAM can be recovered, is not intuitive.

From a nontechnical perspective, too many technologists want to play detective. It is critical to only record facts and avoid opinions. Interviewing people takes great skill. You do not want to lead people into preferred answers. You do not want to intimidate people into shutting down. Some people are highly skilled liars, and it takes equal skill to look for signs of lying. Likewise, some people may fit the stereotypic signs of lying, yet they are just nervous or quirky, and if you do not know how to establish a baseline, you may develop false impressions.

Even people who are involved from other departments need to have relevant skills. Not all lawyers are knowledgeable in all relevant aspects of law. There are special nuances to crisis communications that are not obvious to all communications professionals.

Although it is unlikely you will have the perfect group of people for your team, it is at least important to realize that you do need a highly skilled group of people to assist in the IR efforts. Assuming that you proactively identify response teams, you should also attempt to get those people as much training as possible.

ORDER OF OPERATIONS

Whether the attack begins with the unsophisticated compromise of a human element or it is a highly choreographed or intricate attack involving lateral movements and evasive techniques, eventually an alert fires and kicks off investigative and responsive activities. Once this occurs, IR moves through several different phases intended to act against an attack on an organization:

> Initial investigation: Early and cursory investigative activities begin to identify the nature and impact of the incident. Information is collected and correlated, evidence is gathered, and the response plan is formulated.
> Containment: Once the incident is classified and its impact understood, efforts to contain the attack and limit its spread through the environment begin. Activities intended to maintain evidence, identify additional exposures, and bolster failed controls take place as the organization shores up defenses in the interest of damage control and supporting recovery efforts.
> Remediation and recovery: When the incident and affected systems have been examined and isolated, the response process moves into a phase of corrective action, wherein damaged systems and assets are repaired or restored to the intended function.
> Ongoing investigation: Once the immediate triage and fires are extinguished and the initial incident is resolved, ongoing activities focus on extracting additional detail from the event and monitoring for repeat occurrences or attempts is attempted.
> Post incident: Details and lessons learned from the incident are used to adjust security practices, galvanize security controls, tune monitoring systems, and inform future investigations.

The order of operations associated with IR, from identification of the problem to ongoing resolution, can be defined like many other 12-step programs designed to guide behaviors, control compulsions, and otherwise recover from destructive circumstances.

1. Incident identification: Identify and classify the incident through event or anomaly detection for the purpose of engaging the proper response personnel and stakeholders with whom to communicate.

2. Reconnaissance: Explore the incident to determine a rough order of magnitude of impact and affected systems.
3. Hunting: Gain an understanding of the extent of the compromise and the methods used by the attackers.
4. Gathering: Collect evidence and additional details associated with the incident.
5. Communication and coordination: Engage leadership and IR teams with information about and status of the incident.
6. Containment: Take actions necessary to close off entry points and stop the proliferation and function of the compromise within the environment.
7. Eradication: Eliminate the inciting conditions that brought about and constituted the incident.
8. Remediation: Restore the affected systems to normal operations in preparation for resumption of normal function.
9. Review: Validate that the incident has been resolved and has not persisted or resurfaced and that the updated or augmented security controls are providing the required and intended protection.
10. Recovery and resolution: Restore and resume normal operations.
11. Reporting: Communicate the detailed incident data to involved responders, data and system owners, and those in leadership.
12. Returning to life cycle: Integrate the incident details and lessons learned into event monitoring, analysis, and future response chains and platforms.

So you suspect that you have an incident in progress. How do you know this? Did a small series of alerts fire suggesting that something was amiss? Did myriad bells and whistles go off indicating that half your infrastructure is in a state of dysfunction? Are help desk lines lighting up and users clamoring for attention to systems or processes that have begun to act funny? Is your corporate website now displaying a troupe of clowns dancing to bad techno music? Are you enjoying your morning coffee as your organization's name appears in the crawl across the screen while you watch CNN before heading to office?

You can factor in the subtle nuances and variations present in alert processes later, as well as use them later to flesh out responses, controls, and documentation. Right now, it helps to consider that the ways by which you will become aware that an incident is in progress are actually very few and fairly simple to classify. Whatever the specifics surrounding how you became aware that your day was about to change, traditionally speaking, an organization becomes aware than an incident has occurred through one of the following three basic ways:

■ monitoring systems detect unusual activity and respond by generating alerts,

- an internal party provides information about a change or difference in function or experience,
- an external party reports an issue to the organization.

It is as simple as that. Regardless of how many controls you have in place as part of your unique internal security program, you are going to become aware that something has gone wrong, because someone or something, internal or external to your environment, lets you know that things had changed and you now have an incident on your hands. The more important part is figuring out what to do next.

Once an incident has been determined to be underway, an organization's formal IR process needs to be kicked off. The incident must be declared, an initial definition must be supplied, and the identified teams, responders, and stakeholders must be apprised of the current conditions.

We like to think of IR as being highly mercenary and ordered, much like the surgical strike of a SWAT team deployment or the swift and decisive controlling action we see out of fire departments. Very often, however, IR starts to resemble onlookers staring aghast at a capsizing ship. Containers are sliding across the deck and mowing down rails as they go overboard, waves crash over the sides, and people jump screaming into the water. What do you even do in this situation? Where do you begin to triage, contain, and take appropriate action amidst the chaos?

Step 1: Incident Identification
The first step is to identify the incident. Notice that we did not say classify. A cursory definition of what is being dealt with in order to determine who should be dealing with it and who needs to be made aware of it is as far as we go in the first step because early communications and mobilization of resources is the objective of the first step. Who is in charge? Who needs to be apprised for the purpose of damage control? What infrastructure and services are involved? What customers, internal and external, may be affected and will need to be notified for brand damage control?

Step 2: Reconnaissance
Receiving the incident is the first step and innately involves a high-level triage or consumption of correlates provided by automated processes and systems, but surveying the damage with human eyes and gauging the level of impact to business and operations is necessary to begin mounting real action. Incident responders and investigators need to observe the anomalous behaviors or mount points of an attack and begin working outward to estimate what will be communicated and what countermeasures will need to be called into action in order to get the attack under control.

Step 3: Hunting

Based on information about things such as malware behaviors and spread; affected systems, data compromised, and vulnerabilities; and network attack vectors, investigators can begin hunting activities within systems and environments to identify other impacts and indicators of compromise. If it is a nontechnical incident, the appropriate interviews and forensic analyses provide clues. Looking for indicators of lateral movement of malware and adversary presence or activity often uncovers outlying systems that have sustained undetected damage and provides additional assets that should be brought into the scope of investigations, countermeasures, and containment.

Step 4: Gathering

Gathering evidence and detail is required to inform the communications and containment processes. Trained investigators experienced in IR and forensics are engaged to ensure that the requisite detail is collected in a manner that will not only arm the upcoming and ongoing activities but also aid in interaction with any law enforcement and legal actions that may follow. It is a good idea to begin with at least a cursory checklist of evidence gathering and handling items and processes to begin documenting the IR and investigations activity that has occurred thus far.

Step 5: Communication and Coordination

A formalized process often involving documentation, i.e., war room meetings, and continual updates is critical to ensure that auxiliary teams and stakeholders are apprised of the goings-on and the current impact on the dependent lines of business. This is not the time to have your practitioners taken out of service in a hair-on-fire manner with panicked line-of-business owners. The incident commander and key stakeholders should control the flow of relevant and pertinent information between themselves and their internal customers. Instructions and awareness messaging for the broader user base and any external customers should be considered at this point.

Step 6: Containment

Incident containment has two foundational objectives: to stop the spread and sprawl and to prevent further damage. As such, IR requires containment actions. While addressing an incident, it is important for an organization to decide which modes of containment to employ initially, early in the response. Furthermore, containment strategies should have as a paramount consideration their ability to support incident handlers as they move through all phases of IR. At this point, this is sometimes a consideration to let the attack continue, so you can observe the attacker's actions. Although this can significantly increase the potential loss and damage, it allows you to observe the attack in progress. You might learn of other systems or data compromised. You might better identify the attacker's motives. This is similar to police keeping suspects under observation to know who their accomplices are, to know if they are involved in other crimes, and perhaps, to lead them to more evidence.

Step 7: Eradication

From a technological perspective, the primary goal of eradication is to remove malware and compromising agents from infected hosts and systems. Because eradication efforts are complex and typically involve multiple affected systems, responders should be prepared to use various tools, techniques, and teams simultaneously for different situations. This may include eliminating compromised accounts. If there are physical issues that created an incident, such as flooding or power outages, appropriate elimination of the causation must occur. Security program owners should also consider performing awareness activities that set expectations for eradication and recovery efforts ahead of an incident, as well as during an incident; this is because user behavior modification and a "see something, say something" crisis culture can rapidly tamp down on other areas and mode of spread that may defy ongoing containment and eradication efforts if left unchecked. If user behavior caused the incident, users must be made aware of the behaviors to modify, and how to modify them. Generally, a continuous and layered approach to thwart and remove infectious agents throughout the organization can increase or decrease the efficacy of the response to an incident.

Step 8: Remediation

After you stop an incident, you must then return your systems and environment to normal operations. This may include reinstalling and configuring systems from scratch, hiring new staff, replacing equipment, fixing damaged facilities, etc. Security awareness programs may be required to ensure that people know their expected behaviors. Although this seems very straightforward, depending on the nature of the incident, this could be a very extensive effort.

Step 9: Review

Review of the current state of the incident and any action taken to get it under control are required to determine if incident management has actually been effective and if the incident is ready to be brought to resolution. Additionally, reassessment of each phase of the IR process for completeness and additional action that should be taken is continuous and ongoing, but doing so at this point serves to assemble the lessons learned and state of the incident for activities that surround incident closure. Incidents are more than cases and responses. They have cascading levels of impact to the environment, consumers, adjacent lines of business, external parties, and so on. As such, reassessing and thoroughly documenting the incident, response activities, and what has been learned must be done before the incident can be closed.

Step 10: Recovery and Resolution
Recovery and resolution are the last actual acts associated with the active incident itself. Some examples of routine elements of recovery and resolution are removing any stopgap controls and temporary countermeasures that may be necessary to achieve compliance with normal environmental function and standards, restoring affected devices and systems to their production-ready operating state, and making changes to internal applications.

Step 11: Reporting
Before an incident is truly closed, its state must be communicated and dependent parties must be informed as such. Stakeholders involved earlier in the process must be provided with the updated status and must be informed about any changes made to their ongoing operations that were developed to prevent the return of the cause of the incident.

Step 12: Return to Life Cycle
This final step may be the one that is least implemented or most often overlooked as being part of the IR process, even though it is one of the most critical steps. Regardless of the severity or reach of the incident, a large amount of detail on the behavior of the incident agent was gathered during investigations and several changes were likely instituted to bring it to a close. This can be extremely valuable in improving the monitoring, operations, and IR processes in the future.

At a bare minimum, an opportunity to create a "train as you fight" culture for IR arises from looking back at exactly how you responded under fire. Even if your organization is not quite at the point to develop a vast internal database of indicators of compromise and use that to interoperate in an automated fashion with your security information and event management (SIEM) tools, bringing real, measurable, and material changes into your IR program can begin by answering and documenting questions such as:

- What happened, where, and when?
- How well did the security and technology staff deal the incident? How about the management and leadership?
- Were the documented procedures followed? Were they adequate?
- What would the security and technology staff do differently in a future incident? How about the management and leadership?
- What actions or occurrences inhibited recovery?
- What corrective actions might prevent a similar incident in the future?

- What indicators can be monitored to detect similar incidents?
- How could information sharing with other lines of business be improved? How about with other organizations or law enforcement? What, if shared, would be helpful in resolving this incident?

Here is where you can begin to feedback into your protection efforts. You start assessing where your protection should be improved. You can also determine potential improvements for detection. For example, you can potentially see other opportunities to detect the attack earlier in the kill chain. As we highlight throughout this book, incidents can be the most valuable resources for improving all aspects of your security program. Although we of course recommend that you avoid all incidents, you must fully appreciate the learning opportunities that they provide.

THE IR IMPERATIVE

If you have accepted the notion of embracing failure as part of your security program's success, you will have to forget some of the ideas you have likely held when it comes to incident handling and pick up techniques that have been ingrained into more evolved IR programs. Some are derived from the military, others from law enforcement, and more from other organizations that have been attacked before you. Whatever their etymology, with required response readiness being the new normal, it is time to work on developing an organizational mind-set that has been proved effective in IR.

Tweaking your incident response processes is one thing, but you might be asking why you would want to retool your incident handling policies, plans, and procedures when they were such a beast to put together in the first place. This costs a fortune, irritates nearly everyone involved, and rarely has the up front capital infusion that you see with implementation of tangible programs and solutions that drive fundamental operations. Security is the notorious cost center, so this is going to be a big pain, right? Well, probably. But it is going to help your organization prepare for IR. It will help in the process of IR and recovery. And, it may even help in preventing an incident from happening in the first place.

The prospect of revamping your IR program is admittedly daunting. However, if you are beholden to any of the regulatory compliance requirements from protected health information (PHI), personally identifiable information (PII), Payment Card Industry (PCI), Sarbanes—Oxley (SOX), Service Organization Controls 2 (SOC2), Health Insurance Portability and Accountability Act (HIPAA), international data, and so on, you have very significant responsibilities to properly prepare for, and respond to, an incident. By failing to meet those responsibilities, either through error or purposeful or ignorant omission, organizations can be assessed very stiff penalties.

HOUSTON, WE HAVE A STANDARD!

Thank heavens for the NIST. Security professionals tend to have the ridiculous and unproductive collective habit of not only regurgitating concepts, but also using a host of different terms to refer to the same ideas. This is true for technologies, processes, and roles and functions— lather, rinse, repeat. Fortunately, NIST finally engaged and laid out its *Computer Security Incident Handling Guide* as a set of taxonomic and operational standards defining how to build, classify, and measure a successful IR capability.

It will take a while to peruse and grok the document in its entirety, as the NIST is not a cornerstone of brevity, nor should it be. Contained in the guide are some very well-constructed foundational concepts that will define and drive an effective IR program. Although we recommend that you look at other books and standards to consider in the design and implementation of your IR program, the NIST document can be a strong foundation for your current and future efforts. In short, if you are serious about creating a useful IR program, you should be familiar with the contents of the document. If your program deviates from the NIST recommendations, you should have a purposeful reason for that deviation.

RESPONSE READINESS ASSESSMENT

Attacks and incidents have the annoying habit of appearing at the worst or most unexpected times, and by definition, without warning. It is imperative that an organization is prepared to respond quickly during an incident. It is critical to have a plan in place so that your security team can spring into action, contain the situation, and minimize the damage. In order to create an effective plan that enables and includes the 12 steps previously discussed, organizations should first perform an IR readiness assessment.

The goal of such a readiness assessment is to walk through and shore up the proposed or implemented IR policies, plans, and procedures to ensure that IR capabilities actually exist. This will help in the remediation and recovery efforts by proactively stressing and strengthening your defenses, thereby reducing the risk and level of business disruption, cost, regulatory compliance violation, and overall damage experienced during an incident.

An initial response readiness assessment serves three purposes:

1. assessment of your organization's capabilities to detect, respond to, manage, and recover from security incidents;
2. identification and remediation of gaps and deficiencies in security controls;
3. increasing and improving your ability to identify and stop attacks.

The assessment should include review and exercises that test your organization's event monitoring, IR, and threat intelligence capabilities as a continuum.

FORENSIC READINESS

If you are to be proactive, a response infrastructure is as important to be in place as is a protection infrastructure. To a certain extent, your response infrastructure is part of your detection infrastructure. When you respond to incidents, you need to have forensic data to examine what has happened on your network. You need to know what data has been passed, which systems were involved, what user accounts were used, what is the timing of the incidents, is there lateral movement on the network, what do you not yet know, etc.

To answer these questions, the appropriate monitoring and collection tools need to be proactively in place. In our experience in responding to incidents, we typically find that there is no appropriate forensics infrastructure in place to allow us to hit the ground running, and get a full perspective as to what has been happening to the victim. Even where there might be some tools in place, they frequently are not equipped or set up to collect the full scope of the data that we need. For example, although there might be data collected about blocked attempts to access the network, there is no collection of data that is allowed to egress the network. There might be perimeter controls, but there are no forensic tools in place to watch for lateral movement within the network.

The first thing we need to do is to identify the types of forensic tools we need to fully investigate the incident. Ideally, these tools would have been already available, and collecting data. It is not a surprise that once the tools are in place, we tend to find at least a dozen other potential incidents that were not previously known to the victim.

While your environment, industry, and circumstances determine the optimal forensics infrastructure, it would likely include end point access and monitoring tools, IDS and IPS, logging of all data ingress and egress, traffic analysis tools, behavioral analytics tools, among full access logging. All these tools should ideally report to an SIEM tool for central access and monitoring. Additionally, the tools should provide direct access to the data for IR personnel in demand.

When implementing an IR program, and especially Advanced Persistent Security, it is critical to proactively implement a forensics infrastructure. No matter how strong your protection may be, you will inevitably have many incidents. It is your proaction that will maximize the likelihood that you will stop the attackers from achieving their goals, or at least to minimize the damage created by a malignant threat.

SUMMARY

IR is arguably the most complicated element of implementing a security program; however, it must be done. We cannot say enough that failure of your protection efforts is inevitable, but that does not mean your security program fails. Again, your security program only fails if you fail to properly respond to the incident, and the adversary accomplishes his or her goal and/or damage is done in the case of a malignant threat.

Although detection must occur first, and it is not easy to implement, it is relatively straightforward when compared to IR. There is a major difference between finding an incident and knowing how to fix it. As we mentioned at the beginning of this chapter, we just attempted to set a foundation for IR and strongly recommend that you do further research. If your responsibility is to determine a high-level security program, this chapter might be sufficient for your immediate needs. However, if you have a specific responsibility for designing or implementing IR, you need to do further research.

IR is possibly the cornerstone of an Advanced Persistent Security program, as it provides for the adaptation that is required to evolve as the adversary evolves. Remember that IR does not mean that a full-blown incident has occurred. IR can kick in at the early stages of an attack, and as long as you can disrupt the observe, orient, decide, and act (OODA) loop of adversaries, you can adapt within a reasonable period to prevent them from accomplishing their goals, or at least reduce their success.

Implementation

In this book, we define fundamentals related to security, risk management, intelligence, and cyberwarfare. We identify the foundation of defensive information warfare, which is protection, detection, and reaction. Although we describe high-level strategies that you can implement for each concept, it is important to think strategically about how you should holistically implement our recommendations.

We also want to provide a step-by-step guide to apply the defined strategy. It is important that you coordinate the protection, detection, and reaction strategies into a cohesive program. Just as there is the mantra, "Security should be built in, not bolted on," which implies protection should be built into systems and networks, detection and reaction strategies need to be built into a security program, and not bolted on as well.

This section, therefore, provides a strategy for creating a security program that has cohesive protection, detection, and reaction strategies that are looked at as a part of a whole, and not independent, effort. As you read through the chapters in this section, keep in mind how to apply the guidance to your circumstances. We realize that in many cases, we assume an ideal situation and those ideal situations rarely exist. There should, however, be enough guidance to allow you to adapt our recommendations to your circumstances.

CHAPTER 19

Know Yourself

Before you can take any action, you must know yourself more than any other entity. You need to know what you need to protect. You need to know the resources available to protect an organization. You need to know your people. The list can be almost infinite.

Imagine protecting a medieval castle. To protect it, you need to understand it's strength and weaknesses. Is the castle on top of a tall mountain wall, such as the Salzburg Castle? If so, it reduces the risk from one type of attack. How tall are the walls? How many gates are there? Is there a mote? Are there windows in the wall that allow people to fit through? Are there concentric walls, so an attacker has to make it through multiple walls to breach the actual castle? Are there emergency escape routes? Is someone watching those routes for enemy incursions?

Then there are logistic issues. If the castle is under siege, how long can supplies last? What type of weapons does the castle possess? Does the view from the castle allow you to see an approaching army, with sufficient time to lock the gates and take other required actions to prepare for a siege? If there is a breach, are there still additional areas where defenders can make a stand?

None of these questions are simple to answer. However, unlike computer networks, many castles were designed with security as a primary concern. It is significantly easier to protect a structure that is designed with security in mind.

As you look to defend your enterprise, there are aspects of your enterprise that you need to know and understand. What follows is a basic, but not exhaustive, list of considerations. There are many aspects that are specific to your industry and to circumstances. A seasoned security professional will be able to determine the issues that need to be considered for an organization. It is, however, better to have as many people as possible involved, because experience matters, and the more experienced people are involved, the more considerations will be taken into account.

Advanced Persistent Security. http://dx.doi.org/10.1016/B978-0-12-809316-0.00019-1

IS THERE PROPER GOVERNANCE IN PLACE?

As stated in Chapter 8, proper governance should drive a security program. It should define how security is implemented. A good security program without proper governance is a complete accident.

Review all policies, procedures, guidelines, and relevant standards. Ensure that the relevant standards and/or regulations are embodied properly in the created policies, procedures, and guidelines. If they are, you have your starting point for proceeding forward. If they are not, you have your first strategic task to perform.

Regardless of the state of the documents, you need to ensure that they are complete and also that there is appropriate management support, along with the proper resources, to fully implement proper governance.

HOW MANY PEOPLE ARE THERE IN THE ENTERPRISE?

The number of people within an organization drives a great deal of concerns. Everyone represents a potential security risk, as well as a countermeasure. It is also important to understand where they are located and the job functions. There are social and cultural norms that need to be accounted for.

Some areas of the world present more risk than others, such as war zones or high-crime areas. If people are widely dispersed, it makes it more difficult to consistently implement and enforce policies and procedures. There might need to be more policies and procedures, or at least they might need to be modified to the locations.

WHAT IS THE RANGE OF JOB FUNCTIONS?

Although in some ways this consideration is implicit to the previous question, the type of job functions performed has a very significant impact on security considerations. The legal staff has different considerations than the IT staff. The maintenance staff has different considerations than the executive staff.

Job functions dictate security considerations. Each job has different uses for computers and information. Jobs also create different physical and operational security risks. Even if there are people scattered throughout multiple locations, they might very likely have similar security concerns, if they have the same job function.

WHAT INFORMATION IS INVOLVED?

Different organizations have different types of information and different uses for that information. Different types of information create different security requirements. There needs to be a firm understanding of all the information in use in an enterprise.

The types of information can also create adversaries for you. If money is your information, then criminals will target money. Government information will be targeted by intelligence agencies. Prerelease movies may be targeted by organized crime to facilitate piracy, or in some cases, by foreign governments that are unhappy with the plot of the movie. Intellectual property may be targeted by competitors or governments. It is therefore critical to know the information and who might want to take advantage of its value.

WHAT INDUSTRY ARE YOU IN?

To a large extent, a great deal of your risk, vulnerabilities, information targeted, adversaries, etc., can be predicted solely based on your industry. Although there are, of course, variations from company to company, vulnerabilities within an industry are generally standard.

For example, medical practices need to protect patient information. They have traditional computer systems, and frequently use the same software from one medical practice to the next. Personnel have similar job responsibilities from one practice to the next.

Security practices should likewise be similar from one organization in an industry to another. Again, every organization has unique conditions and information, but there are frequently more similarities than differences.

WHAT IS YOUR TECHNOLOGY POSTURE?

We have seen that even the best technologic environments can be compromised through nontechnical means. However, it is still a very significant concern.

You need to understand your technical architecture. What type of computers do you have? Are networks segmented? What are the communications links?

ARE THERE SPECIAL TECHNOLOGIES IN USE?

A general understanding of the network is critical, but there is also a need to understand special technologies. These might include industrial control systems (ICSs), which are responsible for billions of dollars of operations and might have life-and-death consequences. Anyone who gains control of an ICS can potentially cause critical damage to an organization. There can be special-purpose devices. Special technologies present special security considerations.

ICSs are a high priority target for attackers. They present special security concerns as well. They, therefore, require enhanced protections and detection capabilities. You need to put in specialized reaction strategies, if there is a potential compromise.

Special technologies might also be highly targeted. They are a specific type of intellectual property.

Communications points are critical to attackers, and if there are unusual types of communications, they can be compromised. In general, the more unique a technology is, the more likely it is to be poorly maintained and therefore, poorly secured.

DO YOU UNDERSTAND YOUR NETWORK?

We find that in most organizations, there is not a real understanding of their network. If there is no centralized control of network implementation, it is very likely that there is little knowledge of the overall technology in use. Rogue IT is a phrase that defines the act of people bringing in their own devices. It can also extend to employees acquiring Internet connections.

In one company we assessed, we found that there were more than 1000 Internet connections that they were not aware of, and that was only on the 80% of the network we had visibility into. When the enterprise does not know about the Internet connections, they cannot properly protect them. They provide backdoors into what otherwise would be a reasonably secure network.

Frequently, an enterprise will lose control of its network after mergers and acquisitions. Very rarely is there a full understanding of the network of an acquired company, before an enterprise is attached to the acquiring company's network. Then assuming that there is a formal process for merging IT infrastructures, which is extremely rare, it can take years to complete bringing an acquired network up to the standards.

We will just leave it as a simple fact that you cannot secure a network that you do not understand.

PERFORM A SECURITY ASSESSMENT

Vulnerability assessments are critical to understand how vulnerable you are to technical attacks. Although you can assume that eventually any highly skilled attacker would get through, it is important to understand if you can face basic attacks. There is a continuum of technical security, and you need to know where you fall before you determine how to take action. Understanding this allows you to strengthen your protection, as well as better define your detection and reaction strategies.

If you have a poor technical security posture, you clearly have a great deal of work to do. You would need to focus on implementing basic security measures. If you have a more advanced posture, you can spend time on targeting specific issues that need to be addressed, rather than on implementing a basic security program.

A good security assessment, performed by highly capable people, will usually go beyond just providing the protection levels of systems and will identify issues that were not originally intended. Ideally, a red team assessment will also identify weaknesses, and strengths, in the detection and reaction capabilities of an organizaion as well.

WHAT IS YOUR PHYSICAL SECURITY POSTURE?

You need to take the same action with physical security that you did with technical security. It is easier to understand physical security, as buildings and assets are tangible. A computer should be protected against theft or being physically left vulnerable.

You need to understand all the physical locations within your sphere of responsibility. You need to understand how physical assets are brought into and removed from facilities. You need to understand the surrounding environments of your facilities.

As implied in our discussions of threats, you need to understand the threats that are specific to different locations. Are your facilities within hurricane zones? Are there inherent risks at different locations?

Although you should carefully assess each facility, you should be aware that the information you need should usually be known to people within your organization, and especially your physical security team.

HOW IS DATA TRANSPORTED?

When we assess enterprises, we inevitably find issues with regard to how data is transported and stored, including Internet access. Many enterprises are limiting how data can be exchanged. For example, many enterprises standardize on Box or Dropbox and block access to similar services. USB slots on computers are frequently deactivated, so that people cannot copy large volumes of data from systems and networks.

If data is physically transported via tapes or other mass media, is it encrypted? What are the acceptable measures of transporting large and small amounts of data?

Is there data leak prevention software on Internet connections? Is there a filter on Internet connections? You need to examine egress points to understand how data can potentially be filtered to ensure that you are not losing intellectual property or other critical data.

WHO ARE YOUR ADVERSARIES?

Although we go discuss adversaries further in Chapter 20, here it is important to at least consider who your adversaries might be. You can look through our past discussion of threats to develop an initial list. There are many default adversaries, such as random hackers and insiders, but adversaries who specifically target your organization are driven by issues such as your industry, geographic locations, and general drivers specific to your business.

A consideration of these issues would further refine what information you have is at risk. It, therefore, helps define where you need to focus protections, as well as where to implement detection capabilities. The nature of your adversaries can also tell you the resources that might be used to target your organization.

WHAT IS THE SECURITY POSTURE OF SIMILAR ENTERPRISES?

Although we do not necessarily believe that you should base your security program on those of other organizations, by looking at similar organizations, especially those within your industry, and hopefully in similar geographic regions, you can determine a starting point for your security program. Assuming of course your peers will share information, learn about their successes and failures.

For many industries, there are centers referred to as an ISAC, i.e., Information Sharing and Analysis Center. These organizations allow for sharing of information and also have resources that allow for communications between members. They share information about ongoing threats, as well as other information to assist with improving the security programs of its members. Similarly, they are good for finding peers who want to learn, share, and help.

There are also many professional associations that could provide access to peers in other organizations. Frequently, these organizations and conferences hold events that are specific to CISOs. These are great venues for finding peers who are willing to share information. There are also industry associations, similar to sector-specific ISACs, such as EDUCAUSE in the higher education industry, that allow for sharing of information, as does the FBI-sponsored Infra-Gard organization.

SUMMARY

To create a security program, you need to take complete stock of where you are, your available resources, your vulnerabilities, etc. This sounds obvious, but frequently, people running security programs sink into operational modes and just work with the program already in place, instead of stepping back to get the big picture.

No matter what the intent is, without fully assessing the situation, you cannot create an optimal security program. You need to understand what you need to secure and where you are starting from.

CHAPTER 20

Know Your Adversaries

"If you know yourself, but not the enemy, for every victory gained, you will also suffer a defeat."

Sun Tzu

As potential adversaries have been discussed in Section 1, we will not go into detail about who the adversaries might be. There are clearly many adversaries that all organizations have to deal with. To properly design a security program, you need to understand, or at least expect, the most likely entities that will do you harm.

Also, in the current context, the term adversary implies people, but we mean it to imply any threat, which could include natural disasters and other accidents. They all need to be considered to allow you to design an adequate security program.

As discussed in Chapter 19, you need to understand your vulnerabilities. As Section 1 discusses, threats define the value, a.k.a. information, services, and other resources, most likely to be targeted and the vulnerabilities most likely to be exploited. This information in turn allows you to define the most useful countermeasures to implement, which include protection, detection, and reaction strategies and resources.

LIST THE MOST LIKELY THREATS

Read through the threats listed in the Chapter 6 and list out those that are relevant to your organization. Remember that the list is not exhaustive and you may have additional threats to consider specific to your own industry, location, etc. For example, local crime can be a significant threat in some areas.

As you create the list, create some rating system that indicates the likelihood that the threat will actually attack your organization. For example, you can create a Likert rating scale, in which 1 means there is a very low risk of attack from the threat, whereas 5 means that threats have already attacked or will definitely attack your organization.

217

Advanced Persistent Security. http://dx.doi.org/10.1016/B978-0-12-809316-0.00020-8

It would also help to identify the level of resources that the individual threats will use against you. Again, you can create a Likert scale that rates the level of resources used by the attacker, from 1 to 5. Assuming script kiddies are a threat, they might have unlimited time, but they otherwise have minimum resources to assist their efforts and can be rated 1. Should China be a viable threat, you have to consider that it has the highest levels of expertise, resources, financing, infrastructure, etc. and can be assigned a score of 5.

Based on this exercise, you should get an idea as to the scope of the threat that you face, and it serves as a rational base to go to management to justify the need for a comprehensive security program. Although we realize this sounds basic, we have witnessed many security teams go to their management and could not justify their financial requests, because the security team just wanted to implement security for the sake of security and not because there was a well-thought-out justification for the security budget.

DETAIL THE LIKELY ATTACK STRATEGIES

For each and every threat identified, you need to consciously list the potential attack vectors that will be used against you. This provides a method to begin to determine the vulnerabilities that may be exploited.

For example, if you consider hurricanes as threats, the attack methods may include floods, power outages, and the inability for staff to get to work. If you are a high-tech company that is likely targeted by China, you need to understand that they will use technical attacks, spear phishing attacks, zero-day attacks, and recruit insiders to steal information. You might also have facilities located in China that could be used as a launching point to target information stored in other geographic locations.

Again, you should assign some sort of rating scale to indicate the likelihood of the different attack vectors for each threat. For example, although script kiddies could resort to onsite social engineering attempts, the likelihood of such an attack is low.

DEFINE VULNERABILITIES TO BE EXPLOITED

At this point, you begin to consolidate the information about the different threats. You start by working backward from the attack methodologies to be used against you.

For example, phishing is likely to be used by many malicious threats. However, phishing is an attack, and not a vulnerability. Although most people mistakenly believe phishing specifically targets poor awareness, the reality is that it targets many vulnerabilities.

Poor user awareness is a vulnerability, but phishing also exploits poor spam filters, poor systems security that would allow malware to install on user systems, poor network monitoring to not see communications from installed malware, poor web filters that do not stop users from visiting unsafe websites that steal credentials, poor user authentication that would allow an outsider to reuse user credentials, etc.

As you work your way through the threats, you should begin to see some vulnerabilities that clearly stand out. Some vulnerabilities might not be commonly exploited. Either way, it helps you compile a list that can be used to determine the most useful countermeasures to be used to mitigate the vulnerabilities.

Remember that countermeasures could involve protection, detection, and/or reaction. For example, it might be more feasible to detect the attempted exploitation of a vulnerability than to mitigate the vulnerability.

PRIORITIZE VULNERABILITIES BY POTENTIAL LOSS AND LIKELIHOOD TO BE EXPLOITED

All vulnerabilities are not created equal. The final step is combining the consolidated list of vulnerabilities with the likelihood that the vulnerabilities would be exploited. Then you have to consider the value that could be compromised by the exploitation of the vulnerabilities.

Clearly if a vulnerability is targeted by many threats, it should be seriously considered for mitigation in some way. However, if the exploitation of the vulnerability is not going to compromise value, you need not worry about it.

For example, if there is a computer system that has no security whatsoever, you might be inclined to secure it. However, if the system only stores a cafeteria menu, there would be little reason to mitigate the vulnerability. This of course does assume that the computer is not on a network and could become a launchpad for other attacks.

Similarly, if a vulnerability is not a common target and might result in the compromise of immense value, it must be seriously considered for mitigation. Many companies have suffered significant losses, because seemingly unknown systems created a domino effect. For example, there was a power outage in 2005 that impacted 50,000,000 people, including everyone in the New York City metropolitan area, because a tree fell down in Ohio. Clearly there were many contributing factors, but improper maintenance of remote power lines in the middle of nowhere caused a multibillion dollar loss.

SUMMARY

This chapter has been arranged in a very specific order. Although the topic is about threats, it really is about how threats impact your organization. You must understand the threats with specific regard to how they impact and target you.

There is a systematic approach to understand your adversary and then determine how to consolidate that information to prioritize different aspects of your security program. You will use the information as you step through the remaining chapters of Section 5.

Worksheets to support this exercise can be found at our companion website at: http://www.advancedpersistentsecurity.com.

CHAPTER 21

Define Your Strategy

We want to clearly say that we realize that defining a strategy is not a simple task. This will not be accomplished casually as you work your way through this book. However, we intend to highlight a methodology for defining a holistic security program.

As you can assume, what follows states that you need to identify your protection, detection, and reaction strategies. The previous sections outline high level methods for implementing the disciplines of defensive information warfare. In this section, we identify how you determine where in the kill chain you address vulnerabilities.

We also assume that there is a security program in place. It is likely not ideal to scrap a program and start from scratch. We advocate determining how to improve current programs. For the most part, there will not be significant changes, but many organizations will need to significantly improve their detection and reaction postures.

There are additional materials on our companion website at www. advancedpersistentsecurity.com that assist you in walking through the process.

IMPLEMENT PROPER GOVERNANCE

We cannot understate the importance of good governance. Governance stops the results of a security program from being an accident. Governance specifically defines what a security program should look like, as well as defines the management support and resources required for the program. As we have stated many times, governance is not a set of documents that sits on a shelf between audits.

Start by reviewing any governance documents that exist, such as the policies, guidelines, and procedures. Determine if they are complete. Start with a top-down approach. Determine which regulations and/or standards need to be addressed. Examine policies to see if they meet the standards and regulations.

Then go beyond the minimum requirements and determine the policies for proper governance of the organization. It is critical to understand that

221

Advanced Persistent Security. http://dx.doi.org/10.1016/B978-0-12-809316-0.00021-X

compliance with regulations and standards does not mean that an organization is secure; compliance does not equal security. Fill in any gaps that need to be addressed to define strategic security concerns.

Take stock of procedures and guidelines to determine whether they address all the required concerns. If not, identify and create those documents. Then review all the previous guidelines and procedures and improve them as required.

You then need management approval and commitment to the governance effort. Any effort that is not properly funded is bound to fail. Additionally, it needs executive support to ensure that it gets the promotion required and the support at all management levels.

You can then launch a program that implements the governance. This is not a minor effort. It requires a great deal of promotion. This effort should be combined with your security awareness program, as governance essentially defines proper user behaviors and users need to be made aware of the prescribed behaviors.

Technical procedures and guidelines need to be rolled out through the appropriate technology teams. They need to implement the guidelines and procedures that involve configuration and maintenance of all technology efforts in the organization. If there is a strong centralized technology management infrastructure, it is, of course, easier than in an environment that is decentralized. This has to be done or else you will never control your technical security posture.

ASSESS THE PROGRAM IN PLACE

Regarding the current security program, you need to understand its actual effectiveness. It is very possible that you have a team of strong, security-minded individuals who created a great security program. This could be completely by happenstance of having hired the right people, and it would be something to embrace.

Ideally, a strong program, as it exists, would be very much in adherence to the procedures and guidelines you have in place. If it is not compliant, you need to understand why. Can a strong program be improved through the application of proper governance? Is it possible that governance should be adjusted to account for operational successes? It would be highly desirable to have to make such decisions.

On the other hand, it is possible that the program in place is poor. In this case, you need to assess your strengths and especially, weaknesses. Where there are glaring holes, it is important to understand and study how the holes came into being and why they continue to exist.

The following sections help determine the strength of the security program in place.

REVIEW PAST INCIDENTS

Probably one of the best indicators of the strength of a program is the number and types of incidents previoulsy experienced. Depending upon the organization, the number of incidents previoulsy experienced might not be the obvious measure of security. Strong security programs are better at detecting incidents. They have more stringent reporting mechanisms. So a strong security program will ironically experience a large number of incidents.

In contrast, weak programs may have few reported incidents. They have poor detection capabilities, and even when there is a detected incident, they frequently are not properly reported and recorded. Only when a significantly damaging incident is detected, are there reports to document it. It is possible that significant incidents go undetected.

When you examine the incidents, determine the root cause. Examine the factors that contributed to the incidents. Look where there might have been missed opportunities to detect the incident sooner. Examine how the organization responded to the incident, and how the response could have been improved.

Failures can be the best learning opportunities. They demonstrate what needs to be fixed. They show where threats were able to exploit vulnerabilities. Incidents may ideally identify strengths that led to the detection of the incident.

It is, however, important to keep in mind that incidents will not show all possible vulnerabilities that could have been exploited. You might not have detected all incidents that occurred. Also, just because a vulnerability was not exploited, it does not mean it will not be exploited in the future. So it is important not only to ensure that the vulnerabilities are mitigated, but also to realize that this is just a starting point and there could be more critical vulnerabilities to address.

DETERMINE INFORMATION AND OTHER RESOURCES

Examining sources of value within your organization will allow you to determine the assets that need protection. For the most part, anything of value requires some level of protection. The value of the assets determines the required level of protection.

Value should also drive the level of detection implemented. You must assume failure in protection. As we have previously stated, although your protection may fail, your security only fails when data is exfiltrated or damage is done. If you can detect when protection fails, you can still prevent loss, provided the incident is detected and there is an effective response.

You, therefore, need to take complete stock of your assets and define what protection, detection, and reaction strategies should be applied to each of them.

REVIEW THE VULNERABILITY ANALYSIS

Review the analysis of the vulnerabilities likely to be exploited and the related losses from the results of the adversary analysis recommended in Chapter 20. This will prioritize the vulnerabilities that require mitigation. It is important to consider that vulnerabilities can be mitigated by protection, detection, and/or reaction.

It is asinine to proactively mitigate all vulnerabilities. Note where you believe mitigation is most appropriate for the vulnerabilities to be addressed in the kill chain, i.e., protection or detection.

Vulnerabilities that present little risk may not require mitigation. Although it is ideal that all vulnerabilities will be mitigated, it is not required. In many cases, you will find that even systems not requiring strong security will eventually receive some level of security as a result of the security offered to other systems or assets.

CREATE POTENTIAL ATTACK SCENARIOS

When you examine past incidents, you should also consider what else could have happened. This should be an expansion of the incidents at hand, and hypothetical incidents that are both likely and unlikely to happen. The phrase "failure of imagination" was constantly repeated when there was a post 9/11 attack analysis. Nobody seemed to believe that the Al-Qaeda would use airplanes as missiles.

Consider that the Al-Qaeda used a boat in an attack of the USS Cole in 2000. They regularly used car and truck bombs. They also used a truck bomb in a failed, attempt to blow up the World Trade Center in 1993. Was it that inconceivable that they would use other methods of transportation as a weapon to attack the World Trade Center?

You need to be creative in your scenario design. In many cases, you might not need very original thought, as you can look to attacks on other organizations as fodder for your own scenarios. You can never discount new types of attacks, but attacks that your organization, and similar organizations, experienced are the most likely indications of what you can expect in the future.

When you have identified your scenarios, you can then perform a kill chain analysis on the imagined attacks to determine the likely vulnerabilities exploited. More importantly, you can determine the most effective place in the kill chain to actually stop the attack from being successful. This could mean that you let the attacker in and potentially exploit the targeted system, but you put detection in place that alerts you to the exploitation of the target. There can then be a reaction that allows you to stop the intruder from causing damage.

There are plenty of reasons why this would be the case. As of this writing, one of the most obvious examples is the data breach involving the US Internal Revenue Service (IRS) Get Transcript system. The system allowed taxpayers to download tax documents for a variety of purposes. The IRS has a mandate to provide the function without an overly burdensome process. The IRS implemented an authentication mechanism that used a commercial tool that asked a supposed taxpayer questions from data on their credit report. Criminals were able to obtain information that allowed them to impersonate more than 700,000 taxpayers. Please note that the actual number has been rising for more than a year as of this writing, and the number of compromised taxpayers may continue to increase.

Clearly the authentication mechanism failed to detect fraud; however, it actually could have been sufficient for the level of risk combined with the requirement that the system not be overly burdensome to legitimate users. The IRS failed, because it failed to detect the unusual number of attempts from a common IP address.

It is valid to determine if protection might be too expensive or burdensome to strengthen beyond a given level. Detection can be a legitimate countermeasure, if it can be implemented effectively.

SUMMARY

The purpose of this chapter is to help you start to lay out a high-level strategy to implement, or more likely strengthen, your security program. It is critical to ensure that there is proper governance in place, and although it might not be the traditional way to start, it should be considered the foundation of any security program.

As the purpose of a security program is the cost-effective optimization of risk, it then becomes important to understand the vulnerabilities that are likely to be compromised simultaneously, with the source of the greatest loss. It is then time to decide if the vulnerabilities should be addressed through protection, detection, and/or reaction.

CHAPTER 22

Determining the Appropriate Countermeasures

There is a reason that we step through the process the way we do. Unfortunately, many, if not most, security programs we see have unintentionally evolved to the point where they are. As opposed to designing a comprehensive program that intends to proactively account for the overall risk, security programs tend to be disjointed countermeasures that are bolted on over time.

Every year, budget planning has chief information security officers (CISOs) or other security decision makers looking at their current programs to determine whether or not to renew current contracts, and then if there is extra money available, they might consider additional countermeasures or other capabilities. Although the assumption is that the security program in place achieves adequate risk management, it does not mean that you have an optimal risk management program.

Although it would be great to reevaluate security programs on an annual basis, it is not practical. However, if you have not recently taken a "blue ocean" look at your security program, we recommend that you do so as soon as possible, even if it is as an exercise to examine what should your security program be, if you would start from scratch.

ADDRESSING VULNERABILITIES

If you have followed our guidance to this point, you should have a list of vulnerabilities that need to be addressed, along with information that can be used to prioritize their mitigation. As previously stated, many vulnerabilities can be mitigated with a single countermeasure.

You can create a matrix, organize sticky papers on a wall, or any other method to track the information, but as you go through your vulnerabilities, you need to determine the countermeasures that are the most appropriate mitigation mechanism. For each vulnerability, you need to go through a sort of kill chain analysis. For example, is the vulnerability most effectively, from a cost or difficulty perspective, addressed by protection, detection, or reaction? Depending

227

Advanced Persistent Security. http://dx.doi.org/10.1016/B978-0-12-809316-0.00022-1

on the vulnerability, it may be recommended to implement multiple counter-measures, in all points along the kill chain.

For example, poor awareness should clearly be addressed with improved awareness programs. However, it should also be addressed with protection mechanisms such as limiting access, multifactor authentication, anti-malware software, and other tools. Additionally, there need to be detection mechanisms put in place to monitor access and search for illicit use and malware on the network. Reaction procedures also need to be implemented to rapidly respond to awareness failures.

Many countermeasures can address multiple vulnerabilities as well. Consider that multifactor authentication addresses more vulnerabilities than just poor awareness. For example, it can address the concern of adversaries who have hacked the network and can put in keystroke loggers that can steal passwords. Similarly, it can address poor technical security that enabled password files to be stolen.

EVALUATE THE COMPLETENESS OF PROTECTION, DETECTION, AND REACTION

After determining the required countermeasures, you need to evaluate the completeness of the end result. At this point, you can separate countermeasures by their place in the protection, detection, and reaction chain. You then need to evaluate each link of that chain.

Are there any glaring protection mechanisms that are missing? Are there any new technologies or methodologies that should be included? Are there threats that were not accounted for? Are there obvious attack vectors that were not addressed?

It is also recommended to perform a penetration test with highly skilled testers. Although they will not find all potential vulnerabilities, well-qualified security professionals should be able to find vulnerabilities that you might not have considered. We have written articles about this subject in the past, but it is important to stress that penetration testers are not equally skilled. You should avoid hiring self-proclaimed hackers. Instead, find skilled security professionals, who are also skilled as penetration testers. In short, the goal of penetration testing is improving security. Hackers intend to break security, which is typically woefully easy.

The same procedures should be considered for detection and reaction. You can go "threat hunting" at this point. This is the process of assuming there are threats already inside your network and determining where they would attack and how they would be detected. It is an extremely valuable exercise for determining the design of detection and the sufficiency of the detection capabilities. This also has implications for reaction.

With regard to reaction capabilities, it is also important to perform tabletop exercises, sometimes referred to as war games, where you walk through potential attack scenarios. Although it is a pen and paper exercise that is conducted ideally with stakeholders from all over the organization, it is highly effective for determining what information sources may be required during real incidents.

For example, you may determine that you need information from an Internet service provider (ISP). You may determine that you need to interact with other service providers or vendors, but you might not have a clue as to how to get a hold of them, or you may find that it is impossible to reach them through known communications channels. You might not have visibility into portions of your network. You might want to shut down access to some applications, but shutting down those applications would have a more critical impact than the attack itself.

As you go through these exercises, you should start to understand what your security program should look like. This process is again not simple, but it is not exceptionally difficult either.

PERFORMING A COST/BENEFIT SANITY CHECK

This is the potentially most important section of the book. We have as saying that summarizes this section: "Security professionals get the budgets they deserve, not the budgets they need. Deserve more."

Assuming that you have completed the recommended work to this point, you then need to begin the process of justifying what you want to spend or create. This can ideally be accomplished for a whole security program at once, but it can also be used to identify individual countermeasures.

Specifically, you need to go through the countermeasures and estimate the cost for implementing them, and compare that to the money you can save. As stated in the previous chapters, you need to determine the loss associated with the vulnerabilities. It then becomes a paperwork exercise to determine whether the cost of each countermeasure is significantly less than the loss it prevents. Remember that a countermeasure might mitigate multiple vulnerabilities, and therefore, results in significant cost savings.

You also need to be practical and consider that vulnerabilities might be appropriately mitigated by multiple countermeasures. For example, although you might want to protect against social engineering by implementing multifactor authentication, you may also implement anomaly detection for log-in attempts.

Your goal in the process is to determine the appropriate countermeasures that are going to have the greatest impact. Under the assumption that you have identified countermeasures that provide a complete security program, or improve a program in place, you can approach the management with a strong business proposal to acquire the desired countermeasures.

For example, if you want to implement multifactor authentication, you can state that the implementation will cost approximately $100,000 and will result in a $5,000,000 savings based on decreased operational costs, as well as preventing security compromises.

If management does not approve the budget to acquire and implement the requested countermeasures, you can then specifically lay out that if the recommendations are not approved, it will result in increased risk to the organization. Then they would have to acknowledge assuming a $5,000,000 potential loss to save $100,000.

Although this makes sense from a practical perspective, all too often, security professionals are allocated a general budget and then accept it and allocate funds as best they can. There is typically little proactive effort to influence the budget by laying out a specific business case.

SUMMARY

Although we want to assume that this chapter is irrelevant to most practitioners, from our experience, the information will be one of the most important things that most readers will take away from this book. Most practitioners have not learned to cost-justify their programs beyond what is required to submit internal budget requests.

Without a process to proactively determine the return on investment for their proposed security programs, security practitioners are at the mercy of random events over which they have little control. This should not be considered an inevitable side effect of being a security professional. We urge you to take control of your destiny to the extent possible.

CHAPTER 23

Advanced Persistent Security

Over the course of the writing, we presented the subject matter at several events, including the RSA Conference, and received great feedback. However, we received some comments that stated that the material is too basic. We received similar comments from our technical editor. At a high level, we understand where the comments come from.

There are no technologic breakthroughs presented. We do not endeavor to try to explain how to implement technologies, as a typical Syngress book might. There are plenty of books that explain those topics. We do not intend to compete with those books. On the contrary, we address the arrogance within the industry that believes that implementing advanced technologies is the best way to improve security programs. Books on implementing technology are definitely required and should be consumed and understood. However, without an operational strategy to effectively implement a comprehensive security program that goes well beyond technology alone, the most advanced technologies will quickly fail.

What we intend to do is provide advanced methods for implementing available technologies. To use an academic example, many people want information that would equate to Computer Security 899, which is doctoral research. Based on all the incidents we see and highlight, security programs fail not because there is not enough advanced research, but because there is a failure to implement the material learned in Computer Security 101, the introductory course. We look at this book as more of a capstone course, in which we define how to effectively and practically implement the previous material that should be available to the average security professional.

Consider the example highlighted in the Introduction section, in which a chief information security officer (CISO) stated that the Sony attack was unstoppable. The attack used well-known attack methods and should have been detected, before significant damage was done. Then when the CISO in question was challenged with those facts, he said that the attackers would have inevitably got in, so the damage was inevitable. That again was very wrong.

Advanced Persistent Security. http://dx.doi.org/10.1016/B978-0-12-809316-0.00023-3

Although the technology might not be advanced, many concepts for implementing a security program are unfortunately advanced. This is not because we have people who are ignorant, lazy, or ill intended, but because these concepts are not widely known or taught.

While we hope you learned from this book, and use the content to implement a process, the following are what we believe to be some of the lesser known, but most important, takeaways:

- Security is unattainable and the job of a security professional is actually risk management.
- Security programs are more than protection programs.
- Detection and reaction are as, if not more, important as protection.
- Your security program does not fail when an adversary compromises protection, but when the adversary accomplishes his/her intended action.
- Failure is acceptable, and expected.
- There is too much focus on attributing attacks to specific threats vice figuring out why the attacks were successful.
- Loss is inevitable and acceptable when properly anticipated and budgeted into the security program and overall business.
- Detection deficit disorder involves insufficient and/or poorly architectured detection capabilities.
- Security budgets should be deserved and should result from a conscious acceptance of risk; not from randomly determined budgets.
- Most important, the most devastating threats are not advanced threats, but adaptive threats that expect to run into countermeasures that they will persistently attempt to bypass.
- To respond, your security program must be adaptive and proactively plan for failure, and should quickly adapt to prevent the attackers from being inevitably successful.

Although these seem like relatively simple points, and to a large extent, they are, they are also very powerful concepts that can drastically impact the effectiveness of a security program.

ADAPTIVE PERSISTENT SECURITY

As we have stated many times, the more appropriate title for this book would be Adaptive Persistent Security. We want security programs to be proactive in the anticipation of failure. We want detection and reaction to be as integral to security programs as protection.

Although in many ways this is defense in depth, that term has so far been poorly defined. Typically, defense in depth equates to multiple layers of protection in the minds of security practitioners. Yes, there should be multiple layers of protection, when feasible, so that there is not a single point of failure. However, failure in protection should not result in the threats achieving their ultimate goal, whatever that might be.

Defense in depth includes detection and reaction measures, as much as it does multiple layers of protection. In many cases, detection and reaction countermeasures are both more effective and easier to implement than protection mechanisms. It is also more important to be aware that you are potentially being attacked. If you repel attacks, and are not aware that they occurred, you would not be prepared to respond should they eventually become successful.

The goal is to be able to accept that protections will fail, and your security program should be proactive in that it adapts to a potential compromise, before attackers can accomplish their goals. Unfortunately, this is not how a significant portion of security practitioners have been taught to think. As important, security professionals are frequently judged by the compromise of protection, and not by their ability to protect what is of value. Again, the effectiveness of a security professional is not measured by a perfect perimeter, but by their ability to prevent a loss.

SUMMARY

The goal of this book is to have people implement a more rational approach to designing security programs. This required dispelling a great deal of hype, while establishing some fundamental security principles.

There will always be security-related problems. Even if every malicious party in the world was to magically disappear, there are still malignant problems that will inevitably cause loss in the realm of security professionals. However, there will always be malicious actors, ranging from the technologically inept to the likes of the National Security Agency (NSA) Tailored Access Operations, in both the physical and virtual worlds.

Your security program can be designed and implemented to mitigate the loss caused by malignant issues, as well as the complete spectrum of malicious actors, as long as you have an intelligent and purposeful design for your security program. This means that you design your program to be proactive in all aspects of protection, detection, and reaction. The key issue is that reaction does not imply that you are proverbially stopping the bleeding, but that the bleeding does not occur automatically when protection fails.

Failure of security is expected; however, as long as the security program can proactively adapt to the failures of protection, you may not suffer any loss. Even if loss occurs, proactive adaption can minimize losses. It is our hope that this philosophy and the accompanying guidance will serve you well.

Index

'*Note:* Page numbers followed by "f" indicate figures, "t" indicate tables.'

Printed in the United States
By Bookmasters